Introduction to Transportation Planning

Third edition

Michael J. Bruton

Professor of Town Planning in the University of Wales

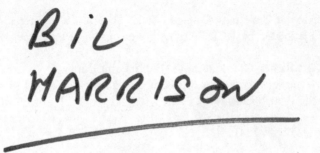

PRESS

First published in 1970
Second edition 1975
Third edition 1985
First published by UCL Press in 1992 as a third impression
Fourth impression 1993

UCL Press Limited
University College London
Gower Street
London
WC1E 6BT

The name of University College London (UCL) is a registered
trade mark used by UCL Press with the consent of the owner.

British Library Cataloguing-in-Publication Data
A CIP catalogue record for this book is available
from the British Library.

ISBN: 1-85728-018-0

Typeset in Times Roman
Printed and bound by Hartnolls Limited, Bodmin, England

Contents

For Sheila and 'Lou',
Suzy and Catherine

Acknowledgements

The author would like to thank all those who gave permission for use of copyright material in the text, in particular:

The City of Cardiff Corporation and Colin Buchanan and Partners in association with W. S. Atkins for their consent to the use in Chapter 3 of trip generation equations derived in connection with the Cardiff Study

Systematica and Wootton Jeffries P L C for their consent to the inclusion of details of MicroTrips and MINITRAMP in Chapter 8

Bruce Hutchinson for agreeing to the inclusion of a number of figures from *Principles of Urban Transport Planning Systems*, McGraw Hill, Toronto (1974).

Preface to the first edition

The land use–transportation planning process can be subdivided in very general terms into four main stages:

1 The estimation of future demands for movement, and the establishment of the shortcomings in the existing transportation system to meet this future demand.
2 The design of a series of alternative transportation plans which accord with community aims and objectives and meet this estimated demand for movement.
3 The evaluation of alternative transportation plans, in both economic and social terms, to derive the optimum solution.
4 The financing and implementation of the chosen alternative plan.

The procedure is complex and highly involved, dealing with and attempting to quantify for some future date the wishes and demands of people.

This book deals only with the techniques of estimating future demands for movement. As such it can be considered to provide an introduction to both traffic estimation procedures, and the transportation planning process. Although methods of evaluating alternative proposals are touched on, the major aim of the book is to outline, in as simple a way as possible, the traffic estimation procedure, highlighting the problems and shortcomings associated with it.

No attempt is made to cover what, in my opinion, constitute the more important and intractable problems associated with route location, the setting up of community goals and objectives, and the implementation of the chosen alternative. The present state of the art is such that the true significance of these aspects is only gradually being recognized. However, the furore aroused by transportation proposals recently put forward in some of the towns and cities of this country, indicates that much more attention must be given to the problems associated with goal setting, public participation and route location, before the transportation planning process as a whole can be considered to be successful.

1970   M J B

Preface to the second edition

The aim of this revised edition is unchanged from that of the first edition, viz. . . . 'to outline, in as simple a way as possible, the traffic estimation procedure, highlighting the problems and shortcomings associated with it'. However, in order to give a broader contextual background, Chapter 1 has been re-written to include a consideration of the methodological approaches which can be adopted in the transportation planning process. Otherwise the revisions are confined to updating the various techniques, and expanding those sections which were incomplete in the first edition. Thus Chapter 3 - Trip Generation has been expanded to include a fuller consideration of multiple linear regression analysis; Chapter 4 - Trip Distribution has been updated to include a consideration of the use of 'generalized cost' and Linear Programming; Chapter 5, formerly Traffic Assignment, has been extended to consider aspects of both Network Planning and Traffic Assignment; Chapter 6 - Modal Split has been updated and includes a consideration of the use of Discriminant Analysis in Modal Split; whilst Chapters 7 and 8 (Computers in Transportation Planning, and Economic Evaluation) have been only slightly modified.

The policy issues involved in transportation planning have again been deliberately avoided - not because they are unimportant but because they constitute an issue which requires more than a generalized textbook treatment.

1975   MJB

Preface to the third edition

Although this third edition has been redrafted to take account of developments in transportation planning since 1975 the emphasis is unchanged. Thus it is concerned '. . . to outline in as simple a way as possible the traffic estimation procedure, highlighting the problems and shortcomings associated with it'. To place the issue of transport into a broader context a new chapter has been introduced – Chapter 1 Transport and society. In addition the chapters on Collection of basic data, Trip generation, Trip distribution, Network planning and traffic assignment and Modal split have been extended and restructured as appropriate to include a treatment of disaggregate behavioural models. The chapters on The evaluation of transportation models and Computers in transportation planning have been extended and updated, while the Conclusions refer to the development of the activity systems analysis approach and the use of transport-related land-use models.

The policy issues in transport have not been given detailed treatment although they are touched on in the new Chapter 1 – Transport and Society.

Cardiff   MJB
January 1985

1 Transport and society

Introduction

Transport is essential to the functioning of any society. It influences the location and range of productive and leisure activities; it affects the location of residence; it influences the range and provision of goods and services available for consumption. It inevitably influences the quality of life. Indeed, it has been argued that developments in society can be closely correlated with the introduction of new or improved transport technology. Holmes, for example, argues that the rapid growth in the economy of the USA in the early decades of this century was, probably, a direct result of the expansion of the transport system arising in part from the introduction of new technology.[1] Morlock, more circumspectly, suggests that '. . . advances in transport have made possible changes in the way we live and the way in which societies are organised, and thereby have influenced the development of civilisation'.[2] Although the relationship between the provision of transport facilities and developments in society is obvious, it is not always a direct cause and effect relationship, i.e. the provision of new or improved transport infrastructure *allows* developments to take place; it does not determine that they *will* take place. Rather any developments that occur will do so as a result of the complex interaction of a number of factors. In this respect, it should be noted that the quality, cost, or level of service provided by the transport system is often of greater significance in triggering off new developments than the basic provision of new transport infrastructure. Two further points should be considered in understanding this interrelationship – it is reciprocal and it is dynamic. Thus, the existence of a range of socio-economic activities in the form of two or more settlements can generate demands for movement. The provision of a transport system to meet this demand can itself generate further demands for movement between the settlements. However, the constantly changing nature of the relationship between transport and socio-economic developments ensures that the system is never in equilibrium for any length of time – advances in technology can lead to cost changes for production, and/or transport and/or the provision of services. These cost changes can lead to changes in the location of activities and, hence, their transport requirements. They can even lead to the development of new activities with a new range of transport requirements.

Take, for example, the South Wales coalfield.[3] From 1760 onwards, the iron and steel industry developed on the northern edge of the coalfield where iron ore and coal were accessible close to the surface. Towns such as Merthyr Tydfil, Aberdare, Hirwaun, Ebbw Vale and Blaenavon expanded rapidly, attracting large numbers of migrants. The production of iron and steel peaked in 1857, but in the succeeding years declined, following the introduction of a new smelting process (the Bessemer process). The locally-produced iron ores were not suitable for this process and, as a result, ore was imported from Spain. The cost of transporting this ore from the coastal ports to the iron and steel centres on the northern rim of the coalfield was such that, between 1857 and 1910, all these centres, with the exception of Ebbw Vale, closed down, to be replaced by new centres on the coast such as East Moors in Cardiff. In recent years, these 'new' plants have been superseded by more modern plants at Port Talbot and Llanwern where, as a result of the need to increase productivity, extensive mechanization and mass production techniques have been introduced. Such techniques require extensive areas of flat land and the ready availability of large supplies of water. Proximity to a deep water port capable of handling the largest ore-transporting vessels is also an advantage. The once modern East Moors plant was demolished in 1978–80.

A number of similar examples can be quoted to show that this relationship characterizes other forms of productive activity, e.g. the decision to locate a significant number of coal-fired electricity generating stations in the Trent Valley in the period 1955–66 was based on the need to have ready access to coal, which is provided by the railway 'merry-go-round' system; proximity to markets; availability of large supplies of water for cooling purposes, and the availability of extensive areas of flat land. Similarly, the location of tertiary or service activities such as shopping, entertainment and specialist health facilities usually depends on their level of accessibility to the catchment area population. For this reason, in the past, town centres developed at transport nodes, where two or more transport facilities intersect. The better the transport facilities, the better the levels of accessibility and the wider the range of tertiary facilities attracted to the location.

But, again, the relationship is not simply one of cause and effect, as the case of Cardiff shows. In 1954, Cardiff, already a thriving and large town, was officially designated the capital of Wales. In the years following the designation the regional offices of many firms operating in Wales moved to Cardiff, while the seat of regional government became firmly established there in the form of the Welsh Office. The enhanced status, and the increasing levels of economic activity, were almost certainly among the factors used to justify the construction of the Severn Bridge and the M4 into Wales. These improvements, in conjunction with the introduction of the 'High Speed Train' link to London, reinforced the position of the city and the improved accessibility encouraged further new developments, especially in the retail, hotel, and entertainment sectors. This improved level of accessibility, allied with the increase in the number and range of facilities available, in turn extended the catchment area of Cardiff to both the west and the east. There have, however, been a number of costs in addition to the benefits involved, in that a number of distribution firms, previously based in Cardiff, have relocated in the Bristol area to take advantage of the significantly better levels of accessibility offered for their purposes where the M4 and the M5 intersect.

While acknowledging the benefits to be derived from improved accessibility, it should be noted that there are often social costs involved. Those who are not mobile (the elderly non-car owners, school children) are often deprived of ready access to services such as the village shop, which closes down in the face of competition from newly accessible places. At the same time, the wider social costs associated with accidents, congestion, noise and pollution should not be ignored.

In the preceding sections, emphasis has been given to the reciprocal relationship between socio-economic development and transport. Since the physical expression of socio-economic development is the use to which land is put, the same reciprocal relationship exists between land use and transport. Indeed, this relationship provides the basis of the travel demand forecasting processes which form the focus of this book. However, it should be noted that transport – the movement of goods and people – is only one aspect of communications. In addition, there is the facility to communicate information through space by telecommunication. Given the ability to link computers into the telecommunications network, it is widely assumed that, in the near future, much routine office work will be decentralized to the home, with savings to both parties involved.[4]

Finally, it should be acknowledged and accepted that transport decisions and politics are highly interrelated. At the broad political level, the maintenance of order (government) often depends on the provision of adequate transport facilities. The Roman roads in Britain are an example of this type of relationship. A more recent example is the construction of the East–West highway from Khota Bahru to Penang in Malaysia. At another level, all decisions relating to investment into transport infrastructure are political in that they are distributive, i.e. the outcome of the allocation of scarce resources means that some people will benefit, while others will lose.

Demographic and socio-economic characteristics and transport

Introduction

The demand for transport derives from the needs of people to travel from one place to another to carry out the activities of their daily lives. In the following chapter, it is shown how this demand for movement is affected by (a) the location of the home, workplace, shopping, educational and other activities;

(b) the nature of the transport system available, and (c) the demographic and socio-economic characteristics of the population. It is the intention of this section to look, in some detail, at the way in which demographic and socio-economic factors can influence the nature of the demand for travel. Experience has shown that the demographic and socio-economic characteristics which are most significant in influencing the demand for transport are:

1   Population size
2   Population structure, by age and sex
3   Household size, structure and formation rate
4   The size and structure of the labour force, income level, which is usually measured by some proxy such as number of cars owned, or owner occupation
5   The socio-economic status of the chief economic supporter of the household.

These characteristics can interact in a complex way to affect demand for transport, while their location or distribution and the way the interrelationships change with time further complicate an already complex situation.

Obviously, the size of population will have a direct and quantifiable relationship with demand for movement. Indeed, the early transportation studies based their analyses and forecasts of travel demand largely on population size and structure, for example Chicago Area Transportation Study 1956. More recently, there has been a move towards analyses and forecasts based on household characteristics. At the risk of stating the obvious, different groups within the population have different demands for travel. These differences can largely be explained by economic, social, and cultural factors; by time, money and effort constraints and personal tastes. By way of illustration, consider the following groups within a population and their different demands for movement.

Infants   As individuals, they do not themselves make demands for movement. However, their particular needs require that a parent or adult makes trips to health clinics, and to specialist baby shops which are not provided locally.

Children   They have specific travel demands which are time specific, e.g. to and from nursery school. Again, a parent, usually the mother, has a heavily constrained day until the children are old enough to make these journeys alone. Some families have access to a car for school journeys, which reduces the constraining impact on the rest of the day, although this facility is usually related to the socio-economic grouping of the family.

Adolescents   They have the time constrained travel demands connected with school and, in addition, after-school activities, e.g. youth clubs, discos, sport. They have no car of their own and are thus dependent on their parents (or parents of friends) for a lift; public transport (if it is available); walking or cycling.

Young workers   They may have a restricted range of employment opportunities available to them. They will be constrained as to the time at which these journeys can be made and are unlikely to have access to a motor car. In addition, they will have a range of after-work activities, e.g. disco, sport, cinema.

Unemployed   Given the limited amount of money available to this group, it is unlikely that much will be spent on travel, although depending on the individual and his/her circumstances a wide range of journeys could be made which are not time constrained.

Workers   They are constrained in the time that work journeys take place. They may have access to a motor car and be able to use it for these journeys (if they can afford to meet the costs involved and have access to a parking space at the work end of the journey). Invariably, the location of home is based on accessibility to work. Shift workers and part-time workers are a special category within this group. In addition to work journeys, the after-work leisure and family activities may generate a wide range of trips.

Pensioners and retired   They do not go to work and, therefore, have greater freedom of choice as to when they make their journeys. They may make a wide variety of trips, many of a spontaneous nature; they may have difficulty in walking long or even short distances or climbing steps. A low income may limit the number of journeys made by some of this group, while failing health and/or eyesight could prevent those owning a car from using it.

Disabled   There are many disabilities which affect an individual's capability for moving, e.g. arthritis, rheumatism, heart and lung complaints. This group may have severe problems in walking, climbing stairs or using footbridges or underpasses.[5]

From these simple examples, an idea can be gained of the complex structure of any population and the potentially complex demands for movement. When the non-home based activities (such as distribution of goods) are added to the list, when locational factors (whether rural, suburban, or peripheral housing estate) are taken into consideration, then it is clear that the factors which could give rise to a demand for movement, and their potential inter-relationships, are complex in the extreme.

Demographic and socio-economic changes in Britain[6]

Population and households
The resident population of Great Britain grew from 53.9 million persons in 1971 to 54.28m in 1981 – a growth of 0.6 per cent. This is in marked contrast to the rate of growth in the previous two decades when the population grew

by 5.3 per cent between 1961 and 1971, and 5.0 per cent between 1951 and 1961.[7] It is predicted to grow by 1.6 per cent between 1981 and 1991, and a further 1.4 per cent between 1991 and 2001 when the resident population is expected to be 55.93m.[8] Thus, in the next twenty years, homes, jobs (or financial support) and services will have to be provided for an additional 1.65 million persons.

Period	Population at end period	Rate of growth (per cent)
1951–61	51.3 m	5.0
1961–71	53.97m	5.3
1971–81	54.28m	0.6
1981–91	55.15m	1.6
1991–2001	55.93m	1.4

Table 1   *Population growth in Great Britain 1951–2001*

Although the rate of population growth has declined, this has not been matched by a similar decline in the rate of household formation. Rather the reverse – the 'baby boom' which occurred after the Second World War has passed through the education boom to the point where the children of that generation are now forming their own households. In effect, the mothers and fathers of the 'boom babies' who had households of say six persons (i.e. two parents and four children), some twenty years ago, are now two person households, while each of their four children could have formed a two person household. In time, these new two person households could become six person households (or whatever the current fashion dictates), while the original parents move on to retirement, pensioner and eventually a single person household. This increase in the rate of household formation at the 'young' end of the age spectrum, coupled with an increased proportion of the retired and elderly living in separate households and a slight increase in the proportion of single parent families, has increased the rate of growth of households to 13 per cent between 1961 and 1971, and 6.4 per cent between 1971 and 1981.[9] The rate of population growth for the same periods was 5.3 per cent and 0.6 per cent, respectively.

The differential rates of population and household growth are reflected in the size of average household which has reduced from 3.09 persons in 1961, to 2.71 persons in 1981. This change has been particularly affected by the reduction of the proportion of married couples with children from 48 per cent in 1961, to 40 per cent in 1981 (see Figure 1).

Housing
Inevitably, these changing demographic characteristics have a direct impact on the demand for and provision of housing, especially housing type and

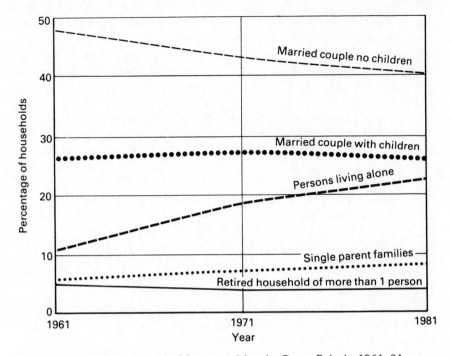

Figure 1   *Trends in household composition in Great Britain 1961-81*

Source: Central Statistical Office, *Social Trends 13*, HMSO, London (1983) Table 2.2

location. A young single professional person invariably seeks different accommodation to that sought by a blue collar married couple with three children of school age. In the period 1961-81, the stock of owner-occupied dwellings in Great Britain increased by 2.13 million from 8.73m to 10.86m, which comprises 55.7 per cent of all households.[10] Of these 10.86m dwellings, 89 per cent are estimated to be single family dwelling houses and 11 per cent flats.[11] The majority of the dwellings constructed between 1961 and 1981 are located on the outskirts of our towns and cities, as part of large, low density estates with a predominance of detached and semi-detached houses.

Employment
The same demographic factors affecting household formation rates are also having an impact on employment in Great Britain. In the period 1971-81, when the population grew by 0.6 per cent, the labour force grew by 4.8 per cent from 25.1m to 26.3m. This increase was due almost entirely to an increase in the female participation rate from 42.7 per cent in 1971 to 47.2 per cent in 1981 and an increase in the married female participation rate from 42.5 per cent to 49.5 per cent in the same period.[12] Currently, however,

female participation rates are static and are expected to remain so in the foreseeable future. The factors giving rise to this trend are complex, but they include a decline in family income in real terms, a continued increase in service sector employment, and the increase in the number and proportion of two person households. The net effect is to increase the number of work journey movements.

In the same period in the U K, employment in primary industries continued to decline as did the number of jobs in manufacturing industry. Indeed, manufacturing jobs declined by 24 per cent, although this loss was offset by a 16 per cent increase in service employment. The greatest decline in the manufacturing sector was experienced by engineering (22 per cent), textiles (42 per cent), the 'rest' of manufacturing (19 per cent) and metals (42 per cent). The largest increases in the service sector were in professional (26 per cent), 'miscellaneous' (32 per cent) and finance (34 per cent). The outcome of these changes was that 28 per cent of the workforce in the U K was employed in manufacturing in 1981, as against 62 per cent in services.[13]

Spatial implications

As an integral part of these demographic changes, population and jobs are increasingly shifting location to suburban and rural areas. The peripheral extension of our towns and cities has already been referred to, the existence of large residential estates such as Thornhill and St Mellons in Cardiff; Woodloes in Warwick, and Eastern Kenilworth in Kenilworth are now commonplace throughout the country. More significantly, the results of the 1981 Census show that in England and Wales during the period 1971–81, there has been a sizeable exodus from the conurbations and towns with a population in excess of 100,000. Indeed, the six conurbations lost 8 per cent of their total population in this period (1.3m), while those towns with a population in excess of 100,000, lost 100,000 persons (1.6 per cent). In the same period, the New Towns, resort and seaside towns, the smaller towns located in the outer metropolitan area, and the more accessible rural areas of the East Midlands, East Anglia, and the South West collectively showed an increase in population of 1.6m (9 per cent).[14]

At the same time, given high land values, old buildings, out-moded technology and problems of accessibility, manufacturing jobs are declining in central city locations. In response to changing technology and the need for single storey factory layouts required by modern manufacturing processes, new manufacturing industries are locating on the outskirts of major towns and cities; in greenfield sites in close proximity to motorway junctions, or in small town locations – a development made possible by the substitution of road for rail as the major mode of freight transport. Similarly, new office, service and retail developments are taking place in the outer metropolitan areas, or in the freestanding towns beyond those areas.[15]

Simmie, in analysing the spatial impact of demographic and economic changes in the London area between 1971 and 1980, establishes in some detail the nature of these changes.[16] He found that, in the area covered by the London Standard Metropolitan Labour Area (SMLA), employment in manufacturing industry declined by 11 per cent to 29 per cent of the total, while employment in services grew by 18 per cent to 66 per cent of the total. Within the SMLA, the decline in manufacturing was most severe in the CBD (Westminster and the City), and the outer areas of the SMLA. The growth of service industry was greatest in the outer areas, and the remainder of the urban area other than the CBD.

These economic changes have been accompanied by population and household change. In the CBD, population fell by 22 per cent and number of households by 19 per cent; in the inner urban authorities, population fell by 12 per cent and households by 7 per cent. By contrast, the population in the outer part of the area (the inner areas of the home counties) remained static with a 6 per cent increase in the number of households. Simmie argues that the dynamic interaction of a number of factors account for these changes including:

1 Decisions taken by economic organizations in the context of the international economy
2 Decisions taken by households to maximize their relative satisfaction from jobs, housing, social and environmental factors, and
3 Decisions taken by government organizations in the context of their politico-administrative responsibilities and the pressures for land in the area.

Income and expenditure[17]
In the period 1975–82 in the UK, nominal household disposable income increased from £68.3 bn to £173.8 bn – an increase of 154 per cent. However, when allowance is made for inflation, the real increase is only 10 per cent. If the actual values are indexed to 1980 (100), then between 1972 and 1982 the real disposable income has increased from 88 to 99, as Table 2 shows.

Year	Index
1972	88
1976	89
1978	94
1980	100
1981	98
1982	99

Table 2 *Real disposable income in the UK 1972–82, indexed to 1980 prices*

Source: Table 5.2, *Social Trends 14*, HMSO, London (1984)

Thus, over the decade referred to, there has been an increase in the amount available for households to spend on transport if they so wished. The following tables suggest that this is, indeed, the case.

Overall average expenditure on transport increased by 18 per cent between 1971 and 1981 at constant 1980 prices. One conclusion which could be drawn from this is that people are making more journeys or travelling further. Indeed, when the indices of expenditure on transport and travel by all consumers for 1972–82 are examined, then this does appear to be the case, with expenditure on travel by the private motor vehicle increasing consistently, while expenditure on 'other travel' has decreased (see Tables 3 and 4). At the same time, it is clear from Table 3 that one and two person pensioner households spend far less than other types of household on transport and, by implication, travel less and/or make fewer journeys.

Year	1971	1981
All house-holds	£16.3	£19.2
1 person pensioner households	£ 0.7	£ 0.7
2 person pensioner households	£ 2.1	£ 3.4

Table 3   *Average weekly household expenditure on transport and vehicles in the UK at 1981 prices*

Source: Table 6.4, *Social Trends 14*, HMSO, London (1984)

Year	Purchase vehicles	Running vehicles	Other travel
1972	115	87	93
1973	110	92	99
1974	84	91	95
1975	87	90	94
1976	91	93	91
1977	82	95	90
1978	101	98	93
1979	117	98	99
1980	100	100	100
1981	102	101	101
1982	105	104	98

Table 4   *Expenditure on transport and travel by all consumers in the UK 1972–82, indexed at constant 1980 prices*

Source: Table *Social Trends 14*, HMSO, London (1984)

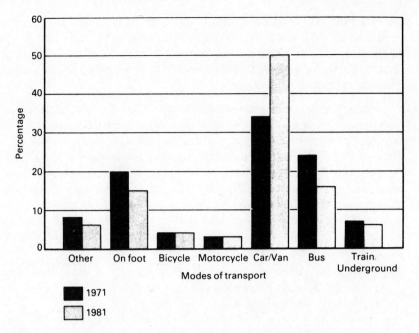

Figure 2 *Principal means of transport to work in Great Britain 1971 and 1981*

Source: Central Statistical Office, *Social Trends 14*, HMSO, London (1984) Chart 9.2

This trend towards increasing car ownership and usage is confirmed by (a) the total passenger miles travelled by different modes between 1961 and 1982, and (b) by the change in the principal means of transport for the work journey (see Table 5 and Figure 2).

Mode	Rail	PSV	Road	Bicycles
Year			Private	
1961	39	67	161	11
1971	35	51	330	5
1981	35	42	420	5

Table 5 *Total passenger mileage (in billions) travelled by different modes in the UK 1961–81*

Source: Table 9.1, *Social Trends 14*, HMSO, London (1984)

Demographic and socio-economic change and transport
The trends in demographic and socio-economic change outlined above and their likely impact on demands for movement can be summarized as follows:

1   Total population is expected to grow – by 1.65m in Great Britain between 1981 and 2001. Thus, jobs, homes, schools, health, welfare and social facilities will have to be provided to accommodate this growth. The growth and the location of the additional facilities required will inevitably increase demand for movement.

2   Currently, the rate of new household formation is greater than the rate of population increase. The trend is, therefore, towards the formation of smaller households. There is no indication that this trend will change in the near future. Experience in North America has shown that, as the size of household increases, the total number of household trips also increases, but the average trip rate per person decreases.[18] Thus, the average trip rate per person in a small household will be larger than that in a larger household – for the reason that in larger households with children there is a larger number of discretionary trips. If this relationship holds good in Great Britain, it can be deduced that:

   (a) There is a minimum number of trips per person associated with running a household and earning a living. These trips will be made regardless of household size.

   (b) With the proportion of adults in the population increasing and grouping themselves into smaller households, the inevitable result will be an increase in the average per person trip making rate, and an increase in the total number of trips made for the reason that a greater proportion of the population will be in small households which exhibit higher average trip rates per person than larger households. However, this increase in trip making will be offset in part by the effect of an increasingly ageing population which has a lower than average trip making rate. Table 4, which summarizes household expenditure on transport in the UK, tends to confirm this latter point.

Similar relationships can also be identified between trip making rates and the location, type of home or employment and density of development. Hillman's work on personal mobility has shown that:

   (a) Car ownership and availability are low in large towns and areas of high housing density.

   (b) High density areas have a much higher proportion of facilities such as shops, banks, clinics and hairdressers, available within a ten minutes walk than low density areas.

   (c) High density areas tend to be dominated by public housing, while low density areas and small towns and villages have a preponderance of owner occupied dwellings.[19]

He argues that the outcome of these relationships is that in low density areas more journeys are made by private motor vehicle, while public transport is more heavily used for motorized journeys in high density areas. The findings of the National Travel Survey confirm that in low density rural and small town locations, the motor vehicle is more heavily used than in large urban concentrations.[20] Thus, the location of new housing developments in peripheral suburban or small town locations beyond the Green Belt is likely to increase further the number of work journeys made, especially by private motor vehicle. When the changing structure of employment is taken into account, with primary and manufacturing industries accounting for relatively fewer jobs than service industries, and the marked preference for a suburban location of service industries, the pattern of work journey movements will inevitably change. An increase in the number of journeys from suburban home locations to suburban work locations can be expected.

3   Given the increase in the possible workforce arising from overall population growth, and the current high female participation rate in the workforce, which can be expected to continue in the future, it must be assumed that there will be some growth in the total demand for work journey movements. While there is speculation that new technology will remove the need for much routine office work to be undertaken in large concentrations of office development, these views are as yet nothing more than speculative.[21] The technology exists to allow this to take place. Whether the pension and insurance funds, with heavy capital investment in city centre office developments, will allow it to take place remains to be seen. Equally, it is by no means certain that the worker will voluntarily give up the social opportunities associated with working somewhere other than at home.

4   Disposable income for the bulk of the population is increasing, as is expenditure in real terms on transport. This suggests that the population at large is both able and willing to pay for the additional journeys antici-pated, as a result of the demographic and socio-economic changes outlined above.

Effects on the transport system
If the changes postulated occur, then the major transport problems of the near future will arise in the suburban areas which are currently experiencing high rates of residential and employment growth, without commensurate increases in highway capacity or public transport services. These suburban communities are being developed on the assumption of the ready availability of the private motor vehicle. Thus, it is reasonable to assume that the growth in demand for travel by the motor vehicle will approximate to the growth in households, which will almost certainly exceed the rate of population growth. Given the relative distribution of residence and workplace in suburban locations, much of this increased demand for travel will be from

peripheral to peripheral locations. This pattern of movement is already evident in the Greater London area.

There is unlikely to be an increase in highway capacity to match this growth in movement demand. The national motorway network is almost completed, and while facilities such as the M25 and the M62 will accommodate some peripheral movements in the conurbations, they alone will not cope with the total range and extent of these additional demands for travel. At the same time, the constraints on public expenditure, the increasing costs of highway construction and improvement, and the extensive maintenance programme required for the existing motorway network, ensure that the rates of highway construction and improvement experienced in the 1960s and 1970s are unlikely to be replicated. These factors, allied with the present high level of environmental consciousness shown by the public, suggests that, even where financial and political commitment for new works exists, public opposition to such projects may prevent their implementation. The Archway improvements in London are indicative of this. Thus, increasing levels of congestion can be anticipated in suburban areas – congestion which may be ameliorated by car-sharing or the provision of 'firm's buses'. The provision of an enhanced level of public transport to meet these new demands is not feasible, given the low density of the residential development and the dispersed location of employment centres. Congestion is inevitable, although it could be a level of congestion which people may be prepared to tolerate.

By contrast, the quality of transport in central city locations may be improved. With population decline, there will be fewer people to transport within these areas. Improvements carried out to the motorway and road networks in the 1960s and 1970s, allied with a decline in the number of jobs in central city locations, suggest that suburban to central radial journeys by private motor vehicle may be adequately catered for. However, the financial situation of public transport services arising out of rapidly increasing operating costs, the declining levels of patronage and the declining levels of service suggest that, even for the concentrated radial to centre corridors of movement, public transport may experience severe difficulties. Thus, transport planning in the future will have to focus on a range of problems with which it is not altogether familiar – problems which could have been avoided if genuine attempts had been made in the past to integrate land use and transport planning.

Transport and the economy[22]

Introduction

Economics is primarily concerned with the production, distribution, and consumption of goods and services on which people place a value. Such goods and services must be provided from natural resources; no one location in the world is endowed with all the natural resources necessary to support the standard of living which exists in the majority of our industrialized societies. As a consequence, very few groups can sustain the standard of living they demand from only local resources. Thus, there is an inevitable requirement to transport raw materials, finished products and knowledge between different parts of the world if the standards of living demanded are to be satisfied. In this context, transport is a means to an end. It is used by firms as an integral part of their commercial operations. It is used by individuals to get to work, to shop, and to visit friends.

In this situation, it is reasonable to assume that those having to make the different types of journeys will choose a system of transport or form of journey which reduces the cost of making that journey to a minimum. Indeed, a crude analysis of the pattern of trip making shows that the cost of travel, as reflected in distance, has a significant effect on the number of trips made. In other words, the number of trips made falls off with distance.

Significant as distance is, it does not fully explain the wide range of trip characteristics of everyday life. Indeed, if the trip making characteristics of the individual traveller are examined, then it is clear that the nearest opportunity for satisfying the purpose of the trip is not always chosen. For instance, a worker will pass many different job opportunities on the way to his/her chosen place of work; a consumer will choose to shop at a major neighbourhood shopping centre in preference to using the local shop(s). The explanation for this is simple – all jobs are not the same, while the facilities offered by different shops vary in range and quality. Thus, the journeys made vary with the perceived benefits to be derived at the range of possible destinations, and the level of accessibility of those destinations. In reaching a decision on which trip (if any) to make, the person making the journey compares the benefits to be derived from the journey with the costs of making it.

As has been noted, this decision is not made solely on the basis of minimizing total time or cost spent on travelling – rather, it is based on a combination of both factors. This combination of the time and money costs of travel is usually termed the *generalized cost* of travel, and it forms just as much a part of the price of a commodity or activity purchased as the direct outlay of money at the destination end of a journey. Thus, the price of a commodity or activity consists of two elements – access to the activity or the commodity and the direct price for it.

Take the following hypothetical illustration. A consumer from a given location (his home) is faced with a range of opportunities for earning his living at different distances (or generalized costs) from his home. He is also faced with a wide range of opportunities for spending his income in the periods of time when he is not earning his living. These opportunities for spending time and money are, again, distributed at different distances (generalized costs) from his home. Any time or money spent on travelling to earn his living, or to spend his time and money, reduces the opportunities for spending time on these activities. He thus has to balance the additional benefits to be derived from travelling to a more distant but more attractive and financially rewarding destination, against the lesser but less costly benefits to be found closer to home.

Changes in the generalized cost of travel can come about in a number of ways. Public transport fares can be reduced through subsidy; private motor vehicle costs can be reduced by the introduction of a new facility such as a motorway. More often, the generalized cost changes as a result of fare increases, or an increase in the price of fuel or labour. To illustrate the consequences of a reduction in the generalized cost of travel on the individual, assume the existence of only one mode of travel. A reduction in the generalized cost of existing journeys will have two effects. First, it will increase the income of the consumer, either directly by leaving him/her more money available to spend on other goods and services, or indirectly by increasing the time available for earning more income. Alternatively, the time saved can be spent on other activities such as recreation. Second, the relative prices of the various commodities or activities on which he/she currently spends his/her

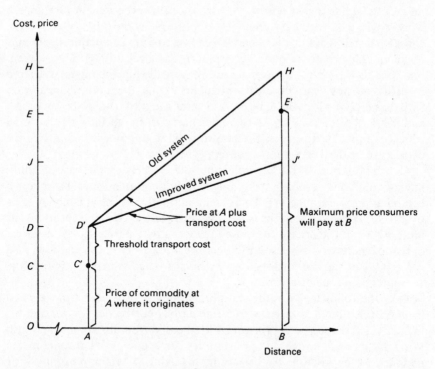

Figure 3 *Total cost of a commodity (consisting of price at origin plus transport cost) and its relationship to place utility*

Source: Reproduced, with permission of the publisher, from Morlok, Edward K., *Introduction to Transportation Engineering and Planning*, McGraw Hill, New York (1978) Figure 2.1

money will change – simply because that part of the price to him/her accounted for by the generalized cost of travel has been reduced. As a result of these changes, he/she may be expected to modify the ways in which he/she spends time and money. He/she may favour those activities whose generalized cost has fallen most and, as a result, change his/her travel pattern to include activities which are further from home than those formerly pursued.

Manufacturing or commercial undertakings are similarly affected, as the following hypothetical examples taken from Morlok show.[23] Assume an existing transport system, and a single commodity produced at *A* with a ready market at *B*, provided the maximum price for the commodity does not exceed *OE*. The cost of transporting one unit of this commodity from *A* to *B* using the existing transport system is *CH* (in Figure 3, the cost of transport is represented by the slope of the line *D'H'*). This cost includes fixed charges relating to invoicing and handling the commodity (*CD*) and the charge for transporting the commodity to *B* (*DH*). In this situation, the total cost per unit of commodity at *B* is *OH*, which is greater than the price the market will bear (*OE*). The result is that the commodity is not produced at *A*.

Assume that a major improvement to the existing transport system is subsequently implemented, such as the introduction of a new motorway. This new facility reduces the cost of transporting one unit of commodity to *DJ* and, as a consequence, reduces the total cost of the commodity to a level

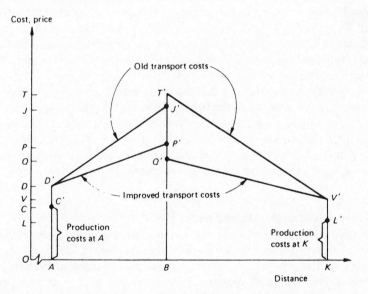

Figure 4 *Differential effects of transport improvements on two production centres*

Source: Reproduced, with permission of the publisher, from Morlok, Edward K., *Introduction to Transportation Engineering and Planning*, McGraw Hill, New York (1978) Figure 2.4

below that which the market at B will bear. In this situation, the commodity is produced at A and marketed at B. In economic terminology, the reduction in the cost of transport between A and B has *place utility* to the goods produced at A.

It should not be assumed that the reduction of transport costs has a uniform or beneficial effect on all locations or sectors of the economy. An extension of the above example illustrates this (see Figure 4). Assume the existence of one market B for one commodity which is produced at two competing locations A and K, with K being located a greater distance from B than A. It costs more to produce the commodity at A (OC) than at K (OL); the cost per unit of distance of transporting the commodity from A to B and K to B is the same, and is represented by the slope of the lines $D'T'$ and $V'T'$. However, given that K is further from B than A, the total cost of supplying the commodity to B from K at the prevailing transport cost is greater than supplying it from A. Thus, the commodity is produced at A and no production occurs at K.

Assume that the unit distance cost of transporting the commodity can be reduced to the slope of the lines $D'P'$ and $V'Q'$. Given the lower cost of production of the commodity at K, the new transport costs result in the total cost of the commodity being cheaper from K than A. Thus, production is carried out at K and ceases at A.

These are simplified examples. However, they illustrate the differential effects of improvements to the transport system – an improvement for one group may result in a loss for another. As a result of what appears simply to be physical improvements to the system, somebody gains and somebody loses. Transport investment decisions are thus distributional and, hence, political. They also serve to show that by reducing the generalized cost of access to facilities and thereby making them more accessible, changes in the location of employment and the home may occur. These changes may result from the spontaneous actions of individuals, or by the planned actions of corporate bodies choosing one location in preference to another, or both. To quote Wingo and Perloff, '. . . the accumulation of these consequences is, in fact, the shape and structure of the metropolitan region, a generation or more hence'.[24]

Regional economic growth and transport[25]
Since the 1930s, successive British Governments have applied policies to redistribute industry and employment between regions. The EEC is currently pursuing similar policies in an attempt to redress regional imbalances within Europe. In the United Kingdom, the concern has been, until recently, to prevent new or expanding industries from locating in the prosperous parts of the country, such as the South-East and the Midlands. Through the availability of grant aid in various forms, the aim has been to encourage new or expanding industrial developments to move to areas characterized by

declining manufacturing and primary industries and high unemployment, such as South Wales, Central Scotland, the North-East. The provision of transport infrastructure has been seen as an integral part of the measures taken to encourage the relocation of industry and to strengthen economic prosperity, for example the construction of the M4 link to South Wales and the Severn Bridge and the construction of the extensive motorway network in Scotland. Such measures, however, have stopped short of offering discriminatory freight rates in favour of development areas.

It is generally accepted that the improvement of transport infrastructure has a consequential improvement on the economy of the region benefiting from that infrastructure. This is, in part, confirmed by the current (1984) concern being expressed by industrialists in South Wales at the likely effect on industrial developments of the restrictions imposed on the use of the Severn Bridge. Yet the evidence to support this firmly held view is not all that strong, although a number of research exercises have been carried out with a view to establishing the strength of any relationship which might exist between regional economic developments and the provision of transport infrastructure. Two basic approaches have been adopted in this work. One attempts to show that transport costs are a low proportion of the total manufacturing costs; that industrialists are not well informed about transport costs, and, as a result, do not make careful comparisons between different locations. Thus, it is argued that transport investments will not affect existing firms in the region, nor will they prove to be a sufficient incentive for new firms to locate in the region. The work of Edwards and Bayliss falls into this category.[26]

The second approach is to show that *overall* the impact of transport investments does influence industrial location decisions. The work of Gwilliam follows this approach and stresses that the overall impact is a complex interaction of a number of factors including cost, quality and reliability of service, and image of the facility and the region.[27] Against this background, it is instructive to review briefly the findings of a number of research projects dealing with this issue.

Two general studies reported by Brown[28] and Rich[29] set the issue in context. Brown attempted to relate regional employment growth at the UK Standard Planning Region level to regional accessibility. He found no significant relationship, although he argued that the effect of road investments may be important in shaping the image of a region as a suitable location for industrial development. More recently, Rich, who examined the pattern of manufacturing change in Scotland between 1961 and 1971, found no evidence to suggest that accessibility influenced employment change between regions. However, he did find that it has a significant effect on the employment change within regions, over and above that which might be expected from the industrial structure of the regions. Indeed, he pointed to the possibility that remote areas are not favoured due to their relative inaccessibility, while the most accessible core areas generally experience congestion and thus may not be favoured in comparison with slightly decentralized locations. Rich's work can, however, be criticized on the grounds that the measure of accessibility used, which was based on physical interzonal distance, is too crude a measure to reflect the complex overall interactions which influence location decisions.

A number of studies have been carried out in an attempt to determine the economic impact of the M62 Lancashire to Yorkshire motorway, which runs across the Pennines from Liverpool to Hull. Dodgson, in attempting to forecast the economic impact of the M62, developed a relationship between regional employment growth and regional accessibility.[30] From this relationship, he then attempted to predict the likely impact of the M62. The first stage of his project involved the development of a transport cost measure for an accessibility calculation in which the cost of transporting a given quantity of freight between each pair of zonal origins and destinations was derived. From this, he assessed the likely impact of the M62. He found that the cost of transport would not drop significantly – 4 per cent at most at the 'epicentre' of the M62 (Huddersfield).

He then went on to test the relationship between regional employment growth and transport costs, labour availability, industrial structure and urban congestion, using multiple linear regression analysis. The relationship derived was weak, with a multiple correlation coefficient of 0.26. Using the derived relationship, he then attempted to predict the employment generating effect of the motorway, which he estimated at 2900 p.a. in an area with 3.4m employees. This work can be criticized on three counts – it used poor quality data; the multiple linear regression relationship developed is weak and fails to take into account the potential impact of developments elsewhere. Nevertheless, the work of Brown, Rich and Dodgson raises doubts as to the employment generating effect of new motorways – a view which is reinforced by the findings of Chymera[31] and Thornton[32], who attempted to assess the impact of the M62, and the M6006 which links Bradford to the M62.

Chymera considered the experience of the Bradford Euroway Industrial Estate which was constructed in 1972 adjacent to the M62 at a cost of £7.0m to accommodate businesses employing 2500 persons. He found that by 1976, some twenty firms employing 300 people were located on the estate. Two of the firms were involved in manufacturing, the remainder were service and retail activities, which were not labour intensive. It can be argued that the absence of public transport links to the estate in an area of low car ownership, and the strictly enforced policy of excluding industries which might be a nuisance to their neighbours, inevitably inhibited the development of the estate. However, the work of Thornton, who considered the impact of the M62 and the M6006 on existing firms in the Bradford area, and the attraction of new firms to the area, suggests otherwise. In fact, he was able to identify only five new companies that had been attracted to the area in the period

1973–7, and even those gave labour availability rather than transport as the reason for their move. For the existing firms in the area that had expanded, transport was not regarded as a factor which had influenced the expansion.

More recently, Judge has completed work on the regional effect of the M62.[33] He based his approach on the assumption that if the M62 has had a significant economic effect, this should be reflected in the use made of the motorway, especially by new trips generated and changes in the pattern of traffic movements. He justifies the use of this approach on the grounds that (a) it is easier to monitor the traffic impact of the M62 than to monitor complex employment changes, and (b) if there has been a significant change in the traffic pattern, then it should be possible to establish spatially whether the observed flows relate to a re-ordering of the existing pattern of movements or to movements which result from the relocation or intensification of activities. Using traffic flow data for movements between Lancashire and Yorkshire collected during the period 1970–7, i.e. before and after the construction of the M62, he found that since the opening of the first stages the M62 has experienced rapid growth in traffic, while traffic flows on the 'other' roads have stabilized or reduced. Indeed, traffic on the motorway increased by 91 per cent in this period, while total traffic flows on all roads surveyed between the two areas increased by 34 per cent. Judge estimates that this 34 per cent increase is greater than the flows which could have been expected without the construction of the M62 – by between 1 per cent and 13 per cent depending on the particular road – and, hence, suggests that the construction of the M62 has probably had an impact on the economic development of the region. However, Judge's findings should be used with caution, given that the traffic flow figures used in the analysis do not differentiate between commercial and other traffic – classified data is available only for the period 1970–73 when there was found to be only a 10.2 per cent increase in commercial vehicle flows between the two areas.

One final piece of research completes the picture – the work of Botham, who attempted to evaluate the longer term indirect effects of the road programme in Britain.[34] His work is speculative in that he attempted to assess what the spatial structure of the British economy would have been if the road programme had not been implemented. He approached the problem by testing the hypothesis that there is a positive relationship between accessibility and economic performance, and used multiple linear regression analysis to evaluate the effects of changes in *relative* accessibility within an overall *absolute* increase in accessibility.

Botham divided Britain into twenty-eight zones and used multiple linear regression analysis to account for differential employment shifts between 1961–6. He then used the regression set derived to estimate two things – first, what the distribution of employment would have been if no road construction had occurred, and, second, what the distribution of employment would have been in 1957 if the 1972 road network had existed then. The difference between the two gives an indication of the impact of the road programme on employment. He makes no attempt to identify the impact of individual projects. A number of different models were derived to estimate the impact of the road programme on economic development, and depending on the model used so the results varied in detail. For example, if the model which includes employment density as an independent variable is used, then the overall impact of the road programme on employment change is small – some 20,000 jobs in all. If, on the other hand, employment density is excluded from the model, then the total impact is greater giving a change of 50,000 jobs due to the road programme. If account is taken of congestion costs in the major towns and cities, then the impact of the road programme becomes more significant, accounting for a change of 117,000 jobs which largely benefit the peripheral regions. The measure of congestion used was an assumed 20 per cent increase in transport running costs. The implication of this particular finding is that the spatial implications of changes in fuel prices are as important as additions to the road programme.

The conclusion that can be drawn from this brief review of research into the relationships between transport investment and economic development, is that there is no evidence to suggest that improvements to transport infrastructure significantly improve the employment prospects of a region. Equally, there is no evidence to show that such improvements do not improve employment. What is certain is that industrialists and politicians believe that the provision of new or improved transport infrastructure is an important plank in policies designed to redress regional imbalance.

Transport and the environment

Introduction

The *Traffic in Towns* Report first presented a coherent account of the ways in which transport affected our living and working environment. It quite forcibly drew attention to the fact that 'The penetration of motor vehicles throughout urban areas is bringing its own peculiar penalties of accidents, anxiety, intimidation by large or fast vehicles that are out of scale with the surroundings, noise, fumes, vibration, dirt and visual intrusion on a vast scale'.[35] It was in this context that the term 'environment' was used to describe the effects of transport upon the surroundings. This concept of 'environment' was used in conjunction with the concept of 'accessibility' – a term used to describe the ease with which vehicle users could move from one part of a town to another, and penetrate close to their final destination. The relationship between environment and accessibility was expressed in a rough and ready 'law' which established that if environmental standards are fixed for any area, then a limit is automatically set to the amount of traffic it can accommodate. However, the traffic capacity can be increased without detracting from the environment by carrying out physical alterations, but at a price. Thus, the amount of traffic an area can accommodate is determined by the environmental standards adopted and the amount of money which can be spent on physically altering the area.

The major environmental elements, which the *Traffic in Towns* team argued should be taken into account in any assessment of traffic proposals or conditions, are neatly summarized in the illustrative cost-benefit analysis included in the Report.[36]

Under the general headings of safety, comfort, convenience, and appearance, they focused attention on the need for:

1   Pedestrians to be able to move about safely in urban areas
2   The segregation of pedestrian and vehicle
3   The removal of the polluting effects of the motor vehicle noise and smell from working and living areas of our towns, as well as
4   The elimination of the overpowering visual intrusion of large vehicles which should not penetrate into those areas unless their destination is there.

This concern with the poor quality of the 'environment', resulting from the unrestrained use of the motor vehicle, was a message which was popularly received. The activities of numerous amenity groups campaigning against major road proposals is one example of how Buchanan's message was absorbed.[37] The widespread introduction of pedestrianized areas for both shopping and residential purposes is another, as are the explicit planning and transport policies adopted in many of our towns and cities to optimize 'accessibility' in ways which do not detract from the quality of the 'environment'.[38]

Despite these many advances in protecting and enhancing the 'environment' against the intrusive effects of the motor vehicle, Buchanan claims, with some justification, that the environmental case as presented in the Report has not been widely accepted by the public at large.

People do not seem to be as steamed up about traffic as we thought they ought to be, they put up with it; people live along the North Circular Road in conditions which I would regard as intolerable, but they don't seem to mind, and their houses are neat and well-maintained and fetch good prices; people park cars, caravans and boats in their front gardens, often blocking out the view from the sitting room; motorists seek assiduously for loopholes in parking restrictions, given the chance they would park in Cathedrals without a qualm of conscience. All the signs suggest to me that people are prepared to trade off their environment in return for motorized accessibility.[39]

Given that it is some twenty years since the Report was published, the disappointment that so little has apparently been achieved is understandable. Nevertheless, advances have been made and it has been claimed that

As a result of 'Traffic in Town' our collective approach to urban development, or redevelopment, is much more sensitive than at any time since the Regency period. We have accepted that, even within tight cost constraints, it is possible to accommodate environmental standards and convenience – although the choice of the standard of environment and the level of convenience is inevitably political.[40]

Indeed, the consistent and widespread opposition to three forms of so-called transport improvements – airport construction or extension, motorway construction and the introduction of the 'juggernauts' – all point to a continuing concern to protect the environment.

Once again, the presentation of a coherent environmental approach in the consideration of proposed airport developments owes much to Buchanan and his activities as a member of the Roskill Commission of Inquiry into the possible location for a third airport for London, 1968–70.[41] After an extensive cost-benefit analysis of alternative locations, the majority of the Commission recommended that the new airport should be located at Cublington in Buckinghamshire. Buchanan produced a note of dissent objecting to all three possible inland sites that had been considered, and which succinctly categorized the environmental and other factors which should be taken into account in considering the proposed airport,[42] viz,

1   The new airport should be used positively to redress regional imbalance by introducing new employment opportunities in area(s) of the country which need such a boost to the economy
2   The location of the new airport in the sector to the west and/or north of London would result in long established policies of restraint being abandoned; would see the disappearance of open countryside and damage a tract of country which is of great interest and value; would involve the loss of several thousands of acres of highly productive agricultural land and would expose many thousands of people to an unwarranted level of noise pollution.

In his words,

To locate the airport squarely athwart the break between the country's two largest conurbations with the noise area extending from the south-west to north-east for forty miles, and with the consequent constraint on all the modest activities that the area so conveniently accommodates at present, and all those that it would accommodate in future, would seem to me to constitute nothing less than an environmental disaster.[43]

The same arguments are being used, some thirteen years later, in the current debate concerning the extension of Stansted Airport as the third London Airport.[44]

In recent years, there has been an equally widespread and vociferous opposition to the increasing use of heavy lorries for the transport of freight in Britain – an opposition based on the potential environmental damage such vehicles can do. Indeed, a recent survey of public opinion in Britain showed that 26 per cent of the population surveyed saw lorry traffic as a serious problem which contributed significantly to noise, road accidents and air pollution.[45] Given that (a) 85 per cent of freight tonnage in the UK was carried by road in 1978; (b) in the period 1950-79, the number of goods vehicles of eight tons or more increased from 2000 to 121,000 approximately, and (c) 60 per cent of the total number of goods vehicles which are less than 1.5 tons carry only 5 per cent of the total freight tonnage, it is quite clear that heavy lorries have a very large share of the road freight market.[46] Indeed, lorries heavier than sixteen tons account for 90 per cent of freight ton-mileage, while the ton-miles carried by road has increased from 53.3 thousand million miles in 1973, to 64 thousand million ton-miles in 1979. These figures serve to dimension the scale of the heavy lorry problem.

Until recently, the maximum size of the freight vehicle that could be operated in Britain was thirty-two tons and four axles; the EEC is proposing to introduce a forty tonne/five axle vehicle, while in 1983 the British government increased the maximum size of road freight vehicle to thirty-eight tonnes. These developments and the recommendations of the Armitage Inquiry into *Lorries, People and the Environment* which proposed that the maximum British lorry weight should be increased to forty-four tonnes, have aroused extensive opposition from the environmental lobby on the grounds of safety, noise, pollution, damage to the fabric of buildings through vibration, and visual intrusion.[47]

Factors affecting the environment

The factors generally seen as having the most significant effect on the quality of the environment are safety and accidents, noise, vibration, air pollution, and visual intrusion. The cumulative effect of these factors can be a disincentive to investment which, in turn, can lead to a deterioration in the fabric of the physical environment. While it is possible to measure these factors, as for example numbers of accidents, recorded decibels, and vibration rate per second, it is a subjective judgement as to the extent to which the environment is adversely affected by these factors. What is acceptable to a householder on the North Circular Road may not be acceptable to a resident of Wiltshire. It is this subjectivity which makes it so difficult to consider fully and to the satisfaction of all the likely environmental consequences of new transport infrastructure.

Safety and accidents

Of all the influences which the motor vehicle has on the environment the question of safety should be foremost. . . . To be safe, to feel safe at all times, to have no serious anxiety that husbands, wives, children will be involved in a traffic accident are surely prerequisites for civilised life.[48]

Safety cannot be divorced from accidents – indeed, victims of accidents can be considered to be the one group which experiences the most significant adverse consequences of transport proposals. Each year, approximately 6000 people are killed on the roads in Britain – the largest single cause of accidental death! In 1982, 6124 persons were killed in road accidents. A further 334,000 casualties resulted from road accidents. In 1981, of those killed or seriously injured, 18,400 (24 per cent) were pedestrians; 5000 (7 per cent) were cyclists and 22,500 (27 per cent) were motor cyclists.[49]

Such figures bring home the vulnerability of the pedestrian and pedal cyclist to the motor vehicle. No amount of improvement to the braking systems of motor vehicles is going to reduce this vulnerability. Only the segregation of these modes of movement from the motor vehicle will improve the situation, which is invariably at its worst in the historic towns and villages with narrow streets and footways designed to cope with the horse and cart and the pedestrian, rather than the motor vehicle. In such circumstances, lorries frequently have to mount the pavement to allow other vehicles to pass or to negotiate tight corners. As Haigh and Hand state 'There can be few more frightening aspects of everyday life than a big lorry lurching over the pavement and casting a pall of gloom, smoke and noise over any pedestrian who happens to be passing by.'[50]

Noise

Noise can be defined as sound which is unwanted by the recipient. This simple definition makes it clear that noise is subjective – it involves people and their feelings. While it is relatively easy to measure the sound level associated with an activity, it is much more difficult to obtain a measure of noise, i.e. unwanted sound. In the words of the Wilson Report on noise 'Not only do people vary in their susceptibility and adaptability to noise, but each of us may be annoyed by one noise but not by another of similar physical characteristics.'[51]

To date, no adequate measures of annoyance levels of noise have been devised. However, by carrying out social surveys in conjunction with sound level measurements, it has been possible to obtain an overall view of the level of annoyance associated with particular sound levels. In carrying out these surveys, it was found that measuring sound levels in decibels, using a weighting system known as the A weighting, gives the best correlation between the objective sound level measurements and the subjective assessment of the associated level of annoyance. For this reason, noise associated with transport is usually measured in dBA.

In 1963, the Wilson Report found that '. . . in London (and no doubt this applies to other large towns as well) road traffic is . . . the predominant source of annoyance, and no other single noise is of comparable importance'.[52] Table 6 shows the range of noise levels experienced under different traffic conditions. The significance of these noise levels is only fully appreciated when they are compared with what were considered by Wilson to be acceptable noise levels inside living rooms and bedrooms, i.e. 40 dBA by day, and 30 dBA by night in country areas; 45 dBA by day and 35 dBA by

Group	Location	Noise climate (in dBA)*		Percentage of the total numbers of points measured falling in each group
		Day (8 a.m.–6 p.m.)	Night (1 a.m.–6 a.m.)	
A	Arterial roads with many heavy vehicles and buses (kerbside)	80–68	70–50	4
B	(i) Major roads with heavy traffic and buses			
	(ii) Side roads within 15–20 yds. of roads in groups A or B(i) above	75–63	61–49	12
C†	(i) Main residential roads			
	(ii) Side roads within 20–50 yds. of heavy traffic routes	70–60	55–44	17
	(iii) Courtyards of blocks of flats, screened from direct view of heavy traffic			
D	Residential roads with local traffic only	65–56	53–45	18
E	(i) Minor roads			
	(ii) Gardens of houses with traffic routes more than 100 yds. distant	60–51	49–43	23
F	Parks, courtyards, gardens in residential areas well away from traffic routes	55–50	46–41	9
G	Places of few local noises and only very distant traffic noise	50–47	43–40	1
			Total	84 per cent

* By noise climate is meant the range of noise level recorded for 80 per cent of the time. For 10 per cent of the time the noise was louder than the upper figure of the range and in the case of Group A attained peak levels of about 90 dBA: for 10 per cent of the time the noise was less than the lower figure in the range.

† In Groups C to F, noise from other sources, such as trains or children's voices, predominated over road traffic noise at particular times, but traffic was the most frequent noise source.

Table 6 *Range of noise levels at locations in which traffic noise predominated*

Source: Final Report on the Problem of Noise (Wilson Report) HMSO, London (1963)

night in suburban areas away from main traffic routes, and 50 dBA by day and 35 dBA by night in busy urban areas.

Work carried out in 1967 on traffic noise rating found that a simple single-figure index, derived from the arithmetic average of the sound levels exceeded for 10 per cent of the time between 0600 hrs and 2400 hrs, gave the best correlation with the levels of disatisfaction expressed by those affected.[53] Subsequent work in 1972 confirmed the reliability of this index.[54] As a result, this L10/18h noise rating index has been widely accepted in the UK as a most suitable measure of dissatisfaction with transport related noise.

Noise is seen as one of the most serious environmental intrusions because of the effect it is claimed to have on the health and efficiency of people. The Wilson Report, in considering this issue, accepted the definition of health used by the World Health Organisation, viz, 'Health is a state of complete physical, mental and social well-being, and not merely an absence of disease and infirmity'. It concluded that '. . . there is no doubt that noise affects health' and drew attention to the fact that repeated interference with sleep is to be least tolerated because prolonged loss of sleep is known to be injurious to health. It also commented on the fact that there was no evidence to suggest that exposure to moderate noise produces any direct and measurable physio-logical effect on the average person. For this reason, it claimed that the general effect of noise on health must be more psychological than physical. In addition to the health implications associated with noise, there is also the irritant of interference with conversation, radio and television.

Traffic noise depends on the interaction of six main factors:

1   Noise from individual vehicles
2   Traffic volume
3   Traffic composition
4   Traffic speed
5   Road gradient
6   Road surface

Individual vehicle noise is the product of the engine, the gearbox and trans-mission, the exhaust, the bodywork and the interaction between the tyres and the road surface. The Motor Vehicles (Construction and Use) Regulations 1978 prescribe the maximum noise level permitted for various classes of vehicle, when measured under specified conditions (see Table 7).

Type of vehicle	Construction limit (dBA)	In use limit (dBA) before 1/11/70	after 1/11/70
Cars	85	88	88
Goods vehicles	89	92	92
Coaches, buses	89	92	92
Motorcycles (125)	86	90	89

Table 7   *Motor vehicle noise limits: Construction and use regulations, 1978*

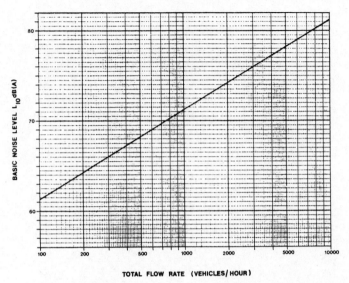

PREDICTION OF BASIC NOISE LEVEL L_{10} IN TERMS OF TOTAL HOURLY FLOW RATE q
(V = 75km/h, p = O, G = O)

BASIC NOISE LEVEL HOURLY $L_{10} = 41 \cdot 2 + 10 \log q$ dB(A)

Figure 5 *Prediction of basic noise level L_{10} in terms of total hourly flow rate q (V = 75 km/h, p = O, G = O)*

Source: Department of the Environment, *Calculation of Road Traffic Noise*, HMSO, London (1975) Chart 3. Reproduced with permission of the publisher

Noise levels increase rapidly with increasing traffic volume as Figure 5 shows. Similarly, the more heavy vehicles in the traffic stream the higher the noise level. So a 50 per cent increase of heavy vehicles in a traffic stream flowing at 50 km/hr will increase the L10 level by 4 dBA – a significant increase when it is realized that an increase of 3 dBA is the equivalent of doubling the sound level.[55]

The relationship between speed and noise is dependent on the proportion of heavy vehicles and the conditions of flow (see Figure 6). Where traffic flow is interrupted and speeds are, therefore, lower, the relationship between speed and noise is complicated. At very slow speeds, engine noise is dominant while movement in low gears is noisier than in higher gears. As a result, there tends to be reduction in noise levels up to speeds of 35 km/hr, especially if the traffic stream contains a large proportion of heavy vehicles. Similarly, the relationship between road gradient and noise is complex. Basically, traffic noise increases on an ascending gradient, but this may be offset by a reduction in noise from descending traffic. At the same time, climbing

CORRECTION FOR MEAN TRAFFIC SPEED V AND PERCENTAGE HEAVY VEHICLES p

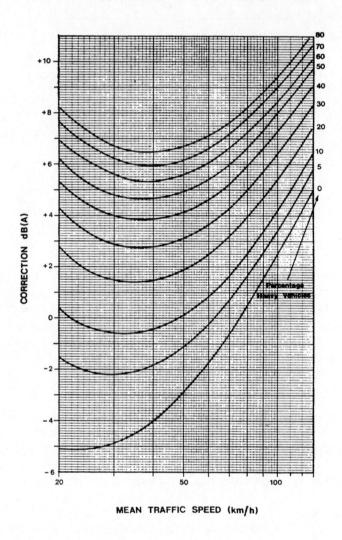

MEAN TRAFFIC SPEED (km/h)

$$\text{CORRECTION} = 33 \log \left(V + 40 + \frac{500}{V} \right) + 10 \log \left(1 + \frac{5p}{V} \right) - 68 \cdot 8 \text{ dB(A)}$$

Figure 6   *Correction for mean traffic speed* V *and percentage heavy vehicles* p

Source: Department of the Environment, *Calculation of Road Traffic Noise*, HMSO, London (1975) Chart 4. Reproduced with permission of the publisher

vehicles lose speed which reduces the noise level until the point is reached when low gear has to be engaged. Finally, different road surfaces may generate different noise levels through interaction with vehicle tyres. These differences are small and, in most cases, can be ignored.

The noise levels affecting a receiver may be significantly lower than the levels recorded at the point of generation. This attenuation of noise can be affected by a number of factors, the most significant of which are the profile of the road (whether it is at grade, depressed or elevated), distance between source and receiver, topography, screening (e.g. planting, earth mounds), weather and the angle of view.

Distance is a most effective attenuator of noise with reductions of 6 dBA being achieved with a doubling of the distance from source to receiver. Similarly, purpose designed screening can reduce levels of noise behind them by as much as 20 dBA. The Noise Insulation Regulations 1975 establish criteria for the insulation of dwellings against construction and traffic noise arising from new or improved roads, while compensation is payable if the value of property depreciates by more than £50 as a result of noise arising from the use of certain public works.

Vibration
It is widely claimed that traffic induced vibration is a cause of structural damage to buildings, but there is no empirical evidence to support this claim. There are, however, social surveys which indicate that vibration is a source of annoyance to people who live or work on major traffic routes. The Transport and Road Research Laboratory found that in Ludlow in 1978 50 per cent of shopkeepers, 31 per cent of office workers and 33 per cent of residents were very much bothered by vibration.

Air pollution
Motor vehicles contribute significantly to the level of air pollution in our towns and cities. Heavy lorries are particularly singled out for criticism in this respect, given the dark and smelly fumes they emit. While lorry emissions are the most noticeable aspect of pollution, the emission from motor car exhausts contains far more carbon monoxide, hydrocarbons, nitrogen oxide and aldehyde than do the diesel engines of lorries.

Lead is a constituent of exhaust emissions which has caused great concern in recent years, given the way in which it can retard the mental development of children who are constantly exposed to air with a high lead content. The normal concentration of lead in the atmosphere in busy urban areas is claimed to be well below the concentrations needed to cause poisoning.[56] Nevertheless, it is some twenty times greater than the level found in more remote areas. For these reasons, most countries have reduced the lead levels in petrol, while in USA legislative controls have been introduced to limit the emission of carbon monoxide and hydrocarbons.

Visual intrusion
There is little doubt that major transport infrastructure, especially urban motorways, changes significantly the visual appearance of the area through which it passes. To many people this intrusion results in a loss of amenity. Equally, there is the much more pernicious intrusion of motor vehicles into parts of our towns and cities where they have no business. Heavy lorries can be particularly intrusive in narrow country lanes or in historic urban streets, or in unassuming residential streets. They are invariably out of scale with their surroundings in such situations. At the same time, the intrusion associated with the indiscriminate parking of private motor cars, caravans and other trappings of modern living in residential areas can detract from the visual attractions of those areas.

As with noise, the judgement of what constitutes unwarranted intrusion is subjective. At a personal level, a householder may trade off the view from his sitting room against the relatively safe parking for his caravan or boat provided by his front garden. At a collective level, the loss of amenity associated with the construction of the M42 through particularly attractive parts of Oxfordshire and Warwickshire has to be weighed against perceived economic and political advantages. At this level, the decisions are political.

Conclusions
In addition to the environmental factors reviewed above, traffic, and, in particular, heavy lorries, can cause damage to buildings and accentuate the effects of urban blight. Arterial roads in inner city areas are particularly affected as heavy traffic flows add to the run-down appearance of such areas and deter those who might, in different circumstances, be persuaded to invest in and maintain property.

Some eight years ago, the government acknowledged the environmental consequences of transport proposals when it offered advice and guidance, in the form of a research report, to those concerned to include environmental factors as part of the evaluation of transport proposals.[57] This report, *The Environmental Evaluation of Transport Plans*, marks a sound state of the art review of the environmental factors, including noise, visual intrusion, severance of communities, land taken, and pedestrians, which should be taken into account in evaluating transport proposals. It also provides advice on the ways in which unrelated aggregated data can be handled as part of the evaluation process. The major drawback with this document is that its application is not obligatory.

Transport and politics[58, 59]

It is important to appreciate that the planning and implementation of transport and traffic proposals form part of a wider and continuous planning process initiated by government to secure social, economic and physical change. The very act of planning carries with it the implication of intervening in market forces to bring about change which would not otherwise happen. Public sector planning, of any sort, is interventionist; it is redistributive; it gives rise to conflicts of interest over the allocation of scarce resources. It is inevitably political. Decisions relating to transport investment and policy form an integral part of this wider planning process. Such decisions are, therefore, inevitably political.

Given the fact of limited resources for the implementation of transport policies and proposals, certain decisions about the allocation of those resources invariably mean that some people benefit from these decisions, while others lose. A further complication which compounds the potential conflicts is that, in any perceived transport problem, there is no single solution. Rather there is a number of different ways of resolving that problem. Depending on one's values and standards, so the preferred solution will reflect those values and standards. Thus, politics in the context of transport is '. . . concerned with the regulation of disagreements about matters of public choice'.[60]

The processes to secure social, economic and physical change are initiated by central government. However, it is important to appreciate that the political party controlling government can be changed at election, or that the ideological stance adopted within a political party can change with time. Thus, the importance that the government of the day places on securing social, economic and physical change, including changes in the transport system, may differ significantly from that of its predecessors. For example, the current (1984) Conservative Government is keen to encourage competition among coach operators and is attempting to achieve this through the removal of certain regulation requirements which had been operative under previous governments – both Labour and Conservative controlled.

At the same time, central government relies heavily on local government to implement or administer policies to secure social and economic change. Yet the administrative units of local government may well be controlled by political parties with different views to those held by the party controlling central government. The policies adopted by South Yorkshire Metropolitan County towards the subsidization of public transport, for example, are very different from those central government would wish to see adopted. Equally, those policies differ from those adopted by other local authorities, such as the neighbouring West Riding Metropolitan County or Oxfordshire County Council. This conflict between the views of the current government, which is determined to cut public expenditure, and a number of equally determined local authorities who are concerned to secure a more equitable system of transport by increasing subsidies to public transport from locally determined tax revenue, highlights the importance of transport as a political issue. Indeed, it could be argued that this conflict between central government and some local authorities has become sufficiently important to lead to proposals for the imposition of rate-capping by central government, and the abolition of those authorities who pose the greatest challenge to central government policies (the Metropolitan Counties).

At another level, experience over the last ten years, with objections to motorway and airport proposals, suggests that plans to change the nature of the physical environment through public investment create significant conflicts of interest, and are seen by the potential 'losers' as being highly susceptible to political pressure to ensure they are not implemented. The third London airport proposed for Stansted in the early 1960s was abandoned temporarily as a result of political pressure from the public. The third London airport proposed by the Roskill Commission for Cublington in 1970 was similarly abandoned; the third London airport now being re-considered for Stansted is, again, being opposed in the same political way.[61] John Tyme's account of the opposition to numerous motorway, urban roads and by-passes in the mid 1970s similarly bears testimony to the conflicts aroused by proposals for investment into transport infrastructure. It also calls into question the democratic bases on which decisions on such matters are made – where government sponsored projects are prepared by or for the government; advocated by the government; and where objections to the proposal are judged by the government prior to the eventual implementation of the project.[62] Indeed, in the words of David Widdicombe QC, the British public inquiry system

. . . as applied to Government sponsored projects like motorways . . . is thoroughly unsatisfactory. This is partly because the Government combines the roles of advocate for the scheme and judge of the objections to it, compounding this unfairness by appointing at inquiries persons such as ex-civil servants who do not strike the public as independent. Far more important, though, is the embargo placed at the inquiry on all discussion on the main thing everyone wants to discuss, namely whether the project should take place at all.[63]

In addition to the potential conflict between central and local government over transport issues, and the inadequacy of the present system for planning and implementing major transport infrastructure proposals, there are a number of other issues which arouse conflicts of interest, the most significant of which are energy, equity, pollution and the environment. Each is capable of separate treatment, but in reality they are closely interrelated.

Energy
The significance of fuel requirements for transport only became an issue of national importance in the industrialized countries of the western world with the oil embargo of 1973–4. This embargo immediately focused attention on the obvious fact that the cost of transport is affected by an increase in the cost of fuel – directly because of the relationship between the price of oil and the cost of transport; indirectly because increased fuel costs result in a lower rate of economic growth, which in turn reduces the demand for transport. At the

same time, the embargo ensured that governments addressed the implications for transport of the gradual reduction of oil and the inevitable price increases which will accompany increasing shortages.

Politically there are a number of ways in which government can react to the implications of a continued increase in the price of oil – at one extreme, market forces can be left to resolve the matter. At the other, the government can intervene in the supply and pricing mechanisms of the oil and transport industries. The situation, however, is not as clear cut as these two extreme positions might suggest. For a start, the issue of energy supply is complex and government intervention may not bring about the type of changes sought. Similarly, attempts to intervene too obviously in a situation where society has grown used to a cheap supply of fuel, and a way of life which centres on the ready availability of the private motor vehicle could well lead to defeat at the ballot box. Thus, governments, alert to the long-term strategic implications associated with a declining supply of oil, are nevertheless constrained as to the transport policies they should pursue in an attempt to reduce fuel consumption.

Certainly, in the West no coherent national energy policy for transport has been articulated. In the USA, the government has intervened marginally with the free-play of the market and imposed a 55 m.p.h. speed restriction on motor vehicles; it has also encouraged the motor manufacturers to produce fuel efficient cars. In the UK, the current national government is adopting a limited low key interventionist role by increasing fuel tax, but given that the demand for oil is generally insensitive to price in the short and medium term, this intervention is unlikely to have any impact on transport energy conservation. When this approach is allied to the continuing construction of the motorway programme; the concern to provide more and more car parking spaces in city centres, and the opposition to the provision of subsidy for public transport to provide a reasonable alternative to the private motor car, then the conclusion is inescapable – nationally, the UK government is largely unconcerned with reducing the energy requirements of transport.

Individual local authorities have attempted to reduce the dominance of the motor car within their area – primarily for environmental and equity reasons, although energy conservation is also quoted in support of such measures. The typical approach adopted is to subsidize public transport; to adopt policies such as park and ride, which encourage the motorist to switch to public transport before entering the more congested parts of our towns and cities; to encourage car-sharing and to increase central area parking charges. Whatever policies are pursued, the decision to pursue them is political.

Equity

In the last ten years in the UK, attention has been focused on the iniquitous elements of the transport policies which have been implemented by different governments since the Second World War. While it is undoubtedly true that for the majority of the population (the car-owning, car-using sector), the transport system has improved enormously during this period, a significant proportion of the population has 'lost' as a result of the policies implemented. The construction of interurban motorways has benefited the motorist; it has, at the same time, disrupted farm units, and destroyed part of our national heritage. The construction of urban motorways and the improvement of the urban highway system has similarly benefited the motorist, but at the cost of disrupting and breaking up communities; of ruining living and working conditions in many parts of our towns and cities. At the same time, the growth in car ownership, and the increasing opportunities to use the car as a result of the construction of new transport infrastructure, has led to an inexorable decline in the provision of public transport services. As a result, the non-car-owning members of the population are restricted in their movements – the elderly, the infirm, and the school children have not featured as significant factors in the development and implementation of transport policies in the UK.

The decisions to adopt the policies which have been implemented were, and are, distributive and political, although, until recent years, no attempt was made to make the political aspects explicit. A generous judgement would argue that the various governments of the day gave the transport needs of minority groups in our society a lesser weighting than they deserve. A more cynical judgement would argue that the political weight of the car-owning population, allied with the oil, commercial and road haulage interests inevitably lead to a road dominated transport policy.

References

1   Holmes, E. H., *Looking 25 years ahead in Highway Development in the United States*, Rees Jeffereys Triennial Lecture No. 6, RTPI, London, 12th April 1965.
2   Morlok, E. K., *Introduction to Transportation Engineering and Planning*, McGraw Hill, New York (1978).
3   See: Humphrys, G., *South Wales*, David and Charles, London (1972).
4   Cooper, J. B., 'The Information Machines', *Town and Country Planning*, Vol. 53, No. 2, February 1984, pp. 33–6.
5   See Hillman, M., Henderson, I., and Whalley, Anne, 'Transport Realities and Planning Policy', *P.E.P.* Vol. XLII No. 567, London, December 1976 for a full discussion of the transport demands of minority groups.
6   A range of statistical sources concerning demographic and socio-economic trends has been referred to which are not always directly comparable, e.g. some figures relate to Great Britain and others to the UK. Thus, any figures used must be seen only as indicating trends.
7   Central Statistical Office, *Social Trends 14*, HMSO, London (1984).
8   Office of Population Censuses and Surveys, *Population Projections 1976–2016*, HMSO, London (1978).
9   Central Statistical Office, *Social Trends 13*, HMSO, London (1983).
10 Office of Population Censuses and Surveys, *Census 1981 National Report Great Britain*, HMSO, London (1983).
11 *Social Trends 13, op. cit.*
12 *Social Trends 14, op. cit.*

13   *ibid.*
14   Office of Population Censuses and Surveys, *Census 1981 Preliminary Report for Towns: England and Wales*, H M S O, London (1981).
15   Eversley, D., 'Can planners keep up if the flight from the cities continues to accelerate?' *Paper delivered to the Annual Conference of the Royal Town Planning Institute*, May 1982, R T P I, London (1982).
16   Simmie, J., *Planning and the Decline of London*, Town Planning Discussion Paper No. 40, University College London, October 1983.
17   *Social Trends 14, op. cit.*
18   *National Personal Transportation Survey 1977*, U S Department of Commerce, Bureau of Census.
19   Hillman, M., Henderson, I. and Whalley, A., *op. cit.*
20   Department of Transport, *National Travel Survey 1975/76 Report*, H M S O, London (1979).
21   Cooper, J. B., *op. cit.*
22   See Harrison, A. J., *The Economics of Transport Appraisal*, Croom Helm, London (1974), and Glaister, S., *Fundamentals of Transport Economics*, Basil Blackwood, Oxford (1981).
23   Morlok, E. K., *op. cit.*
24   Wingo, L. and Perloff, H., 'The Washington Transportation Plan: technics or politics?', *Proceedings of the Papers of the Regional Science Association* (1961).
25   See Button, K. J., and Gillingwater, D. (eds), *Transport, Location and Spatial Policy*, Gower, Aldershot (1983).
26   Edwards, S. and Bayliss, B., *Operating Costs in Freight Transport*, Department of the Environment, London (1972).
27   Gwilliam, K. M., 'Transport Infrastructure Investments and Regional Development' in Bowers, J. K. (ed.), *Inflation, Development and Integration*, Leeds University Press (1979).
28   Brown, A. J., *Evidence to the Expenditure Committee on Regional Development Incentives*, House of Commons Paper No. 5, London (1973).
29   Rich, D. C., 'Population Potential, Potential Transportation Costs and Industrial Location', *Area*, Vol. 10 (1978) pp. 222–6.
30   Dodgson, J. S., 'Motorway Investment, Industrial Transport Costs and Sub-regional Growth: A Case Study of the M62', *Regional Studies*, Vol. 8 (1974) pp. 75–91.
31   Chymera, A., *Motorway Investment and Regional Development Policy*, unpublished; Department of Town Planning, Leeds Polytechnic (1976).
32   Thornton, P., *Roads: The Price of Development?*, Occasional Paper No. 3, School of Science and Society, University of Bradford (1978).
33   Judge, E. J., 'Regional Issues and Transport Infrastructure: Some Reflections of the Effects of the Lancashire–Yorkshire Motorway' in Button & Gillingwater (1973), *op. cit.*, pp. 57–81.
34   Botham, R., 'The Road Programme and Regional Development: The Problem of the Counterfactual' in Button & Gillingwater (1983) *op. cit.*, pp. 23–56.
35   Buchanan, C. D., *et al., Traffic in Towns*, H M S O, London (1963).
36   *ibid.*
37   Tyme, J., *Motorways Versus Democracy*, Macmillan, London (1978).
38   See special issue of *Built Environment* 'Buchanan Twenty Years After', Vol. 9, No. 2 (1983).
39   Buchanan, C. D., 'Traffic in Towns: an Assessment Twenty Years After', *Built Environment*, Vol. 9, No. 2, pp. 93–8.
40   Bruton, M. J., 'The Traffic in Towns Philosophy: Current Relevance', *Built Environment*, Vol. 9, No. 2, pp. 99–103.
41   Roskill, Lord Justice, *Report of Commission of Inquiry into the Third London Airport*,

HMSO, London (1971).

42　Buchanan, C. D., 'Note of Dissent', *Roskill Report, op. cit.*

43　*ibid.*

44　Buchanan, C. D., *No Way to the Airport*, Longman, Harlow (1981).

45　Marplan, *Survey of Public Opinion on the Lorry*, Marplan, London (1980).

46　Armitage, A., *Report of the Inquiry into Lorries, People and the Environment*, HMSO, London (1980).

47　Haigh, N. and Hand, C., *Assessment of Society's Transport Needs: Goods Transport*, Paper delivered to the Ninth International Symposium on Theory and Practice in Transport Economics, Madrid, 2–4 November 1982.

48　Buchanan, C. D., *op. cit.* (1963).

49　*Social Trends 14, op. cit.*

50　Haigh and Hand, *op. cit.*

51　Wilson, Sir Alan, *Final Report of the Committee on the Problem of Noise*, Cmnd. 2056, HMSO, London (1963).

52　*ibid.*

53　Griffiths, I. D. and Langdon, F. J., 'Subjective Response to Road Traffic Noise', *Journal of Sound and Vibration*, 8(1), pp. 16–32 (1968).

54　Langdon, F. J., 'Noise Nuisance Caused by Road Traffic in Residential Areas: Part 2', *Journal of Sound and Vibration*, 47(2), pp. 243–63 (1976).

55　Department of the Environment, *Calculation of Road Traffic Noise*, HMSO, London (1975).

56　Ashby, Sir Eric, *Report of the Royal Commission on Environmental Pollution*, HMSO, London (1971).

57　Lassiere, A., *The Environmental Evaluation of Transport Plans*, Department of the Environment, HMSO, London (1976).

58　See Wistrich, E., *The Politics of Transport*, Longman, London (1983).

59　See Altshuler, A., *et al., The Urban Transportation System, Politics and Policy Innovation*, MIT Press, Cambridge, Mass. (1978).

60　Rose, R., *Politics in England Today*, Faber and Faber, London (1974).

61　See Cook, Olive, *The Stansted Affair: A Case for the People*, Pan Books, London (1967) and Buchanan, C. D., *No Way to the Airport*, Longman, Harlow (1981).

62　Tyme, J., *Motorways Versus Democracy*, Macmillan, London (1978).

63　*ibid.*, p. vii.

2 An introduction to travel demand forecasting and transportation planning

The land-use/transportation planning process

At first sight the purpose and content of transport planning appear obvious. The problems and difficulties associated with moving about within the towns and cities of the industrialized world are readily apparent and publicized and feature daily in the lives of urban dwellers. Although these problems are not new, they have taken on more dominating dimensions with the growth of urban populations and the rapid increase in motor vehicle ownership and usage, and the transport planning process has been developed in an attempt to alleviate these problems, while at the same time utilizing the full range of transport modes available for movement. The aim of this process until comparatively recently has been purely traffic functional. That is, it has aimed both to ameliorate those obvious inefficiencies of the current transport systems such as congestion, delay and accidents and to produce proposals for capital investment and construction in existing and new transport facilities, which will improve the operating conditions of the estimated future movement flows where they are expected to overload most seriously the existing transport networks. Because it is quite clearly seen to be an attempt to correct visible and foreseeable ills, this approach is attractive both to the political decision-makers, and to those members of the public not directly affected by the proposals put forward.

More recently, however, transport and land-use planners have come to realize the potential of transport to shape the urban environment by influencing the accessibility of locations within the urban area. Although progress in this direction has been slow, transport planners are gradually moving from the position where a consideration of land use is incorporated in the transport planning process merely as an input control in the preparation of estimates of future travel needs. Now to shape and change urban structure, attempts are being made to utilize the long-term influence of accessibility and changes in accessibility brought about by the implementation of transport proposals. This has led to the development of 'new' approaches to the transportation planning process in an attempt to improve on the traffic functional approach adopted in the first round of major studies, e.g. the systems approach; the 'cyclic' approach. Yet it is essential that this dual function of transportation planning be recognized and implemented if the efforts of planners are to be successful in creating an environment which is an efficient, attractive and pleasant place in which to live and work. It is important that the traffic functional problems, which are primarily short- or mid-term problems, be dealt with as an integral part of the transport planning process. Equally it is essential that the long-term influence of transport and accessibility on shaping and changing the structure of urban areas, be considered as an integral element of transport and land-use planning.

The basis of transportation planning process
The urban transportation planning process is based on a range of assumptions and principles the most basic of which are that:

1   Travel patterns are tangible, stable and predictable.
2   Movement demands are directly related to the distribution, and intensity of land uses, which are capable of being accurately determined for some future date.

In addition to these fundamental assumptions, it has been found necessary in the light of experience to assume that:

1   Decisive relationships exist between all modes of transport and that the future role of a particular mode cannot be determined without giving consideration to all other modes.
2   The transportation system influences the development of an area, as well as serving that area.
3   Areas of continuous urbanization require a region-wide consideration of the transport situation.
4   The transportation study is an integral part of the overall planning process, and cannot adequately be considered in isolation.
5   The planning process is continuous, and requires constant up-dating, validating and amendment.

Given these principles and assumptions it is evident that if transportation planning is to be effective it must be comprehensive and co-ordinated with other aspects of the overall planning process. It must therefore reflect the views of all the specialists involved in planning – the engineer, the traffic and transportation specialists, the town planner, and the economist – as well as meeting the requirements of the population at large. To achieve this, teamwork of the highest order is required.

Early developments in North America
Prior to the early 1950s problems of movement were seen largely in terms of road traffic, and the accepted method of assessing the future demand of movement by road was to examine or count the then existing flows, and extrapolate these to some future date by applying an appropriate growth factor.

In 1953 a major breakthrough was achieved with the work of Robert Mitchell and Chester Rapkin of the University of Pennsylvania.[1] Following an analysis of movement and land-use data for Philadelphia, they expounded the thesis that different types of land use generate different and variable traffic flows. This approach brought about fundamental changes in the study and understanding of movement. It shifted the emphasis from the study of road traffic flows to the study of the land uses that give rise to the flows. It underlined the basic dictum that movement desires can be manipulated by controlling the land uses that represented the origins and destinations of journeys. The approach was successfully applied in the Detroit Area Traffic Study (1953), the Chicago Area Transportation Study (1956), the Penn–Jersey Transportation Study and the Tri-State New York Metropolitan Transportation Study, and now dominates the large urban transportation studies supported by the US Bureau of Public Roads. Indeed, to qualify for financial assistance in road construction, the 213 urban areas of over 50,000 population in the USA must, under the Federal Aid Highway Act 1962, carry out a continuing, comprehensive land-use/transportation study.

The objectives adopted by these studies were however largely traffic functional; they aimed only to ameliorate the various elements of the transport problem such as congestion, delay, poor accessibility and accidents, by producing proposals for capital investment in new transport facilities, or in supporting existing transport services such as public transport. Indeed the prime objective of the Chicago Area Transportation Study is typical of many of the early studies and emphasizes how much attention was focused on the traffic functional elements of the problem, viz. '. . . what then is the dominant objective of a transport facilities plan? It is to reduce travel frictions by the construction of new facilities so that people and vehicles . . . can move about within the area as rapidly as possible, in a manner consistent with limitations of cost and safety'.[2]

During the 1960s this 'traffic functional' planning process was gradually modified to incorporate a consideration of alternative future land uses, and Figure 7 illustrates the approach generally adopted since that time. Although this approach indicates that the process is a continuous and co-operative planning process incorporating both transport and land-use planning, in actual fact practitioners generally held the view that 'urban transportation planning is designed to develop and continuously evaluate short- and long-range highway and transportation plans'.[3]

Early developments in Great Britain
In Great Britain the development and application of the transport planning process received its first major impetus in the late 1950s, when the Ministry of Transport encouraged the local authorities in the major conurbations to co-operate in producing long-term highway plans for their areas. The objectives

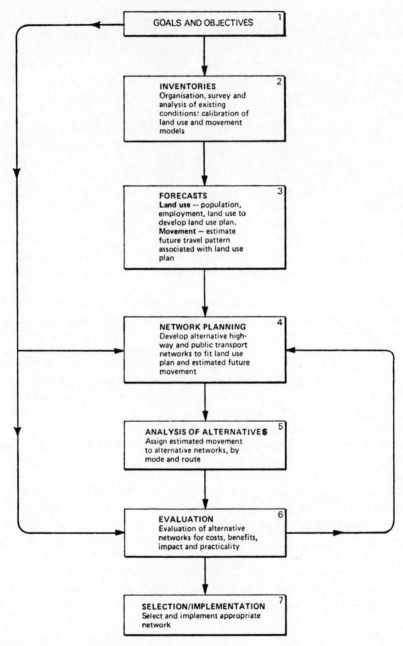

Figure 7   *The traffic functional transportation planning process*

Source: Bureau of Public Roads, *General Information and Introduction to System 360*

adopted for studies such as the *London Traffic Survey* (1960) and the *SELNEC Highway Plan* (1962) were limited and purely traffic functional. For example the objectives of the London Traffic Survey were basically:

1 To survey the origins and destinations of traffic movement within an area extending beyond the boundaries of the then London County Council.
2 To survey journey times.
3 To develop a method to estimate the amount of traffic on a road network.
4 To indicate areas where travel capacity was limited and travel conditions poor.
5 To present the results in a form suitable for the preparation of a comprehensive road plan for the County of London.[4]

Although these objectives were limited, the significance of developments in transport planning in the United States was realized in the early stages of the studies. Gradually amended objectives were incorporated which required land-use and public transport analyses to be carried out as part of the process. Following the publication in 1963 of the *Traffic in Towns Report*[5] which established the need for comprehensive movement studies involving land-use analysis, the then Ministries of Transport and Housing and Local Government issued a joint circular in 1964 advocating the use of land-use transportation studies to achieve a co-ordinated approach to land-use and transport planning.[6]

In April 1964 the first of these land-use/transport studies (the West Midlands Transportation Study) was commissioned, and was followed in later years by the studies for Greater Glasgow (1964), Teesside (1965), Belfast (1965), SELNEC (1965), Merseyside (1966), West Yorkshire (1967), Tyneside (1967), and many other studies for smaller urban areas such as Worcester, Colchester, and Brighton and Hove. The objectives generally adopted for these studies were again traffic functional, although the interaction between land use and movement was seen to be an integral element in the process. The objectives for the West Midlands Transportation Study and the Belfast study are perhaps typical of this type of study and illustrate quite emphatically that their aims were to produce solutions to the traffic functional elements of the transport problem, viz,

1 *West Midlands* 'to undertake a comprehensive survey of all forms of transport in the West Midlands conurbation, and to analyse its relationship to types of land use and all other factors affecting the demand for and movement of transport; and to make forward projections with the aim of providing guidance on the desirable pattern of road development and public transport facilities'.[7]
2 *Belfast* 'to carry out a transportation study which would lead to the preparation of a long-term transportation plan for the improvement of communications in Belfast, i.e. a plan to provide for the efficient movement of persons and goods by all forms of transport.'[8]

Criticisms of the transportation planning process

The transport planning process, as it has been applied in North America and Great Britain, has been criticized on both operational and conceptual grounds. At the operational level it is said to be too concerned with the technical problems associated with traffic estimation and network planning, and too little concerned with the transport needs of the community at large. In the eyes of many politicians and the public generally it has led to proposals favouring the motor vehicle and ignoring the possibilities of public transport, while the level of public involvement has been woefully inadequate. At a technical level the process is criticized for considering too few (if any) alternative plans and policies; for inadequately defining goals and objectives and basing the evaluation of alternative proposals solely on economic grounds.

Although the operational deficiencies of the traffic functional transport planning process are serious enough, fundamental conceptual deficiencies arise as a result of the extremely narrow viewpoint adopted by most practitioners.

Despite the requirements both in Britain[9] and the United States[10] that the transport planning process should be comprehensive and incorporate on an integrated area-wide basis the considerations of economic and population factors, land use, social and community values and the role of different transport modes, what generally tends to emerge is a highway plan designed to fit one particular land-use plan. A comprehensive approach tends to be interpreted as full coverage of the technical aspects of the planning process in relation to highway networks, with lip-service being paid to the needs and values of the community, while public transport demand becomes a residual after motor vehicle trips have been estimated. This attitude has resulted in the development of a comparatively sophisticated methodology to estimate future traffic flows and derive alternative networks. At the same time it has led to the production of proposals which threaten jobs and houses and are totally unacceptable to the public.

A panel of experts brought together in Paris by the OECD in 1971 to consider the strengths and weaknesses of transport planning emphasized that the narrow conceptual approach adopted on the part of practising transport planners was perhaps the greatest weakness in the process. They found that investment in transport proposals derived from land-use transport plans tends to be evaluated against six main traffic functional criteria.

1   The satisfaction of observed demand.
2   The reduction or elimination of bottle-necks in the existing network(s).
3   Enhanced efficiency in the existing or proposed network(s).
4   Net user benefits.
5   Capital costs involved in the construction of the network(s).
6   The economic return on investment.

They argued that although this:

allows for the satisfaction of internal, system specific demands, it ignores the wider external effects of transport. Yet transportation is only a part of a larger urban or regional complex and every change within the transport system reverberates throughout the larger complex, producing multiple impacts that reach out beyond the confines of the transportation system.[11]

This comment highlights what is perhaps the most significant criticism which can be levelled at transport planners – the failure to recognize and utilize transport planning as one of the most important tools for guiding and shaping the development of the urban environment. Rather than take the opportunity of designing a framework of interaction for urban communities, urban transport planning has been seen and applied as an engineering exercise to design a physical transport system. Indeed Wingo and Perloff state quite categorically that 'the choice of a transportation system is the core developmental decision that the metropolitan region can make . . .'[12] and it is surprising that, with notable exceptions, planners have made little attempt to use this tool to shape the physical urban environment.

Perhaps the root of the problem lies in the definition generally implied or adopted for a transportation system. For example, the definition of a transport system adopted by the Washington transportation plan is typical, 'a set of facilities for the movement of goods and people, including highways, parking facilities and public transit'.[13] The definition may be acceptable as a definition of a physical system, but the transport system of any urban area is something more than a physical system. Its performance can have far-reaching consequences for all individuals, businesses and other bodies relying on it. These consequences can be both long- and short-term. In the short-term they influence the origin and destination, the time, the mode and route, of all trips made. In the long-term they can result in a change of location of activities in order to adjust to the transport system. In the transport studies completed to date, changes in the location of activities (and ultimately land uses) in response to the implementation of transport system proposals are not considered as part of the process. The reasons for this are:

1 The physical transport system is designed to 'fit' a predetermined land-use plan
2 It is argued that little can be done in twenty years (the normal target period for transport studies) to change current trends and commitments in the distribution of activities.

This state of affairs leads to the anomalous situation of recommending long-term proposals based on an analysis of the short-run transport behaviour of the users of the system, and inevitably policy is implemented on a project by project basis.

Such an approach, although often self-correcting, is wasteful. Specific problems may be rectified as they arise, but the long-term consequences for the locational behaviour of businesses, individuals, and hence the structure of urban areas, are haphazard and unpredictable.

Arising from this narrow outlook other 'lower-level' conceptual defi-ciencies can be identified. For many years the complex nature of the transport planning process and the difficulties involved in applying the methodology were underestimated. This tended to lead to the operational deficiencies already identified, and the production of over-simple plans and proposals. For example, plans were produced for an 'end-state' situation some twenty years in the future, with no real attempt to assess how the area was likely to evolve during the plan period or after the target date was reached. At the same time, the narrow conceptual basis led practitioners to think of plans and proposals in terms of a physical plan form – social and economic activities were seen in terms of physical land-use systems, while the transport systems were seen solely in physical terms as, for example, highway networks and public transport systems. Although this makes it relatively easy for alter-native proposals to maintain a consistent approach, it can be argued that a reliance on the physical plan form inhibits a full exploration of a wide range of policies that one might expect in a set of alternative plans.

New approaches to the transportation planning process

In an attempt to offset the many deficiencies associated with the traditional traffic functional approach to transport planning, a variety of alternative approaches have been put forward. The most significant of these new approaches are the systems approach, and the cyclic approach.

The systems approach towards urban planning evolved from the work of engineers and planners involved in the early transportation studies, such as the Chicago and Detroit studies, and from the work of Mitchell and Rapkin.[14] In the view of these men, the city was seen as a set of interconnected parts – a system of component parts (land uses) connected by different forms of communication, especially road traffic. As we have seen, a series of trans-portation plans was produced based on the view that if the land-use pattern of a town or city could be defined for some future date, then the associated traffic pattern could also be determined and a suitable transport system designed to fit it.

In the early 1960s objections were raised to this view. People like Wingo and Perloff argued that the city should be seen as a system which evolves, where land uses and traffic flows are interdependent. Thus, they contend, it is not realistic to define land-use distribution for some period of time twenty years into the future and derive a traffic pattern for it, for this approach fails to recognize that traffic flows alter in response to changing land-use patterns and vice versa.

In an attempt to overcome the preoccupation with physical form, Wingo and Perloff claimed that a transport system should be seen as 'a set of faci-lities and institutions organized to distribute a quality of access selectively in an urban area'[15] that the 'locational behaviour of businesses and individuals is affected by the implementation of transport proposals', and that 'these induced locational changes affect the performance of the transport system in the long run'. Indeed they are of the opinion that 'the accumulation of these consequences is in fact the shape and structure of the metropolitan region a generation or more hence'.[16]

In an attempt to utilize the systems approach and to encourage the use of transport as a 'structure-forming' tool, Wingo and Perloff argue that:

1 Transport facilities fulfil a 'market role' in determining the amount of land that is available for development at different levels of accessibility.

2 A transport system should not be chosen exclusively on its ability to meet travel demand, as the side-effects from this sort of choice may be so over-whelmingly negative in the field of public services, that the short-term benefits on which the choice was based are cancelled out. At the same time the locational consequences of business and individuals may accumulate in such a way as to impair the performance of the transport system as a whole.

3 The design of a transport system should be achieved by a process of suc-cessively constrained choices. The first constrained choice – the setting of long-run developmental objectives for the region – being the most critical, and concerned with policies to influence the productivity of the region, the form and organization of the region and consumer satis-faction relating to living and working conditions.

Figure 8 taken from Bieber[17] illustrates the systems approach in abstract. Wingo and Perloff indicate that this approach can be made operational in the transport planning field by applying the following sequence of constrained choices.

1 Specify the long-run developmental objectives for the region, e.g. make town X the regional capital, with a strong central area and avoid low-density peripheral areas.

2 Identify the location and investment decisions which cumulatively move in the direction of the first level objectives, e.g. to achieve long-run development objectives housing investment would have to be diverted from peripheral areas into the existing built-up area.

3 Specify the levels of accessibility needed to induce the locational and investment changes required to achieve the long-run developmental objectives, e.g. ensure poor accessibility to the peripheral areas, and good accessibility within the built-up area.

4 Designate the levels of service implied by the accessibility conditions, e.g. high-speed public transport within the built-up area, with low-speed motor vehicle access on dual-purpose streets from peripheral areas.

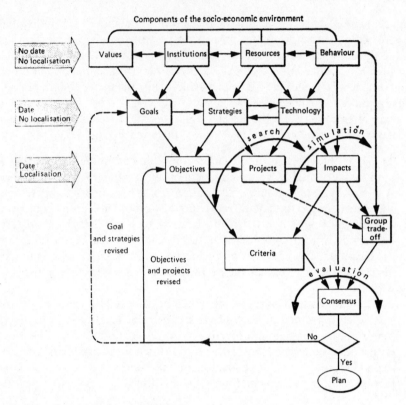

Figure 8   *The systems approach*

Source: Bieber, A., 'Transportation planning and systems analysis', in *Urban Transport Planning Process*, OECD, Paris (1971)

It can be seen that this approach is characterized by the desire to identify and define the objectives of the overall urban system, including the transport system. At the same time a rational evaluation and decision-making procedure is essential to assist the assessment of whether the original objectives are met. This procedure is based on the use of criteria and standards which are related to the original objectives.

Figure 9, which extends the Bureau of Public Roads flow chart for the traditional transport planning process, illustrates how this approach might be implemented.

The advantages associated with the use of the systems approach are that it allows the implementation of transport proposals to be used positively as a determinant of urban form. It can be applied to assess the impact of transport proposals on both the short-term movement habits and the long-term locational behaviour of firms and individuals. At the same time it enables modifications to be made to the preferred urban structure in the light of the impact

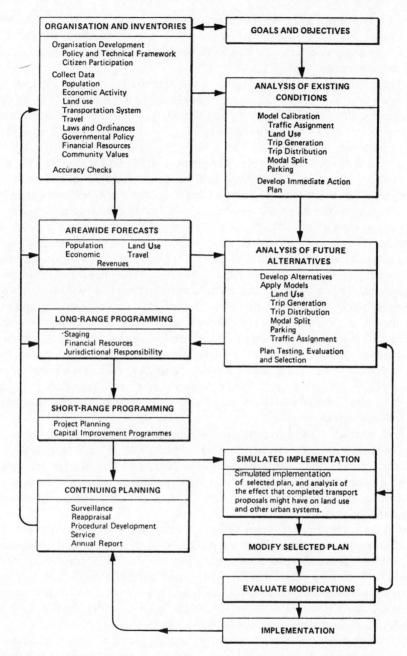

Figure 9 *Transportation planning process incorporating the systems approach*

of the implementation of transport proposals. In short, it distinguishes between 'urban transport planning as an engineering exercise, on the one hand, and as the design of a framework for the interaction for a viable urban community on the other'.[18]

There are two major drawbacks to the approach. It is very difficult to develop true alternative structures and policies if the starting point of the exercise is one set of common objectives, while the complex interrelationships involved in its application could well be self-defeating unless handled by experienced professionals.

The cyclic approach put forward by Boyce, Day and McDonald[19] is concerned primarily with the development of true alternative sets of plans or policies. They argue that a revision is required of the traditional and basically linear progression from a common set of objectives to alternative sets of plans and policies to evaluation and selection. In substitution they propose that a cyclic planning process be adopted, with each cycle commencing with the formulation (or re-formulation) of design criteria, standards and proposed policies for each alternative to be tested. At the end of each cycle conclusions are drawn and decisions made in order to determine which aspects of the alternatives should be considered further and only in exceptional circumstances is an alternative carried forward intact from one cycle to the next. Figure 10 illustrates the broad procedure, and at least three to four cycles are required to produce an effective final plan. As the cycles advance, so the plan-production and evaluation methodologies should develop. For example, in the early cycles broad tentative patterns of development are suitable with some *ad hoc* elaboration, while later cycles utilize allocation and simulation models.

The alternative plans considered should not be restricted to comprehensive, physical, end-state, twenty-year plans. Rather the whole range of alternatives should be explored, including 'both near and far time horizons, metropolitan and sub-metropolitan configurations, comprehensive and individual facility-service system schemes, as well as divergent assumption and staging'.[20]

Land use and transportation alternatives should be explored at the metropolitan scale only if there are proposals for major shifts in the relative location of population and employment groups, or if over a long-term period (thirty-five to fifty years) there is a large increment of growth. This type of alternative should be prepared in a broad, generalized way. Other, more detailed alternatives need to be produced for the specific facility-service systems and for representative sub-metropolitan areas.

This approach has the advantage of ensuring that different goals and objectives can be derived for each alternative (in contrast to the traditional and systems approaches which rely on the formulation of one set of common goals). This in turn makes it easier to develop plans and policies which are true alternatives. The problems associated with operationalizing this

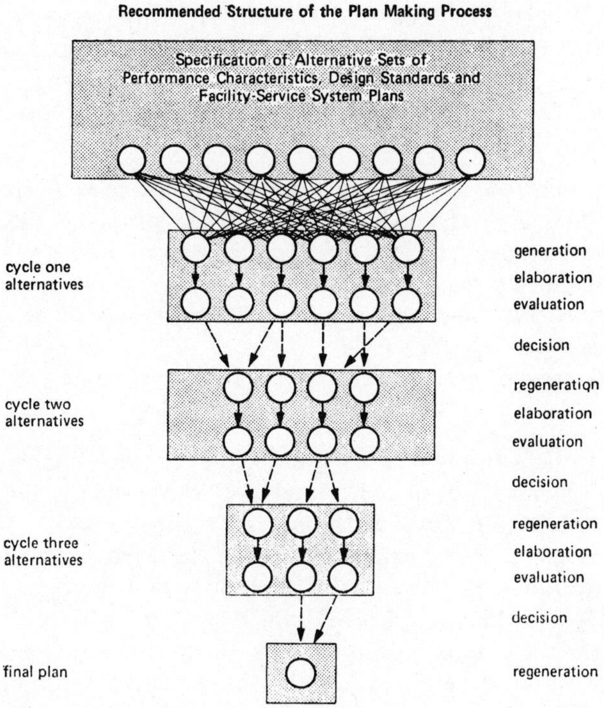

Recommended Structure of the Plan Making Process

Figure 10   *The cyclic approach to plan making*

Source: Boyce, Day and McDonald, *Metropolitan Plan Making* (1970)

approach are severe, although it would seem that the systems approach could be incorporated as part of this cyclic approach.

In spite of the fact that there have been these varied conceptual approaches adopted in applying the land-use/transport planning process in different countries over the past twenty years, a study of the work done shows that basically similar techniques have been applied to develop alternative land-use plans, to estimate the future pattern of movements associated with the land-use plans, and develop and evaluate alternative network proposals.

Land-use and transportation planning as part of planning in the public sector

Land use and transportation planning form part of a wider and continuous process of planning (generally referred to as strategic planning) which is undertaken in the public sector. The extent to which this wider planning process is undertaken varies from country to country and with political ideology. Similarly, the detailed operation of this strategic approach to planning also varies from country to country. However, the principles underlying the process and the general framework within which it is operationalized have been clearly established.[21]

In outline, the principles underlying this strategic approach to public sector planning include the following.

1   Establishment of the socio-economic change the government of the day wishes to achieve, and acting purposefully to achieve that change
2   Recognition that strategic policy decisions are interconnected and cannot be treated in isolation
3   Acceptance that uncertainty is an essential element of all decisions about the future
4   Co-ordination of decisions and actions of different agencies with related objectives

The framework within which these principles are operationalized ideally consists of a hierarchy of planning levels with each level forming a strategic function for the level below it and, conversely, being constrained by the level above. This hierarchical arrangement of choice and policy formulation allows the relationships between policy options to be worked out at each level separately, but within a framework which provides an explicit means for handling the vertical relationships between them. In this way, at one level, a comprehensive but generalized overview of the issues and policies can be maintained and developed into more specific and detailed policies at other lower levels to offer guidance to the agencies concerned with implementation. Figure 11 illustrates this general hierarchical relationship.

The adoption of a hierarchical structure to attempt to cope with complex interrelated problems is an essential feature of this framework, for the reason that such structures are more robust in adapting to change. At the same time, they require the transmission of less information among their parts than other systems. Indeed, Simon, in writing on decision making and the design of business organizations argues that large and complex organizations will inevitably evolve towards a hierarchical structure for these reasons.[22]

This general hierarchical framework has been amplified by Chapin and Kaiser with particular reference to land-use planning.[23] Their framework develops a five-stage policy and plan formulation process and incorporates both spatial design (plans) and programmes for action leading to implementation. Figure 12 illustrates this structure. From the diagram, it is clear that there is interaction between (a) the different levels of planning, and (b) the plans and programmes. There is also interaction between the plans and programmes and the community at large through the political decision-making processes which, in conjunction with the activities of planning, determine the plans, policies and programmes to be adopted. This interaction occurs at all five levels of the land-use planning framework illustrated here.

Within the general hierarchy of land-use planning levels identified by

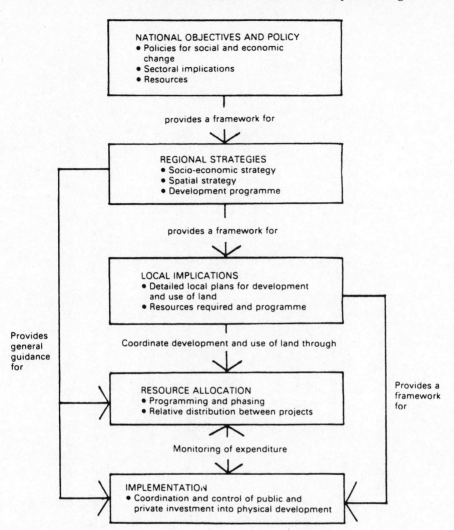

Figure 11 *An idealized framework for strategic planning and implementation in the public sector*

Source: Bruton, M. J. and Nicholson, D. J. 'Strategic Land Use Planning,' *Town Planning Review*, Vol. 56, No. 1 (January 1985). Reproduced with the permission of the author.

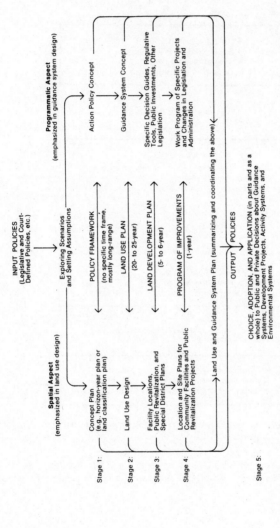

Figure 12   *Five-stage policy/plan formulation along parallel spatial and programmatic tracks. Each stage features both spatial aspects (left side) and programmatic aspects (right side); earlier stages emphasize the former, and later stages, the latter*

Source: Chapin, F. S. and Kaiser, E. J., *Urban Land Use Planning*, third edition, University of Illinois Press, Urbana (1979) p. 90. Reproduced with the permission of the publisher

Chapin and Kaiser, there is also a parallel hierarchy of transport levels. At the top of the land-use hierarchy is the *concept plan* which provides a policy framework for socio-economic and physical change for the region (or country) under study. The contribution of transportation planning at this level is restricted to the provision of estimates of future travel demand by major corridors of movement.

At stage two in the land-use hierarchy, the *land use plan*, the process is concerned to produce long-range strategies for (a) the region as a whole, and (b) the urban areas within that region. At the regional level, policies and proposals are produced to shape the broad pattern of urbanization and the impact this might have on the environment. As part of the output from this level, policy constraints are established for the constituent urban areas in the form of target populations; the types and levels of employment to be provided; the location and programming of the introduction of basic infrastructure such as water and sewerage. The transportation contribution to this stage of the process derives estimates of future travel demand on major transport routes. This is achieved through the application of simplified travel demand models used in conjunction with land-use allocation models.

At the urban strategy level, alternative development concepts are analysed to establish the respective transport and servicing implications. Comprehensive forecasts for population and employment are produced on a zonal basis and major land-use areas are defined using generalized land-use zones. It is at this stage that estimates of future travel demand are derived using comprehensive transport models in conjunction with land-use allocation models. In addition, route location studies are undertaken.

The output from this stage of the process takes the form of (a) a general plan for the desired spatial distribution of population, employment, shopping, recreational and social welfare facilities, and (b) a plan for road and public transport construction and improvement, which can be used as a basis for making decisions on future investment into physical transport infrastructure. It is at the regional and urban strategy levels that the transportation planning process outlined later is central to the planning process. With the more detailed land development plans and programmes of improvement, the contribution made by transportation planning is less significant. At the *land and development stage*, detailed local plans are produced which vary in form and content with the problem(s) being studied. In terms of forecasting travel demand, information derived from the previous urban or regional strategy stage is usually supplemented by detailed traffic and travel analysis. The type of supplementary information collected is again dependent on the problem under review, and can include, for example, vehicle turning movements at major junctions, pedestrian flows and car parking. Preliminary design studies for new and improved facilities are also undertaken at these stages as a basis for preparing programmes for implementation.

Travel demand forecasting and the transportation planning process

Proposals resulting from the transportation planning process can take many different forms. Road improvements or traffic management schemes could result from a limited transportation study. Rail improvements, such as the electrification of the Euston–Manchester line and the reconstruction of Euston Station, could result from another form of transportation study, while new roads, such as the M1, could result from yet another form of transportation study. Such limited studies usually involve the consideration of only one mode of travel. Urban transport studies, on the other hand, involve the consideration of several modes of travel, and their interaction one with another, and are consequently much more complex. Traditionally these different types of transportation study, although they are designed to meet different objectives, have the same basic framework. Each one involves the following.

1   A survey and analysis stage which establishes the present demand for movement and how this is met, and the relationships between this demand for movement and the urban environment.
2   A prediction and plan formulation stage, which projects for some future date the likely travel demand – based on the data collected and the relationship established in the survey and analysis stage – and puts forward proposals to meet this demand.
3   An evaluation stage which attempts to assess whether the transportation proposals put forward satisfy the projected demand for travel with adequate safety, capacity and levels of service, and provide the maximum benefits to the community for minimum costs.

These three stages are an essential part of any transportation planning process. However, the urban transportation planning process, because of its complexity, is the most comprehensive example of the procedures and techniques involved. Consequently, to obtain as complete a picture as possible of the transportation planning process, it is essential that the urban transportation study be outlined in full. The more limited studies, with limited objectives, generally tend to consist of part of the overall urban process.

The principal stages in the urban transportation planning process can be identified as

1   The explicit formulation of goals and objectives.
2   The collection of land-use, population, economic and travel pattern data for the present-day situation.
3   The establishment of quantifiable relationships between present-day movements and the land-use, population, and economic factors.
4   The prediction of land-use, population and economic factors to the target date for the study, and the development of a land-use plan(s).
5   The prediction of the origins, destinations and distribution of the future

movement demands, using the relationships established for the present-day situation, and the predicted land-use population and economic factors (trip generation and trip distribution).

6 The prediction of the person movements likely to be carried by the different modes of travel at the target date (modal split).

7 The development of alternative highway and public transport networks to fit the predicted land-use plan and accommodate the estimated pattern of movements.

8 The assignment of predicted trips to alternative co-ordinated transport networks/systems (traffic assignment).

9 The evaluation of the efficiency and economic viability of the alternative transport networks in terms of both economic and social costs and benefits.

10 The selection and implementation of the most appropriate transport networks.

Although the individual steps in the transportation planning process can be readily identified and isolated in this manner, the relationship and interaction between them is vitally important '. . . for they are inter-dependent and individually almost meaningless'.[24]

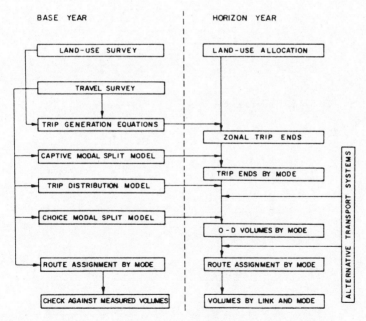

Figure 13 *Sequence of activities involved in transport analysis*

Source: Hutchinson, B. G., *Principles of Urban Transport Systems Planning*, McGraw Hill, London (1974) p. 20

Trip generation, trip distribution, modal split and traffic assignment form the core of this process, and collectively are referred to as the travel demand forecasting stages. Figure 13 illustrates the interrelationships between these activities for both the base and target years. In essence, the travel demand models are calibrated to the base year (the year in which the land-use and travel data is collected) and then used to predict the travel demands arising from a preferred land-use allocation for the target date of the study.

Figure 14 sets out, in greater detail, the interrelationships between the various activities undertaken as part of the travel demand forecasting process for the target year. This particular version of the process incorporates a 'choice' modal split analysis phase. In those medium- and small-sized urban areas with limited public transport systems, the use of a 'choice' modal split analysis would not be warranted as the bulk of public transport users would be 'captive'.

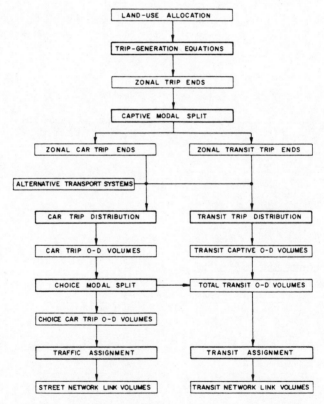

Figure 14   *Travel demand forecasting activities for horizon year*

Source: Hutchinson, B. G., *Principles of Urban Transport Systems Planning*, McGraw Hill, London (1974) p. 23

The formulation of goals and objectives

In any systematic planning process the formulation of explicit goals and objectives is essential, as the objectives become the criteria against which the alternative plan proposals are evaluated. Once formulated many decisions will follow naturally from them, and without a clear idea of goals and objectives the choice of courses of action to follow become indeterminate. Indeed Branch puts the argument for goal formulation most succinctly: 'Since the purpose of planning is to provide a rational direction of activities toward established goals, a plan cannot be drawn without objectives.'[25]

The type of goals adopted in traffic functional transport planning tend to reflect the traffic functional characteristics of the 'transport problem'. Thus goals relating to safety (reduction of accidents), the saving of travel time, the reduction of operating costs, the increase of efficiency and mobility tend to dominate, while the basic aim of this type of study is generally 'to test the forward route capacity of an area and to propose new urban routes with a view to reserving feasible alignments'.[26]

Collection of basic data

Before land-use, population, economic and travel pattern data can be collected it is necessary to define the area for which the transportation study is to be carried out. Basically the study attempts to develop a pattern of travel relating to a typical weekday which is repetitive, and varies little from weekday to weekday. The boundary usually chosen to define the area of study approximates to the 'commuter-shed' associated with the urban centre, and is referred to as the external cordon.

For the purpose of grouping the origins and destinations of movements the areas within and beyond the external cordon are divided into zones known as traffic zones. Data relating to the present-day patterns of movement is collected as part of a home-interview study or at roadside interviews carried out on the external cordon.

The home-interview study is carried out solely within the area bounded by the external cordon, and consists of a sample survey of movements associated with the home, and commercial vehicle operating deports. Questions are asked about all the previous day's movement concerning the origin, destination, purpose and method of completing the journey.

The roadside interviews carried out at the external cordon are designed to collect data about movements originating outside the area of study, but which pass through the area of study or have a destination within the external cordon. Questions are asked about the origin, destination and purpose of the journey, and the mode of transport is noted by the interviewer.

Land-use, population and economic data relating to the present-day situation is collected for each zone of the survey, within the external cordon, and should provide zonal estimates of the total population, the employed population, the number of dwelling units, the number of motor vehicles, median household income, the number of jobs available, the volume of retail sales, school attendance and the area of land given over to different uses.

In addition to the planning and movement data, an inventory of the existing transport facilities must be carried out. This should include parking surveys, travel time surveys, and highway capacity and volume studies.

Establishment of quantifiable relationships between movement and land use

Relationships between land-use and movement data for the present-day situation are established and quantified by using statistical and mathematical techniques. For example, multiple linear regression analysis can be used to establish the relationship between the number of person or vehicular movements produced by a defined traffic zone and the characteristics of that zone such as total population, population density, and income. For the same zone the number of trips attracted to that zone can be estimated by the same technique, but this time relating the movements to such factors as the number of jobs available, the volume of retail sales, and school attendance, within the zone. This stage of the process is generally referred to as trip generation. Similarly the present-day pattern of movements, that is the distribution of movements within and beyond the area under study, can be reproduced by applying mathematical models such as the 'gravity model' while the actual routes taken by present-day movements can be reproduced by using traffic assignment models such as the 'all-or-nothing' or 'capacity-restraint' assignment procedures. The trip generation and trip distribution relationships thus established are used to forecast the future origins, destinations and distribution of movements associated with the developed land-use forecasts, while the assignment relationships are used to evaluate alternative network proposals.

Prediction of future land-use, population and economic characteristics, and preparation of land-use plan

Demands for movement are related to activities pursued by people and these activities are reflected in the distribution and characteristics of a range of different land uses. By using the relationships established between land use and movement for the present-day situation, and applying them to future estimates of land-use distribution and characteristics, it is possible to derive estimates of the future pattern of movements associated with a particular set of land-use proposals. Thus the development of estimates of the future land-use characteristics and distribution, and the preparation of a land-use plan are fundamental aspects of the transport planning process. Indeed, it is essential to have estimates, on a zonal basis and for some future date, of population, economic activity, vehicle ownership and land-use characteristics. In the United States, where there is little history of strong regulatory planning powers, the forecasting of future land-use distribution and characteristics has for some time been based on the use of land-use distribution models, such as the Garin-Lowry residential allocation model. In the absence of land-use controls, these models attempt to estimate the effect on urban areas of incremental growth resulting from the actions of individuals and corporate bodies intent on maximizing their own benefits.

In Britain, however, with its long history of comparatively strong land-use controls, the approach to the forecasting of future land-use distribution and characteristics has been somewhat different. Indeed, with notable exceptions, such as the Teesside study, it could be argued that in Britain no real attempt has been made to forecast, on a systematic and comprehensive basis, estimates of the future land-use characteristics and distribution. Rather, *ad hoc* estimates of land-use distribution tend to be produced, based on generalized and rather crude predictions of population and employment.

The end product of the land-use forecasting stage of the process, in both Britain and the United States, tends to be similar – one land-use plan or set of land-use estimates, relating to a date some twenty years in the future.

Prediction of future origins, destinations and distribution of person movements

This part of the procedure can be subdivided into two stages – a trip generation stage, and a trip distribution stage.

Trip generation can be defined as the determination of the number of trips associated with a traffic zone, area of land, or other unit of generation, and consists of trips produced by, and attracted to, the generation unit. These are referred to as trip productions and trip attractions.

Trip distribution is the allocation of a given number of trips between each pair of traffic zones, or unit of generation, in the study area.

To predict the number of trip productions and attractions associated with each traffic zone in the study area, it is necessary to utilize the mathematical relationships established between land use and patterns of movement for present-day conditions. On the assumption that these relationships will not alter materially in the future, the predicted land-use, population and economic data (e.g. population, numbers in employment) are substituted in the formula, and the equation is solved to derive the predicted trip productions and attractions for each traffic zone.

In the trip distribution stage of the process the number of trip productions and attractions estimated in the trip generation stage is used in conjunction with recognized mathematical techniques, to achieve a distribution of future trips between specific zones of origin and destination.

Two basic methods are used to achieve a satisfactory distribution of future trips – growth factor or analogous methods and synthetic or inter-area travel formulae. The growth factor methods were the first to be developed for major use in trip distribution forecasts. They are simple to understand and use, and require little basic understanding of the underlying reasons as to why persons and traffic move. In general the growth factor methods calculate the future distribution of trips by multiplying the present-day pattern of movements by a growth factor, which can be derived in a variety of ways – usually from some combination of estimated total area or zonal growth rates. The most widely used growth factor methods are the uniform factor, the average factor, Fratar and Detroit methods.

The synthetic methods used to predict future trip distribution vary widely in detail, but in general terms fall into four main categories – the gravity models, the opportunity models, the electrostatic field models and the multiple linear regression models.

The gravity model as applied in transportation planning is based on Newton's Law of Gravity and assumes that all trips originating in a particular zone will distribute themselves among all other zones in accordance with the attractiveness of the competing destinations (usually indicated by some measure of size such as the total number of jobs available within the destination) and in inverse proportion to a measure of the travel resistance between the zones (typical measures of travel resistance are distance and journey time).

In mathematical terms the gravity model is expresed:

$$T_{i\text{-}j} = \frac{P_i \dfrac{A_j}{(D_{i\text{-}j})^b}}{\dfrac{A_j}{(D_{i\text{-}j})^b} + \dfrac{A_k}{(D_{i\text{-}k})^b} + \ldots + \dfrac{A_n}{(D_{i\text{-}n})^b}}$$

where $T_{i\text{-}j}$ = number of trips produced in zone i with a destination in zone j

P_i = total number of trips produced in zone i

$A_j \ldots A_n$ = total number of trips attracted to zone $j \ldots n$

$D_{i\text{-}j} \ldots D_{i\text{-}n}$ = measure of spatial separation between zones i–j and i–n

b = empirically determined exponent which expresses the average area-wide effect of spatial separation between zones on trip interchange

It should be pointed out that the measures of attraction and travel resistance used vary with trip purpose, e.g. people are generally prepared to travel much further to work than to shop. Consequently the gravity model is used to distribute trips stratified by different purposes, rather than to distribute total trips.

Opportunity models were first developed and used on the Chicago and the Pittsburgh Area Transportation Studies, and use the theory of probability in deriving estimates of future trip distribution. Basically these models assume that the probability that a trip will go to a particular destination depends on the relationship between the opportunities for satisfying a trip in the destination area and the other opportunities acting in competition with the chosen destination zone. Thus the attracting power of a zone of destination is conditioned by the number of trip opportunities in that zone (such as the total number of jobs) and by the number of trip opportunities within the same time or distance from the zone of origin.

The 'electrostatic field' method of trip distribution was developed in an attempt to eliminate the need for expensive home-interview studies. It is based on Coulomb's Law of electrostatic force, and assumes that movement occurs within a system because of an initial imbalance between the number of jobs (which are regarded as positive charges) and the number of people looking for employment (which are regarded as negative charges). However, the model is similar in form to the gravity model, and although it has been tested in research projects has not been widely used in transportation studies.

The multiple linear regression model is an empirical attempt to determine the distribution of future trips from the mathematical relationship which exists between present-day trip distribution and land-use and socio-economic characteristics of the population. Using this relationship and predicting the future land-use and socio-economic characteristics, the future number of trips between pairs of zones can be estimated.

This method of trip distribution is easily understood, and has the advantage that any variable thought to influence trip distribution can be included in the basic relationship. However, the method is expensive of computer time and for this reason has not been widely used in transportation studies. More recently the use of linear programming has been advocated in trip distribution.

Estimation of future person movements carried by different modes of travel

The estimation of the future person movements likely to be carried by different modes of travel can occur at different stages in the transportation planning process. It can be introduced at the trip generation stage when estimates of person movement made by different modes of travel are derived, in addition to the total person movements generated. Alternatively the future modal split can be estimated at or before the traffic assignment stage and after the trip distribution stage, when the appropriate proportions of the total person movements are allocated to the different modes of travel such as public transport and the private motor vehicle.

Considerable work has been carried out on the modal split stage of the process, and it is generally understood that factors such as income, the availability and convenience of alternative modes of transport, and length of journey all affect an individual's choice of mode of transport for a particular journey. However, these relationships are only imperfectly understood, and much more research into the motivation behind people's choice of transport mode is necessary before the modal split stage of the process can be applied with any confidence.

Network planning

The network planning stage of the processs involves the development of alternative transport networks for the selected land-use plan. These alternative networks generally take the form of complete systems serving the whole of the area under examination, and include networks for both public transport and the motor vehicle. Each alternative network should ideally reflect different policies regarding the extent, location, characteristics and cost of the network.

The procedure generally adopted in the traffic functional transport planning process involves the consideration of such factors as the density of trips produced by or attracted to an area, trip length, land-use characteristics, network design criteria and investment costs, although the way in which these factors are considered, and the influence they have on the design of the alternative networks varies from study to study.

Assignment of future trips to the proposed transport networks

From an analysis of the distances and journey times on each section of the different transport systems in the area under study it is possible to estimate the routes most likely to be taken between each pair of zones. Total person or vehicular movements derived at the trip distribution stage can then be assigned to these routes.

A variety of assignment techniques have been developed, the most significant of which are the diversion curve, all or nothing and capacity restraint assignment procedures.

The diversion curve was the first assignment technique to be developed. It is based on empirical studies and in general terms estimates the proportion of persons or vehicles likely to transfer to a new or improved facility. The proportion of diverted traffic is generally related to such parameters as distance, cost or speed.

The all or nothing assignment is based on the assumption that all movements between each pair of zones will take the shortest route between the zones. All the trip interchanges between zones derived from the trip distribution stages are allocated to this shortest route, and the total traffic volumes on each section (or link) of the system are then summed to estimate the traffic volumes assigned to the network. The most recently developed traffic assignment technique is the capacity restraint assignment. This technique is similar to the all or nothing assignment in the early stages, in that movements between each pair of zones are assigned to the shortest route. However, in an attempt to simulate the real-life situation, this technique also takes account of the congestion which builds up with increased traffic volumes, and as the capacity of each section of the transport networks is reached, so movements are assigned to the next shortest route.

Evaluation of efficiency and economic viability of alternative schemes

The evaluation stage of the transportation planning process is probably the most important stage. As yet it is only imperfectly understood and often ignored except for initial, intuitive judgements. On the traffic side, and within the limitations imposed by the numerous assumptions made in the process, it is a comparatively straightforward matter to assess whether the proposed transport networks fulfil the estimated travel demand with adequate capacity, safety, and standard of service. However, the problems associated with the assessment of the economics of alternative proposals are considerable. Although the cost of implementing and operating transport proposals can be estimated reasonably adequately, the price mechanism cannot be used as an investment criterion as 'vehicle-miles' is not a commodity which is directly bought and sold. In addition many of the benefits derived from a particular proposal are 'social' benefits and as such cannot be valued reliably.

In an attempt to overcome these problems a technique known as cost-benefit analysis has been developed to guide investment. In theory, the application of this technique is a comparatively simple exercise in which costs (including capital, operating and maintenance costs) and benefits (including savings in time, accidents and operating costs) are assessed for future years and discounted back to the base year, so that a rate of return on the investment might be calculated. In practice, however, it is extremely difficult to apply this technique except in a most general way, because of the problems associated with the assumption of values of future savings and costs, and for social and environment costs and benefits.

Evaluation techniques are now receiving considerable research attention, and with time should become more sophisticated and reliable. Even today, however, and despite the crude approaches adopted, evaluation of alternative proposals should be undertaken as an integral part of the transportation planning process. If nothing else, the use of such techniques attempts to rationalize the investment decision-making process.

The selection of a balanced transport system

The decision as to which transport system best serves the needs of the community cannot be made by the transportation planning process. Future traffic estimation is an important and powerful tool which can only be used to rationalize the decision-making process, and to help people make decisions which are sound and logical rather than intuitive. It is important to realize that the transportation planning process is no more than this. The often sweeping assumptions which are fundamental to the different stages of the process and the lack of knowledge concerning the prediction of future land uses ensure that accurate results are impossible except by coincidence. But, equally important, accuracy for its own sake is valueless since forecasts to the nearest traffic lane width are all that are required. The transportation planning process is basically an aid to orderly decision making, and not the precise instrument that some people like to think it is.

A further problem which must be faced in selecting the most appropriate form of transport system is to ensure that any proposals put forward are not so rigid as to prejudice the course of progress. In the last half-century change has been occurring at a tremendous rate – in the technological field advances in transportation have been enormous; demographically, changes in family size, age of marriage, size of the working population and its age and sex structure make it impossible to predict accurately population trends for more than 5–10 years ahead; economic advances have led directly to changes in the pattern of industrial growth and indirectly to changes in the skills, demands and standards of the employees.

Changes of this sort can be equated with progress, and it is important that plans are flexible enough to accommodate any changes brought about by progress. Flexibility can be achieved by presenting the range of long-term possibilities that might develop out of the present situation, and ensuring that by picking a path common to the range in the short term, nothing is done to prejudice these possibilities. However, no plan can have infinite flexibility for decisions have to be taken in the light of the best advice and information available at the time. In the words of the South Hampshire Study:

Planning . . . is becoming less and less a matter of precise propositions committed to paper and more and more a matter of ideas and policies loosely assembled under constant review, within which, every now and then, some project is seen to be as ready for execution as human judgement can pronounce.[27]

In transportation planning this 'constant review' is part of the process. Although policies are laid out for the long-term, projections are made for the short-term (five years) and interim periods (up to 10–15 years). Checks are made against these short-term projections by actually observing what happens at those dates and comparing them with the projected trends. If the comparisons are good, then no changes to the policies are made. If the comparisons are bad then the assumptions made at the outset could well have been wrong and must be reviewed and up-dated.

Disaggregate behavioural travel-demand modelling and the activity approach

The approach to travel demand forecasting outlined above, which is often known as the conventional four stage or aggregate sequential approach, is criticized on the grounds that it is concerned more with simulating or reproducing known situations, than predicting the way travellers behave now or will behave in the future. It is argued that the traditional models described here are naive and simplistic, and that the implied assumption on which they rest is fallacious, i.e. the assumption that the trip-making process can be broken down into a series of independent elements which can be treated separately and sequentially – trip generation, trip distribution, modal split and assignment. Despite the contention of Davinroy, Ridley and Wootton that each of these elements is interdependent and individually almost meaningless, nevertheless practice over the last twenty-five years has implicitly treated them separately.[28] Attempts have been made to develop behaviourally-based individual choice models, especially for the modal split stage of the process. However, the fundamental criticism remains; this aggregate sequential approach, by treating the trip-making process as a series of independent elements which can be treated separately and sequentially, is fallacious.

An alternative approach which has found favour in the last 10–12 years is the development of *disaggregate behavioural models* to represent or forecast the individual unit of travel behaviour – the individual unit being either the individual or the household. It is argued that this type of model has explanatory powers rather than correlative associations, and that by using disaggregated data relating to the household or person level a procedure can be developed whereby demand for travel can be represented in a single simultaneous model rather than through the application of a series of sequentially and conditionally linked aggregate models. It will attempt to forecast future demands for movement in a way which acknowledges that the trip maker often has a choice of: trip frequency; time of day when the trip is made; mode of travel, destination and route followed; and that by changing any of these elements the character of the trip may well be changed. In effect it breaks from the approach which

1 Produces at an aggregate (zonal) level the number of trips generated by or attracted to each zone; then
2 Distributes those trips between origin and destination; then
3 Allocates those trips to different modes of transport and to different routes between origin and destination. Disaggregate behavioural travel demand models attempt to consider the interrelated nature of all these elements, usually simultaneously, on the demand for travel.

This disaggregate behavioural approach has also been criticized on the grounds that 'It is difficult to see how one might formulate a finite set of mathematical equations capable of capturing the complex processes of choice.'[29] As an alternative to the disaggregated behavioural models, it is claimed that it is more realistic (a) to accept that all-embracing models of travel behaviour are not feasible, and (b) to attempt to develop a more pragmatic approach, which utilizes a mixed qualitative/quantitative description of behaviour to define specific aspects of travel behaviour where more limited econometric techniques can then be applied, e.g. define the limiting assumptions for forecasting new journeys by bus by developing a descriptive understanding of travel behaviour, and then apply a small econometric model using standard elasticity concepts to quantify potential new journeys. A more radical alternative approach (the activities approach) is put forward by the Transport Studies Unit in Oxford. Here a model of household travel behaviour (activities) has been developed which allows for interaction between different household members; takes account of existing constraints on household behaviour and confronts the household with discrete and realistic changes in travel circumstances, in attempting to forecast future travel demand patterns.[30]

Transport equity and politics

Implicit in the preceding sections is the view that transportation planning is an integral part of what is primarily an engineering operation, heavily under-pinned by a concern with economics, i.e. the main problem is seen as a need to provide for the efficient movement of people and goods, while the main objective is to remove impedances to the free flow of traffic, in a way which utilizes scarce resources to best effect in reducing the real cost of transporting people and goods. Such a view dominated the whole field of transportation planning until the early 1970s. In some places it is still the dominant view.

An alternative view of transportation planning can be advanced – a view which sees the problem as one of providing a transport system which serves effectively the needs of the community as a whole.[31] Thus, from this per-spective, transport problems cannot be considered separately from the wider environment in which they occur, for any attempt to solve them separately could lead to disbenefits in other areas. Rather it is argued that as an integral part of the transportation planning process, the interrelationships between transport and non-transport problems should be carefully evaluated to ensure that either (a) no such disbenefits result, or that (b) such disbenefits are acknowledged and accepted as a consequence of improving the trans-portation system. The proponents of this view of the transportation planning process argue that it should address simultaneously the problems of:

1 *allocative efficiency*, i.e. the need to provide for the efficient movement of goods and people
2 *social equity*, i.e. the need to ensure that certain groups in society are not disadvantaged through the implementation of transport proposals, and
3 *environmental impact*, i.e. the need to protect the physical and built environment from the adverse effects of transport systems.[32]

Intellectually and pragmatically this view of the transportation planning process has much to commend it. Certainly experience of objections from the public to major highway and airport proposals in the 1970s and 1980s confirms that, in practical terms, large sections of the population see the interrelated nature of transport and other problems, especially when proposals to improve the allocative efficiency of the transport system directly affect the social and/or environmental condition of those objecting.

Arising out of these intense and often prolonged objections to transport proposals, it has gradually been accepted that transportation planning, like land-use planning, is concerned with the distribution of scarce resources; that conflicts of interests inevitably arise in reaching transport planning decisions and that such decisions are political in both senses of the word. Bell and Held remind us that '. . . politics arises in the first instance when one realises that there is no such thing as the people – that no single decision can please all people. There are only peoples with contradictory and conflicting ideas and interests.'[33] Gyford puts this situation more graphically when he states '. . . given the fact of limited resources certain decisions about their allocation mean that some people will win and others will lose',[34] while Rose succinctly summarizes the role of local politics as '. . . the regulation of disagreements about matters of public choice'.[35] Against this background it can be argued that in reality the complexities of political decision-making processes are more central to the implementation of transport proposals than the engineering (or traffic functional) approach to transportation planning. At the same time, however, the transportation planning process, as outlined in the following chapters, forms an important part of those political processes. It attempts, as far as is possible, to quantify future demands for movement and to evaluate alternative ways of meeting that demand. As such, it provides the raw material against which other conflicting needs of the community can be articulated and argued out in the political arena.

References

1   Mitchell, R. and Rapkin, C., *Urban Traffic – A Function of Land Use*, Columbia University Press (1954).
2   *Chicago Area Transportation Study. Final Report. Vol. I*, State of Illinois, County of Cook & City of Chicago (December 1959).
3   *Bureau of Public Roads, Urban Transportation Planning: General Information and Introduction to System 360*, Washington (June 1970).
4   *London Traffic Survey, Vol. I*, The London County Council (1964).
5   Buchanan, C. D. *et al.*, *Traffic in Towns*, HMSO, London (1963).
6   Ministry of Transport & Ministry of Housing and Local Government, circular 1/64, *Buchanan Report on traffic in towns*, HMSO, London (1964).
7   Freeman Fox, Wilbur Smith and Associates, *The West Midlands Transport Study* (1968).
8   R. Travers Morgan and Partners, *Travel in Belfast*, Belfast Corporation (1968).
9   Ministries of Transport and Housing and Local Government, *op. cit.*
10 Highway Act 1962.
11 *The Urban Transport Planning Process*, Consultative Group on Transport Research OECD Paris (1971) (available through HMSO).
12 Wingo, L. and Perloff, H., 'The Washington Transportation Plan: technics or politics?', *Proceedings and Papers of the Regional Science Assoc.* (1961).

13　*ibid.*

14　Mitchell and Rapkin, *op. cit.*

15　Wingo and Perloff, *op. cit.*

16　*ibid.*

17　The Urban Transport Planning Process, *op. cit.*

18　Wingo and Perloff, *op. cit.*

19　Boyce, D., Day, N. and McDonald, C., *Metropolitan Plan Making*, Regional Science Research Monograph No. 4, Philadelphia (1970).

20　*ibid.*

21　See the following for a consideration of the strategic approach to planning:

　　Bruton, M. J., 'Strategic Planning and InterOrganizational Relationships' in Bruton, M. J. (ed.) *Spirit and Purpose of Planning*, 2nd edition, Hutchinson, London (1984) Chapter 4, pp. 78–94.

　　Friend, J. K., and Jessop, W. N., *Local Government and Strategic Choice*, 2nd edition, Pergamon Press, Oxford (1977).

　　Friend, J. K., Power, J., and Yewlett, C. J. L., *Public Planning: the Intercorporate Dimension*, Tavistock Publications, London (1974).

　　Solesbury, W., 'Strategic Planning: Metaphor or Method?' *Policy and Politics*, Vol. 9, No. 4 (1981), p. 421.

22　Simon, H. A., 'Decision Making and Organisational Design' in Pugh, D. S. (ed.), *Organisation Theory*, Penguin Education, London (1971) pp. 201–5.

23　Chapin, F. S. and Kaiser, E. J., *Urban Land Use Planning*, 3rd edition, University of Illinois Press (1979) Chapter 3, pp. 68–104.

24　Davinroy, T. R., Ridley, T. M. and Wootton, H. J., 'Predicting Future Traffic', *Traffic Engineering and Control* (1963).

25　Branch, M. C., *The Corporate Planning Process*, American Management Association, New York (1962).

26　Solesbury, W. and Townsend, A., 'Transportation Studies and British Planning Practice', *Town Planning Review* (1970).

27　Buchanan and Partners, *South Hampshire Study*, London (1966).

28　Richards, M. G. and Ben-Akiva, M. E., *A Disaggregate Travel Demand Model*, Saxon House Studies, Farnborough (1975).

29　Heggie, I. G., 'Behavioural Dimensions of Travel Choice' in Hensher, D. A. and Quasim Dalvi, *Determinants of Travel Choice*, Saxon House, Farnborough (1978) pp. 100–25.

30　*ibid.*

31　See Bayliss, D., 'Urban Transport Research Priorities', *Transportation* 6(i) (1977) pp. 4–7; Heggie, I. G., 'Transport Studies Research in U K Universities', *Transportation* 6(i) (1977) pp. 19–44; Hillman, M., 'Social Goals for Transport Policy', in *Transport for Society* (1975) London, Institute of Civil Engineers, (1975) pp. 13–20.

32　Banister, D. and Hall, P., *Transport and Public Policy Planning*, unpublished Final Report to S S R C, London (Grant H G154/23) (1980).

33　Bell, D. and Held, V., 'The Community Revolution', *Public Interest 16*, (1969) pp. 96–110.

34　Gyford, J., *Local Politics in Britain*, Croom Helm, London (1976).

35　Rose, R., *Politics in England Today*, Faber and Faber, London (1974).

3 Collection of basic data

Introduction

The 'aggregate sequential' transportation planning process involves the accumulation of a considerable amount of basic data. Characteristics of the present-day travel pattern in the area under consideration must be collected, the future distribution of land use and population derived, the adequacy or otherwise of existing transportation facilities determined and spare capacity estimated. Although the amount of basic data collected, and the detail in which it is presented, varies according to the purpose of the study and the size of the area under consideration, the principles governing the gathering of this data are broadly similar.

The different surveys necessary to collect the basic data are time-consuming and expensive in both staff and money. Consequently careful programming of this collection process is required, and it is standard practice to analyse each element in the process, allocate an estimate of the time necessary to complete each element and from this data prepare a critical path diagram, to ensure that the required data is assembled as quickly and efficiently as possible.

Definition of study area

To ensure that all travel-pattern and land-use data relating to the transportation planning process is collected in an efficient and economic manner the area to be studied is defined by a boundary known as an external cordon. Basically, the area within the external cordon is surveyed intensively – present and future land uses are analysed in some detail and travel-pattern data is assembled by means of a 'home-interview' study. Movements originating outside the external cordon, but crossing the cordon, are surveyed at the point at which they cross it.

Outside the external cordon changes in the land-use pattern are considered to be less significant, and therefore are examined in a less detailed manner. No home-interview studies are carried out beyond the external cordon.

In defining the study area, three main criteria must be met:

1   The external cordon should isolate those problems of movement which

are crucial to the daily life of the urban centre being studied. To achieve this, it should circumscribe the zone of systematic daily movement oriented towards the urban centre. Generally, this means that suburban and semi-rural areas which generate a regular flow of trips, especially work trips, to the urban centre are included within the study area. Details of these movements are most easily surveyed by a home-interview study. Those residents who live further out make fewer trips to the urban centre, with the result that there comes a point when it is easier and more economic to survey these movements at a roadside interview rather than use a home-interview study. External cordons therefore tend to be drawn at the 'commuter-sheds' between urban areas.

2   The external cordon should include the area into which future urban development will probably extend during the period for which the transportation facilities are to be planned.

3   The external cordon should meet certain technical requirements for roadside interviewing of traffic, viz. to reduce the number of survey points at the cordon, the cordon line should be located in the fringe area of the urban region where movements are channelled on to a reasonably small number of roads. It should cross roads at a point where it is safe to carry out roadside interviews; it should be continuous, and it should be uniform in its course so that movements (with the exception of movements passing through the area) cross it only once.

An interesting development in the process of defining the external cordon has been the use of census data by the *Tri-State New York Metropolitan Transportation Study* to determine the extent of urbanization. On the basis that the external cordon should include all continuous urban development, as well as the expected future population increase, the Tri-State Study determined the extent of urbanization by plotting population density and car ownership per acre for each municipality. This gave a good indication of population dispersion from high intense urbanization to suburban and then rural conditions, and provided a visual idea of the area which should be encompassed by the cordon. Alternative cordon lines derived from this exercise were tested with 'pilot' roadside interviews, and the broad effect of future land-use changes within these cordon lines was evaluated. Finally, the most suitable cordon line was chosen.[1]

For free-standing towns this method would appear to have little advantage over the more traditional approach as outlined above. However, in the more complex built-up areas of the conurbations this method might well be used with advantage.

Subdivision of area into traffic zones

The objectives of the survey and analysis stage of the 'aggregate sequential' transportation planning process are to

1 Determine where journeys begin and end
2 Determine the factors which influence trip generation
3 Establish the main 'corridors of movement'

However, the mass of data collected relates to individual journeys, households and centres of employment, and in its crude form is difficult to analyse and interpret. To overcome this problem the area being surveyed, and indeed the whole country, is divided into zones, for the purpose of '. . . (grouping) the data so as to make it intelligible, amenable to analysis, and suitable for the assignment of journeys. . . .'[2] The procedure is similar to choosing class intervals for a histogram – which do not oversimplify the data, but which bring some order to it.

To ensure that information is collected in sufficient detail to enable meaningful conclusions to be drawn about trip generation rates, and trip distribution, two main types of traffic zone are distinguished:

1 *External zones* Traffic zones outside the external cordon boundary.
2 *Internal zones* Zones contained within the external cordon. These zones are further subdivided into central area zones, and non-central area zones.

External zones
The traffic zones defined beyond the external cordon cover the whole country. As the influence of traffic generators tends to decrease with distance away from the study area, so the size of external traffic zones is increased with distance from the study area. In these outer areas population centres, the communications network, and topographical features must all be taken account of in defining the external zone boundaries, but the basic principle to be followed is that those centres of population close enough to the study area to generate significant traffic flows to that area, should be separately zoned.

Internal zones
For internal traffic within the study area the aim is to define zones small enough to give accuracy of movement, and to allow reliable trip generation rates to be established. This is normally achieved by dividing the area bounded by the external cordon into sectors one of which is the central area. The other sectors are defined working outwards from the central area and using topographical barriers, such as rivers, canals, railways, in conjunction with natural traffic catchment areas, to delineate boundaries.[3]

The sectors are then further subdivided into zones and sub-zones, on the basis of the predominant land use, e.g. residential, shopping, recreational, industrial. The zonal boundaries used by other bodies for the collection of information related to the travel-pattern data must be taken into consideration if it is to be used in the analysis stage of the transportation planning process.

Traffic movement will certainly be related to population. Therefore it is always advisable to relate these zones as far as possible to Enumeration District boundaries.

Land-use data collected by the local planning authority is often processed for street blocks or units, and if it is intended to relate traffic movement to land-use or floor-space characteristics, then the street block boundaries should be taken into consideration when defining traffic zones.

Employment data relating to firms employing five persons or more is available from the Ministry of Labour for Employment Exchange areas and Employment Districts within the Exchange Area. If this is to be used in conjunction with travel-pattern data then the boundaries of these areas must be taken account of when drawing up traffic zones.

In addition to considering land-use, population and employment 'zone' boundaries when drawing up traffic zones, the more recent transportation studies also take account of environmental areas and groupings.

The size of traffic zone required varies with the different stages of the transportation planning process. The zones required for the establishment of trip generation rates are generally smaller than those required for trip distribution. This is largely because to establish reliable trip generation rates it is necessary for the particular land use to exhibit similar characteristics, so that it might reasonably be assumed that the traffic generation rate is also similar. Thus as far as possible households of similar types will be grouped together – owner-occupied properties at a low density of development are not as a rule grouped with high density council-rented property. This principle is applied to other land uses.

Trip distribution, which simulates travel patterns in a general way, often requires larger zones because of the comparatively small amount of travel-pattern data relating to the trip generation zones. It is usually found necessary to combine these smaller trip generation zones to derive a reliable distribution of trips.

The size of zones required for the trip assignment stage of the process will vary with the computer program used. However, the zones chosen for trip generation are invariably satisfactory, and for assignment purposes these are either used as they stand or are aggregated to form larger more suitable zones.

The capacity of the computer available to analyse the data will often prove to be the limiting factor in the number, and therefore the size, of the traffic zones to be used.

Central area zones

The definition of zones within the central area sector is based on the same procedure as that adopted for the internal zones. Factors of especial importance here are land use, and the local planning authorities street block method of recording floor-space statistics for the various land uses.

Coding

If the transportation study is to be analysed by computer then the zoning and coding of the area tends to follow a standard pattern, to simplify the coding and data punching procedures. The external zones are usually prefixed by the digit 9. The area within the external cordon is normally subdivided into nine sectors, one being the central area, which is given the prefix 0. The remaining eight sectors are then given the prefixes 1–8 numbering clockwise and outwards from the central area. The sectors are then subdivided into 10 zones numbered 0–9 using land-use and traffic catchment areas as guide lines, and if necessary these zones can be further divided into 10 sub-zones numbered 0–9, numbering outwards from the central area. Thus the reference 481 can be immediately recognized as Sector 4, zone 8, sub-zone 1.

The central area, with the prefix 0, can similarly be divided into 10 zones numbered 0–9, and based on the predominant land use. Further division into sub-zones can be carried out if necessary.

Zones defined in this manner are usually plotted on maps of different scale depending on the type of zones. It is normal practice for central-area zones to be plotted at 1:2500 or even 1:1250 scale. Internal zones are usually plotted at a 6-inch to 1-mile scale, although if the selection of the sample of households to be interviewed is based on a map of the internal zones, then they are plotted at 1:2500 scale. External zones are plotted at the scale of 10 miles to 1 inch.

Zoning by National Grid references

Traffic zones defined in the conventional method outlined above depend almost entirely on the judgement of the engineer, since they are defined without knowing the full facts necessary to draw a balance between conflicting requirements. In addition the need to index and code by zone number all place names likely to occur as origins or destinations, is a costly and time-consuming process. But perhaps the most significant disadvantage is the inability to alter zone boundaries after the preliminary analysis, without recoding all the place names in the data.

Because of the disadvantages associated with the conventional method of zoning for traffic surveys, attempts have been made in recent years to develop alternative techniques. In 1963 Worcestershire County Council, after consulting with the Ministry of Transport and the Road Research Laboratory, successfully carried out two Origin and Destination Surveys using National Grid Reference Numbers to define traffic zone boundaries.[4]

Basically the procedure adopted involved the following.

1   Coding of all place names in the survey area by the grid reference listed in the Ordnance Survey Gazetteer.

2   Preliminary computer analysis of:

(a) all journeys originating within each 1 km², within an area extending just beyond the County boundary.

(b) all journeys originating within each 10 km^2 surrounding the County, and within an area measuring 300 km by 200 km on its outer boundary.
(c) all journeys originating within each 100 km^2 for the remainder of Great Britain.

3   Defining zone boundaries, around groups of squares using as guide lines the approximate optimum number of origins of each zone that experience in other surveys had shown was desirable, and other factors such as administrative boundaries, and the road network.

Because of the problems associated with manually specifying curvilinear boundaries, all zones in the two surveys conducted were straight lines. The zone boundaries were specified for computer input by listing against each zone number the grid reference for every change of direction going in clockwise order round the zone.

4   Traditional distribution of origins and destinations to the zones was then carried out by the computer, and normal journey analyses undertaken. The main operational advantages claimed for this method of zoning are:

(a) 'Zoning can be related to the actual location and density of journey origins as disclosed by the survey.
(b) Errors in the coding of place names are minimized by reducing the task to its simplest possible form . . .
(c) Zoning can subsequently be changed without the need to recode the place names in the original data'.

In addition the adoption of this method on a wider basis would enable the results of diifferent surveys carried out by different authorities to be collated and combined to make up a regional survey. It would also facilitate the accumulation and use of basic travel data for research purposes.

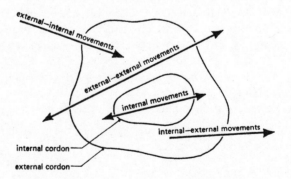

Figure 15   *Diagrammatic representation of the four basic movements for which data is collected in the transportation planning process*

Travel-pattern data

Travel-pattern data is required for four basic movements illustrated in Figure 15.

1 *External-external* (or *'through' movements*) with an origin and a destination outside the area defined by the external cordon. Depending on the purpose of the study these movements are sometimes subdivided into: (a) through movements stopping in the town or area defined by the external cordon, and (b) non-stop through movements.
2 *External-internal movements*, with an origin outside the external cordon, and a destination within the cordon.
3 *Internal-external movements*, which originate within the area defined by the external cordon, and have a destination beyond it.
4 *Internal movements* with both their origin and destination inside the area bounded by the external cordon.

All these types of movement can be made by different modes and depending upon the purpose of the study this movement data may be collected for private motor vehicles, public transport, commercial vehicles, and even walking. For example, the transportation studies undertaken in the conurbations of this country, which are designed to produce a plan for a 'primary' communications network, collect comprehensive movement data for all the above major modes. On the other hand, a limited transportation study carried out to determine whether or not a by-pass is required to a small country town, would be concerned primarily with the movements made by private motor vehicle.

Data relating to these different types of movement is collected in a variety of ways. Through movements and external-internal movements are invariably surveyed at the external cordon. They are also picked up on an internal cordon or screen line survey, if this is considered necessary.

Internal-external movements are surveyed in the home-interview study, if this is carried out, and are also picked up on the internal and external cordon surveys. Movements occurring within the area defined by the external cordon are surveyed in the home-interview study. In addition an internal cordon or screen line survey is sometimes carried out as a check against the results of the home-interview and external cordon surveys.

The home-interview study

The home-interview is concerned with the collection of basic facts relating to present-day movements for all trips on a typical day within the town or urban region defined by the external cordon. The survey includes home interviews, commercial vehicle and public transport surveys to determine movements originating within the area. Roadside interviews are carried out on the external cordon line to cover trips passing through or into the area.

These surveys provide the essential facts on present-day travel desires and habits, and in combination with data from land-use and economic studies serve as a basis for projecting future travel patterns.

Home interview – sample size

Travel is an expression of an individual's behaviour, and as such it has the characteristics of being habitual. As a habit it tends to be repetitive and the repetition occurs in a definite pattern. In addition, travel habits of different individuals . . . are similar for work, shopping, recreation and other types of trips.[5]

Because patterns of movement exhibit these characteristics it is not necessary to obtain travel information from all residents of the area under study, for a long period of time. Statistical methods can be used with confidence for the sampling of movement in urban areas.

To ensure that a sample is representative it is necessary that the persons included in it are distributed geographically throughout the survey area in the same proportion as the distribution of the total population. Experience has shown that the dwelling unit is the most reliable and convenient sampling unit to be used in home-interview studies.

The size of sample to be interviewed depends upon the total population of the area under study, the degree of accuracy required, and occasionally, on the density of population, e.g. a small town of primarily low density residential development will require a larger sample than a large, densely populated town. The adequacy of various sample sizes has been tested, and this has led to recommended sample sizes related to the population of the area under study. These are given in Table 8.

Population of area	Recommended sample size	Minimum sample size (dwelling units)
Under 50,000	1 in 5	1 in 10
50,000–150,000	1 in 8	1 in 20
150,000–300,000	1 in 10	1 in 35
300,000–500,000	1 in 15	1 in 50
500,000–1,000,000	1 in 20	1 in 70
Over 1,000,000	1 in 25	1 in 100

Table 8   *Recommended sample sizes to be adopted in home-interview studies*

If the purpose of the study is to determine long-term proposals then the minimum sample size is used. If a greater degree of reliability and accuracy is required then the recommended sample size is used.

The *Greater Glasgow Transportation Study* used a 1 in 30 sample for the home-interview study.

Home interviews – selection of sample
The frame from which the sample of households is selected can be set up from either the electoral roll or the rating lists. The electoral roll (or register of electors) is compiled annually and includes a list of the names and addresses of those persons who are qualified electors. It does not include any addresses at which all residents are under eighteen years of age, or alien.

The rating (or valuation lists) which are compiled by the inland revenue and held by local authorities, comprise a list of all separately rated units, including those occupied by aliens and persons under eighteen years. Although rateable units contained in the rating register tend to identify quite closely with individual households, there are problems associated with its use as a sample frame, e.g. buildings used for other than residential purposes, such as shops, offices, public buildings, are included in the register, among the dwelling unit records. Consequently these 'non-dwellings' must be eliminated before the sample of households is derived. A further administrative problem occurs when the study area includes several local authorities. This can be overcome by conducting primary sampling at the offices of the local authorities concerned. Unless great inconvenience is experienced in gaining access to the valuation lists it is recommended that they be used for the sample selection of households for home interview.[6]

The sample of residential buildings not occupied as single family dwelling units, such as hotels, institutions, and boarding houses, can usually be derived from the valuation list. However, in those cases where it is difficult to determine the number of rooms or dwelling units in such buildings the procedure adopted for sample selection is somewhat different. Whenever a hotel, or institution or boarding house is encountered in the valuation list it is omitted from the sample frame. A separate record of its particulars, including location, is made, and on a subsequent date, often near the completion of the home-interview study, the number of 'dwellings' or rooms in each building is determined by a field inspection. The actual sample to be interviewed is derived from this.

Home interview – interview procedure
Once the selection of the dwelling unit sample is completed, then the collection of data relating to internally generated movements can commence. Specially trained field interviewers, under the close guidance of a supervisor, are used for this purpose. They are given a list of addresses at which they are to call on a particular day. Three or four days before the intended visit a letter is sent to the householder explaining the reasons for the survey, and warning him that the interviewer will call on the appropriate day.

The information requested by the field interviewer covers basic household

WYCOMBE AREA TRANSPORTATION STUDY
HOME INTERVIEW SURVEY — PART 2

Zone .... Code No .... Page .... of ....

CODING COMPLETE	Card type	1
	Traffic zone	2
	Code No.	5
CODING CHECKED	Expansion factor	8
	Seasonal factor	11

PERSON INFORMATION

Person No.	Person identification	Journeys made	Direct interview	Sex	Age	Employment	Normal place of employment	Type of employment	Regular train travel	Departure station
		YES	YES	Male	Over 21	1 Full time	1 High Wycombe	1 Industry	1 High Wycombe	
		NO	NO	Female	Under 21 (state age)	2 Part Time	2 Remainder Study area	5 Offices (state business of firm)	2 Beaconsfield	
						3 Unemployed	3 Slough		3 Great Missenden	
						4 School or college	4 Beaconsfield	8 Shops	4 Amersham	
						5 Housewife	5 Marlow	9 Other (state)	5 Saunderton	
						6 Retired	6 Wooburn, Bourne End		6 Other station	
					14	7 Pre-school age	7 Greater London		7 None	
						16	8 Elsewhere 17	18		19

SURVEY DAY   SURVEY DATE

JOURNEY INFORMATION

Journey No.	ORIGIN Precise address if in Study Area	DESTINATION Precise address in Study Area	TIME			JOURNEY PURPOSE Ring appropriate letters		MODE OF TRAVEL Ring appropriate number	TRIP TYPE
			Start	Finish		From	To		
				A.M.	A.M.	A Work	A 1 Drove car, light van	
						B School or college	B 2 Drove goods vehicle	
						C In course of work	C 3 M/C, Scooter, moped	
				P.M.	P.M.	D Shopping personal business	D 4 Rode pedal cycle	
						E Social sport, entertainment	E 5 Passenger in car, van, taxi	
						F Serve passenger	F 6 Private coach or bus	
						G Home	G 7 Public service bus, coach	
20	21	24		27		H Change mode 29	H 8 Train 30	
							H 9 Walk or other	
				A.M.	A.M.	A Work	A 1 Drove car, light van	
						B School or college	B 2 Drove goods vehicle	
						C In course of work	C 3 M/C, Scooter, moped	
				P.M.	P.M.	D Shopping personal business	D 4 Rode pedal cycle	
						E Social sport, entertainment	E 5 Passenger in car, van, taxi	
						F Serve passenger	F 6 Private coach or bus	
						G Home	G 7 Public service bus, coach	
33	34	37		40		H Change mode 42	H 8 Train 43	
							H 9 Walk or other	

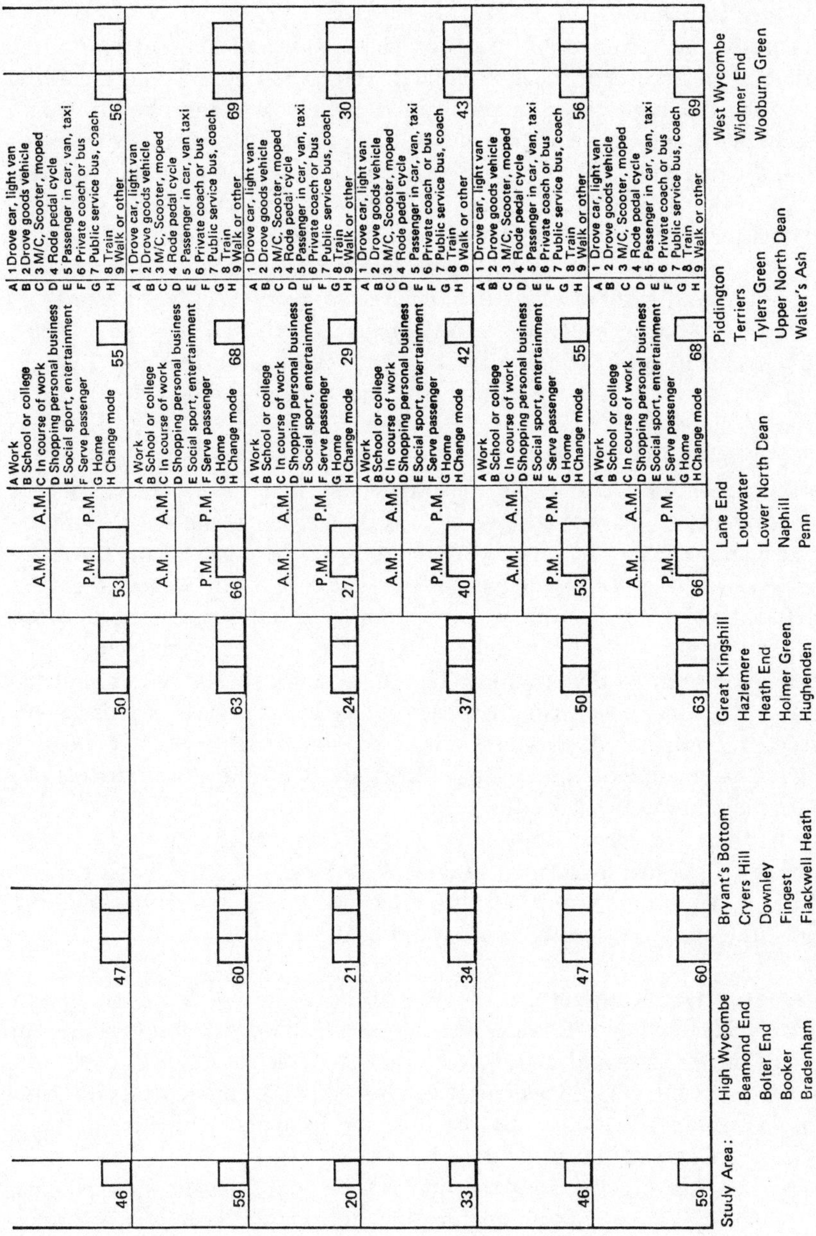

Figure 16 *Typical home-interview study form*

characteristics, and all the journeys made by each member of the household of five years of age and above in the previous twenty-four hours. This data is recorded on the home-interview form, a typical example of which is illustrated in Figure 16.

Basically, the household information gathered includes the address of the dwelling unit, the size of the household, and the age and sex structure of the occupants; the numbers economically active, their job, and place of work; the number of motor vehicles owned; the household income; the place of school/further education for those occupants of school age; and the day and date of the journeys to be reported, i.e. normally the previous day and date.

Often questions concerning income are omitted because of the reluctance of people to answer reliably such personal questions. However, an assessment of the household income can be derived from an analysis of the number of vehicles owned, the type of dwelling occupied, and the job of each employed member of the household. In these cases additional questions are asked about whether the property is owner-occupied, council-rented, or privately rented.

The information required from each member of the household of five years of age or more, about *all* the journeys made in the previous twenty-four hours includes the precise address of the origin and destination, the time of the start and finish of the journey, the purpose of the journey, and the mode of travel. Up to ten different journey purposes are distinguished, the most significant being to or from work, school or college, in course of work (including employer's business), social, sport or entertainment, serve passenger, home and change mode. The most significant modes of travel distinguished are car driver, car passenger, goods vehicle driver, goods vehicle passenger, motor cycle/scooter, rail, bus, coach, taxi, pedal cycle and walking. Depending on the nature of the study some of these modes may be amalgamated or even omitted.

If the field interviewer cannot make contact with the householder on the appointed day, then he or she should call back on the following day. If no contact is made on the second visit, then no further attempt is made to contact the occupants until seven days after the appointed day.

Cordon surveys – external

The only satisfactory method of determining the origin and destination of through movements and external–internal movements across the external cordon, is to question the persons actually making the movement. In transportation studies this is normally done by direct interview, or issuing pre-paid business reply postcards at the roadside.

Other methods, relying on the observation and identification of each movement across the cordon line, are sometimes used. However, the reliability of 'match registration' and 'tag and disc' surveys in anything but the smallest area leaves much to be desired, while the fundamental disadvantages of an incomplete knowledge of origin and destination cannot be overcome. Consequently direct interview or pre-paid postcard surveys tend to be favoured.

Road traffic movement (a) postcard surveys

Pre-paid business reply postcards, with return address and questionnaire to be filled in by the road user, are distributed at the external cordon survey point. They are usually accompanied by a request for co-operation, the location of origin and destination, purpose of trips, and type of vehicle. The time, location and direction of travel are entered on the card by the staff operating the survey, as they are distributed to the road users.

This method requires few enumerators and site organization and delays to traffic are kept to a minimum. However, the response rate to such surveys is variable, and usually ranges from 10 to 50 per cent of those issued with the postcards. In addition there is a danger that the 'returns' received form a biased sample. Experience in the United States of America shows that lower percentage returns are usual for commercial traffic and night drivers, while drivers making more than one trip through the cordon are often reluctant to complete and return more than one card.

Nevertheless postcard surveys can be reasonably successfully utilized in heavy traffic conditions, pilot surveys, and where they are used in conjunction with some direct interviewing. They can also be successfully utilized in major transportation studies, as the experience of Buchanan and Partners with the *Bath Study* shows – a 72 per cent return was achieved, but only after extensive and repeated publicity was given to the importance of the study in the local press.[7]

Road traffic movement (b) direct interview

In the direct interview method, a sample of road users are stopped at the external cordon survey point, and questioned by an interviewer, who records the answers on specially prepared forms. Figure 17 illustrates a typical cordon survey form. The information recorded includes general information about the date, time, location of the survey point and the identification of the interviewer. The class of vehicle being interviewed is identified and entered on the form in code, as is the number of occupants in the vehicle. This information is normally recorded as the vehicle approaches the survey point.

Questions are then put to the driver of the vehicle about the origin and destination of his journey. Because the study area is divided into zones for the purposes of a transportation study all origins and destinations within the external cordon must be recorded in detail (e.g. street name and number, or the name of a well-known shop or firm). For points outside the study area, the name of the town or village, and the county is normally sufficient. The origin and destination of a trip must never be recorded as the same point. For round trips the farthest point reached from one end of the journey should be recorded as either the origin or destination of the trip.

WYCOMBE AREA TRANSPORTATION STUDY

CORDON INTERVIEW SURVEY

INCOMING VEHICLES

Coding completed	Date	Sheet No.	Card type 1
	Interviewer		Cordon Station 2
			Time period 4
Coding checked			Sheet No. 6
	Cordon Station	Half-hour beginning	Expansion factor 9
			Seasonal factor 12

Vehicle class	No of occu-pants	ORIGIN Name of Town or Village	DESTINATION Precise address if in Study Area	PURPOSE		INTERMEDIATE STOP		Trip Type
				From	To	Precise address	Ston purpose	
15		18	21	24			25	
27		30	33	36			37	
39		42	45	48			49	
51		54	57	60			61	
15		18	21	24			25	
27		30	33	36			37	
39		42	45	48			49	
51		54	57	60			61	

Figure 17 *Typical external cordon interview form*

The driver is next questioned about the purposes of the journey and what he or she was doing before starting the trip (e.g. going home from work; going shopping from home). A typical transportation study in a conurbation would subdivide the journey purposes into as many as eleven classes. However, for a small or medium-sized town fewer classes of journey purpose are usually defined. Basically these are similar to the journey purposes distinguished in the home-interview study.

In certain cases additional questions concerning a possible intermediate stop within the area under study and the reasons for it are asked of people making through trips.

While the interviewers at the survey point are questioning the sample selected for interview, a continuous record of all vehicles passing through the point is kept by enumerators. This count is a classified vehicle count, and is usually recorded on the standard Ministry of Transport Enumerators Form, although in certain cases tally counters are used.

Both interviews and the total vehicle enumeration are carried out for a set time interval – usually fifteen or thirty minutes. As soon as this chosen period of time elapses a fresh count for the next time period is commenced, regardless of the number of entries recorded.

Each cordon station is usually in operation for sixteen hours daily, from 6 a.m. to 10 p.m., and is operated by staff working in two shifts. The numbers required to operate the station depends on the traffic volume, the number of questions asked, and the size of sample selected. As a rule of thumb it is estimated that one interviewer should be able to cope with approximately eighty vehicles per hour.[9] It is standard practice to have a police constable on duty to direct traffic and select the vehicles for interview on the instructions of the site supervisor. The size of sample interviewed varies with the accuracy required in grossing up, and the volume of traffic on a particular route.

Sample selection at cordon surveys
Three main types of sampling procedure can be employed on a cordon survey.

1 *Time cluster sampling* During each hour or time interval of the survey a period of time is selected when all vehicle drivers are interviewed, and a further period of time when no interviews are carried out. This method allows the interviewers to alternate interview directions to cover both inward and outward movements.
2 *Volume cluster sampling* The number of vehicles to be interviewed is predetermined, depending on the sample size adopted. Similarly a predetermined number of vehicles is allowed to pass without interviewing.
3 *Variable rate sampling* This method of random sampling was developed by the Road Research Laboratory and is the method normally used at

cordon surveys.[9] Interviewers are employed at a constant rate, and the size of sample selected varies with the volume of traffic flow. Depending on the characteristics of the stream, sample rates are calculated for either half-hour or one-hour periods. To reduce bias different sample rates are usually calculated for different classes of vehicle.

Public transport trips
Public transport trips by bus or rail which originate outside the external cordon, but have a destination within it, may form a small proportion of the total travel in the area under study. However, they are usually of sufficient importance to warrant the collection of full information about them.

A variety of techniques can be adopted to assemble this information. Because of the problems associated with interviewing on a crowded bus or train the most favoured method is the pre-paid business reply postcard. These are issued to passengers as they board either bus or train and they are requested to complete the questionnaire and return the postcard to the survey headquarters. The survey of rail passengers undertaken as part of the *London Traffic Survey* adopted a variation on this theme by asking rail passengers to complete the questionnaire while travelling into the central London termini, and hand it in at a 'collection point' on arrival. However, problems associated with the low returns and a biased sample still remain, although in an attempt to overcome this, more recent transportation studies use the pre-paid postcard as lottery tickets so that for each card correctly completed and returned the person interviewed stands a chance of winning a prize.

Another technique adopted with some success, especially in West Germany, is to use an interviewer with a tape recorder to collect information about public transport trips across the external cordon. This method allows a large sample to be interviewed, and coding to be undertaken the same evening.

In areas where the volume of bus passenger traffic across the external cordon is light it is possible to use an interviewer, boarding the bus, noting the number of people on the bus and interviewing a sample of those present.

The information required from both bus and rail passengers is similar to that required at the roadside interview – namely place of origin and destination, purpose of journey, and (depending on the purpose of the study) mode of travel adopted prior to boarding the bus or train, and mode of travel to be adopted on leaving the bus or train.

Internal cordon or screen line counts
Volumetric counts of traffic crossing an internal cordon or screen line are made, to compare the estimated number of trips derived from grossed-up interview returns, with the trips actually observed on the road. These counts can be carried out automatically, or manually.

If only one screen line is chosen it should divide the study area into approximately two equal halves, but should not pass through the central area. To minimize the number of survey points on the screen line it is best to utilize a barrier to movement such as a river or a railway.

In exceptional circumstances the procedures used at the external cordon are also adopted on the screen line or internal cordon. However, because of the congestion and delays to traffic and the additional expense involved, this happens only rarely.

Commercial vehicle survey

To obtain full information about commercial vehicle trips taking place within the external cordon it is necessary to take a sample of all the commercial vehicles garaged within the area, and interview the owner or driver responsible for the vehicles chosen. No definite guidance is available about the size of sample to be selected, but it is generally accepted that for a small town a sample approaching 100 per cent could well be necessary, whereas in a larger area a sample of less than 30 per cent would be considered satisfactory.

The sample frame from which the vehicles are selected is usually the record of vehicle excise licences for the area under consideration. This should relate to the same period of time as the household interview sample. There are several problems associated with using this sample frame. Vehicles registered in the study area but used continuously elsewhere present a problem which is especially associated with fleet operators: vehicles recently transferred to new owners outside the study area, or recently scrapped or out of service for repair can upset the sample frame.

The vehicle owner or operator might refuse to supply the information requested, or the vehicle selected for interview might not have been used on the day for which travel data is required. These problems can only be determined at the time of interview, when the appropriate course of action is to record the situation on the interview forms, so that appropriate adjustments can be made for these vehicles when the expansion factor is calculated.

Figure 18 shows a typical Commercial Vehicle Survey Form; the information normally collected consists of

1 *Vehicle information* This includes the registration number of the vehicle, name and address of the firm or owners (these are usually entered in the office before the interview is undertaken), and the name and address of the depot from which the vehicle operated on the survey date and the vehicle type.

2 *Journey information* This relates to one-way travel between two essential stops. It does not include stops for traffic jams, accidents and other delays. Journeys should be numbered consecutively for each vehicle, beginning with No. 1 for the first trip, No. 2 for the second and so on, and information about the origin and destination and the time taken

WYCOMBE AREA TRANSPORTATION STUDY

COMMERCIAL VEHICLE SURVEY

Zone .... Code No ...... Page .... of ....

ADMINISTRATIVE RECORD

INTERVIEWER

LETTER SENT			TEL.	
	CALLS	DATE	TIME	RESULT

INTERVIEW COMPLETED

INTERVIEW NOT COMPLETED

COMMENTS

FIELD CHECK	OFFICE CHECK
CODING COMPLETED	CODING CHECK

VEHICLE INFORMATION

	Card Type	1
	Traffic zone	2
Registration No.	Code No.	5
	Expansion factor	8
SURVEY DAY SURVEY DATE	Seasonal factor	11

NAME & ADDRESS OF FIRM (OR OWNER) — 14

VEHICLE TYPE
(Tick appropriate box)
- ☐ Car with 'C' licence
- ☐ Light goods (under 30 cwt. unladen)
- ☐ Heavy goods (over 30 cwt. unladen)
- ☐ Private coach or bus
- ☐ Taxi

ADDRESS OF DEPOT (FROM WHICH VEHICLE OPERATED ON SURVEY DAY)

JOURNEY INFORMATION

Journey No.	ORIGIN Precise address if in Study Area	DESTINATION Precise address if in Study Area	TIME		JOURNEY PURPOSE Tick appropriate box	Number of PASSENGERS including driver	TRIP TYPE
			Start	Finish			
	15	18	A.M. / P.M. 21	A.M. / P.M.	☐ Firm's business ☐ To or from home ☐ Personal business 23	25	26
	28	31	A.M. / P.M. 34	A.M. / P.M.	☐ Firm's business ☐ To or from home ☐ Personal business 36	37	39
	41	44	A.M. / P.M. 47	A.M. / P.M.	☐ Firm's business ☐ To or from home ☐ Personal business 49	50	52

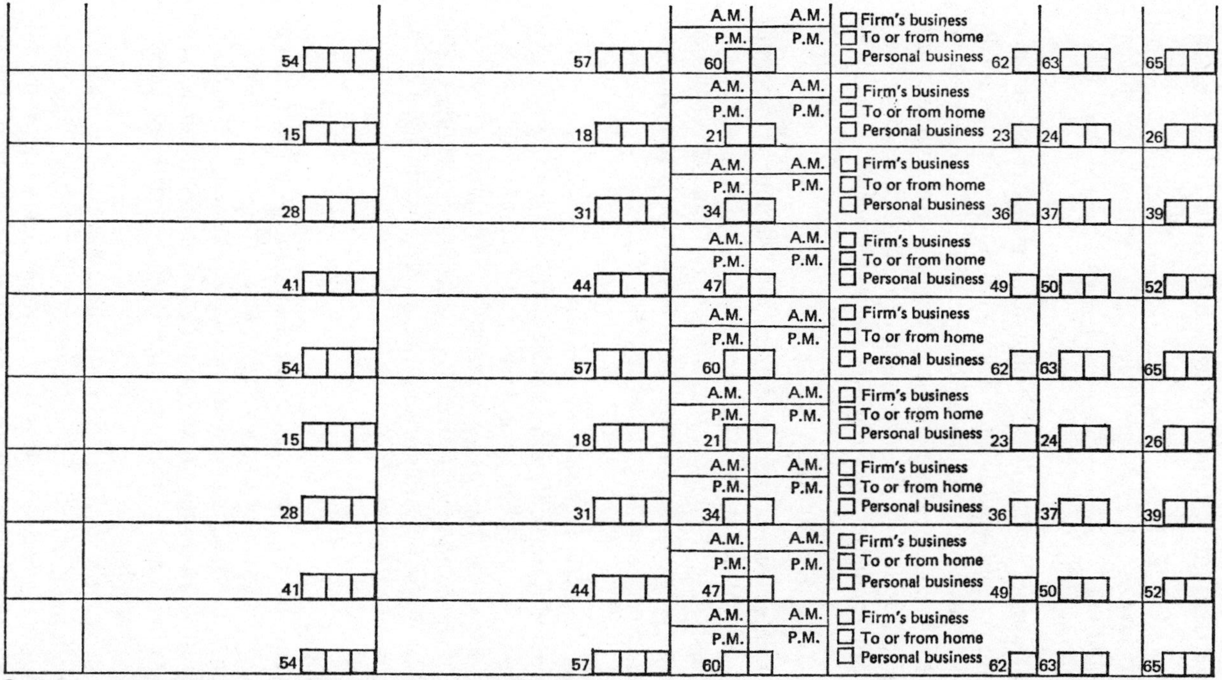

Figure 18 *Typical commercial vehicle interview form*

for each trip must be collected. As with the external cordon count exact addresses for origins and destinations within the study area must be given. In the larger transportation studies as many as ten commercial journey purposes may be defined, although it is usual to consider only three main purposes:

(a) Firm's business
(b) To or from home
(c) Personal business

Difficulty may sometimes be encountered in obtaining exact information about the movements of a particular vehicle on the survey day, especially when the vehicle has made a number of different journeys. To overcome this problem log-books are sometimes issued to the drivers of the appropriate vehicles at the start of the survey day, so that the correct journey information can be entered as each journey is completed.[10]

Taxi survey
In large towns or cities where taxis are an important element in the public transport system, a separate survey of taxi movements is usually carried out. The procedure adopted is identical to that used in the Commercial Vehicle Survey, although owing to the comparatively limited size of the sample population the sample size adopted tends to be larger.

Survey of existing transport facilities
An important element of the collection of basic data is the survey of existing transport facilities. It is, in effect, a stocktaking of the major highway and public transport networks, the existing demand for and supply of parking accommodation, and the present-day traffic volumes and travel times. This data is required for use in the trip distribution and assignment stage of the transportation planning process.

Main road inventory
The limited capacity of the computer, and the amount of work involved, normally results in the survey of the physical characteristics of the road network being restricted to the main or primary network. The designation of this primary network is based on the volume and nature of traffic carried, the existing road classification, and the requirements of the traffic assignment procedures to be adopted.

Following the designation of a primary network, its basic characteristics in terms of local, regional and national functions are determined. Within the survey area the nature, extent and density of development adjacent to, and fronting on, the network are examined. Particularly important are the number and frequency of frontage accesses. Carriageway widths, traffic regulations, visibility conditions, junction spacing and capacities, especially at critical points, are also important. Analysis of this survey data will high-light those parts of the road network operating at less than capacity. In addition the number, location and extent of any bottlenecks on the network will also be revealed.

Public transport inventory

The designation of public transport networks is slightly more complicated than the designation of road networks. In the large urban areas both rail and bus facilities will be available for internal movements, but for the smaller built-up areas only bus transport will be of interest.

The identification of the railway network is a comparatively straight-forward matter, which can be done from a route map and time-table. The capacity of the various services can only be obtained by field studies, or with the co-operation of British Rail. It is usual for the public transport operators to participate in the transportation planning process, and in addition to current passenger volumes carried, they also provide details about fare structure and future proposals.[11]

A similar procedure is adopted in identifying a bus network. Principal routes, stopping places, and travel times can be derived from route maps and the operator's time-table. However, buses are invariably delayed by traffic congestion, especially during the peak periods, and to obtain the actual rather than the scheduled running time of the services, a check is made in the field. In addition, links must be added into the public transport network to represent time spent walking and waiting at the terminal and interchange points.

Traffic volume census

Traffic volume counts are made at the external cordon, the internal cordon if operated, the internal screen lines, and any other position considered neces-sary. The purpose of the counts is to establish typical patterns of hourly, daily and seasonal variations in the traffic flow. These counts can be made manually, using the standard Ministry of Transport Enumeration Form, or banked tally counters, but the more normal practice is to use automatic recording counters in conjunction with sample manual classified counts to determine the composition of the traffic flow.[12] Pedestrian counts of move-ments across the carriageway are sometimes undertaken at conflict points.[13]

Travel-time survey

Travel times, and speed-flow relationships for both peak and off-peak periods are used as a basis for determining the present level of service per-formed by the system, and in the distribution and assignment stages of the transportation planning process. The 'moving-observer method', devised by the Road Research Laboratory, is considered to be the most efficient and reliable way of collecting this information for motor vehicles.[14] Basically the procedure involves an observer in

1   Making a trip in a motor vehicle over a specified length of the road network, both with and against the traffic stream he or she is surveying.
2   Counting the number of oncoming vehicles when travelling against the stream of traffic being surveyed.
3   Counting the number of vehicles overtaking the test car, and the number of moving vehicles overtaken by the test car.
4   Measuring the times taken for the journey with, and against, the stream being surveyed.

From the formulae

(i) $q = \dfrac{(x + y)}{(t_a + t_w)}$ (Flow)

q = flow vehicles per minute
t = mean journey time
x = vehicles met when travelling against the stream

(ii) $t = t_w - \dfrac{y}{q}$ (Mean journey time)

y = vehicles overtaking test car minus vehicles overtaken by test car
t_a = time against stream
t_w = time with stream

the flow of vehicles in the stream (in vehicles per minute) and the mean journey time can be calculated.

The run over each leg is repeated for a minimum of six times and x, y, t_a and t_w are replaced by the average values for the total number of runs.

Mean journey times are be obtained for different classes of vehicle if x and y are counted for the different classes of vehicle.

Parking survey
'It appears absolutely essential that the public authority should retain complete control of

1   the amount of parking space that is provided
2   its location, and
3   the charges that are levied

and it should be prepared to use this control methodically as part of the transportation plan.'[15]

As part of the transportation planning process parking investigations are undertaken to collect information about the physical location, type, capacity, layout and operating characteristics of existing on- and off-street parking facilities within the central area.[16] The number of legal parking spaces is determined by a field survey – as are other factors such as specially reserved spaces for lorry loading, bus stops, taxi stands, hotel entrances, and areas within the vicinity of junctions, pedestrian walks, and driveways where parking is prohibited. Time limits and other restrictions on the use of legal metered and non-metered parking spaces are determined. The rates charged for metered on-street spaces and off-street facilities are recorded. This data is then processed to determine the total parking supply in the central area.

The existing parking demand within the central area is determined by means of a count of parkers within the district. The method usually adopted is to record the licence plate of each legally and illegally parked vehicle at intervals of not exceeding thirty minutes, between the hours of 7 a.m. and 7 p.m. on a weekday. This data when analysed will indicate the occupancy and turnover of parking spaces within the area.

In addition parking information collected in the field is used in conjunction with the information collected in the home-interview study, on destination, type of parking and distance walked after parking, to determine the existing parking demand.

Planning and economic data

The *Traffic in Towns Report* quite clearly demonstrated that the movement of goods and people by either public transport or private motor vehicle is inextricably linked with the distribution and intensity of land use.

Vehicles do not of course move about the roads for mysterious reasons of their own. They move only because people want them to move in connection with activities which they (the people) are engaged in. Traffic is therefore a function of activities . . . and traffic is concentrated in towns because activities are concentrated there. It is characteristic of activities in towns that they mainly take place in buildings or in places such as markets, depots, docks and stations. . . . In towns therefore traffic can be said to be the function of buildings.[17]

It is this relationship which forms the basis of transportation planning, whereby present-day trip generation rates are established for different land-use, population and economic characteristics. These planning factors are then predicted for the target date, and future trip generation rates estimated using the predicted planning data, and the present-day relationship between trip generation and planning data.

Population and employment data

The type of planning data collected varies with the size, purpose and organization of the study being carried out. However, certain elements are fundamental to all studies. For each internal traffic zone, basic population statistics are essential. Experience has shown that the total zonal population is a significant factor in estimating trip generation. In addition some indication of the age/sex, and household structure of the zonal population is required. In some instances this can take the form of a simple indication of the number of persons of five years of age and above. In other cases the age structure can be given in considerable detail covering the groups 0–4 yr, 5–14 yr, 15–24 yr, 25–44 yr, 45–59 yr, and 60 and over, although fewer number categories would probably be more satisfactory. The household structure of a zone can similarly be given in an unsophisticated way such as the total number of households, or can be subdivided into categories based on different household sizes.

Information relating to the size and structure of the labour force is also required for each internal zone. This data can be simply the crude total of residents who are in employment, or it can be presented in more detail by breaking it down into significant groupings by age and sex.

The most comprehensive source of this data is the Census of Population which provides all the above information for Enumeration Districts, parishes and wards throughout the country. However, there are two basic problems associated with using the census as a source of population data:

1   Enumeration Districts are arbitrarily defined areas, based broadly on the amount of information it is possible for a census enumerator to collect in one day. They rarely coincide with traffic zone boundaries. Consequently, difficulty is experienced in providing reliable population statistics for each traffic zone.
2   The Census of Population is carried out decennially, with the result that any data used is often several years out of date.

Consequently, the Census of Population tends to be used in transportation studies largely as a check against population data collected in the home-interview study, rather than as a basic source of data.

The incompatibility of Enumeration Districts and traffic zones could be overcome if the census information were to be collected for areas related to National Grid References. Attempts have been made in recent years to overcome this problem and perhaps the most successful method has been that adopted by Essex County Council. In several studies they have conducted, Enumeration Districts were used as traffic zones. In those instances where traffic zone requirements were in conflict with the Enumeration District, planning data and movements were coded to both the Enumeration District and a superimposed traffic zone.

For all internal zones employment data is required which relates to the total number of jobs, and the break-down of these jobs into the type of employment. This grouping of employment data should be based on the Standard Industrial Classification, although the number of classes used can vary with the purpose and scope of the study.[18] It is usual to identify at least three types of employment category distinguishing between extractive/primary, manufacturing, and service employment. In the larger transportation studies the types of employment are often classified into as many as nine groups covering manufacturing industry, non-manufacturing industry, retail trade, personal services, business and professional, wholesale trade and storage, public service, recreation and others.

The Department of Employment carries out a triennial Census of Employment which is available locally through the Manpower Services Commission, who act as the regional representative of the Department of Employment. The census is based on a one-third sample of firms above a certain size, although the size cut-off point varies from area to area depending on the size of firms in the area. The data is coded by post-code and can be amalgamated by ward, district and county if necessary.

There are a number of problems associated with using this census as a basic source of employment data, for example it is not a complete record of employment; the data can be up to three years out of date; establishments with branch offices may have all their employees registered at the head office, despite the fact that they may be dispersed throughout the country. As a result the census is only rarely used as a source of employment data in transportation studies. It is usual practice to carry out a special survey to derive the required information.

This survey can be a sample survey or a complete coverage, and the sample frame is usually derived from the Valuation Rolls. Special investigations are also initiated to determine employment premises not listed in the rolls. Information from the home-interview study relating to destinations for employment is used as a check against the employment survey data.

The inclusion of journey to work questions in the Census, and the availability of this data at Enumeration District level provides another source of employment data, in a form which could be used in the transportation planning process. Detailed information is provided concerning the destination of all those in employment, the industry of employment by Standard Industrial Classification, and the mode of travel to work. However, the problem of the probable incompatibility of Enumeration Districts and traffic zones remains.

Income

The level of income in a household affects the number, frequency and mode of trips made by the residents. Consequently, as part of the transportation planning process, data is required about the income levels in each traffic zone. One method of obtaining this information is by asking a direct question about household income as part of the home-interview study. However, the population at large is generally reluctant to answer such personal questions and if answers are given there is a strong possibility that they will be incorrect anyway.

An indication of levels of income in each zone is therefore derived indirectly from an analysis of those factors which reflect income and for which information is more readily available. Levels of car owner-ship – derived from the excise licence records kept by the local authorities – the proportion of owner-occupied dwellings in the zone, or alternatively the proportion of council-rented properties – derived from valuation rolls, or local authority records – the socio-economic group of the chief economic supporter – derived from an analysis of occupation by socio-economic group – are all popular and generally adopted indicators.

The Census provides the bulk of this information, at Enumeration District level, giving details of the following.

1   The total number of cars owned, the number of households with nil, one and two or more cars.
2   The number of owner-occupied dwellings, council-rented dwellings, other rented dwellings furnished and unfurnished, and 'other' dwellings.
3   The socio-economic group of the chief economic supporter of the household.
4   The social class of the chief economic supporter of the household. How-ever, the problem of incompatibility of Enumeration Districts and traffic zones still remains to be overcome.

Retail sales
The number of trips made to the central area for shopping purposes is reflected in the volume of retail sales, and/or the retail floor area. Data relating to these two factors is therefore required in the transportation plan-ning process; in some instances all that is required is the crude total for all shopping centres within the survey area. In the more sophisticated studies, the volume of retail sales is classified into sales of day-to-day goods, and durable goods; and the retail floor area into 'selling' space and storage space. Floor-space data can be derived either from a land-use survey or an exami-nation of the valuation rolls. Statistics relating to sales in different categories of retailing over the UK can be obtained from the *Retailing Enquiry* pro-duced by the Business Statistics office of the Department of Trade and Industry. Unfortunately this information is not available on a local basis, although local information on retail floor space use may be available from private firms e.g. URPI or major Chartered Surveyors.[19]

Attendance at schools, colleges and other educational establishments
Information about the location, and number of attendances at primary and secondary schools and further education establishments is required for each internal zone. This data is obtained from local authority records. If necessary the home-interview study results can be used as a check.

Other land-use data

It has been found that both the amount and the characteristics of travel are influenced by the intensity of development of land. For residential areas – the areas from which the bulk of travel is generated – this intensity of use is measured in terms of residential· density. Net residential density is the measure most typically used and is defined as the ratio of the resident population or the number of dwellings or the number of habitable rooms to the acreage of all land used for residential purposes, plus half the width of the surrounding roads up to a maximum of twenty feet.

For employment zones and the central area – the areas to which most trips are attracted – the intensity of use is measured in terms of Plot Ratio or Floor Space Index. The former is defined as the ratio of usable floor space to the net site area. The latter is defined as the ratio of total space to the site area plus half the width of roads up to a maximum of twenty feet.

Evaluation of survey accuracy

It is desirable to check the accuracy of the survey data before the process of analysis is completely under way. This is done by comparing it with facts that are either already known, or obtained as part of the survey process.

Home interview

The accuracy of the dwelling-unit sample selection can be estimated by comparing the population of each Enumeration District or traffic zone, as determined from the expanded home-interview data, with the population derived from census data. The census data, however, must be adjusted to take account of changes which may have occurred since that information was compiled.

To avoid unnecessary expense a preliminary check should be done manually before the tabulating cards are punched. If at all possible it should be carried out as the interviewing is completed in each zone or area, so that if the comparison is not satisfactory the source of the trouble can be determined immediately and steps taken to rectify the situation before the work is too advanced.

Expanded home-interview data should not vary by more than $\pm$ 15 per cent of the adjusted census data. If an unsatisfactory comparison does result then the two possible causes are:

1 An inadequate or poorly selected sample.
2 Unsatisfactory work on the part of the interviewers.

The cause can be determined by carrying out spot checks at sample dwellings previously interviewed, and if this shows the interviewers to be at fault then they should either be given further instruction on interviewing procedure or they should be replaced by other trained interviewers. If necessary, parts or all of the zones showing unsatisfactory comparisons should be re-interviewed.

If the spot checks indicate that an inadequate or poorly chosen sample is the cause of poor comparisons, then the procedure of sample selection should be re-examined and if necessary a modified sample chosen.

Travel-pattern data

The accuracy of travel-pattern data recorded in the home-interview study and the roadside interviews can be checked in a variety of ways each of which involves preparatory work before the survey commences. Perhaps the most satisfactory method of checking motor vehicle trip data is the use of a screen line. The object of a screen line is to divide the area bounded by the external cordon into two, and to compare the actual traffic flows across the line with those reported in the home-interview study. The screen line chosen should preferably be a natural barrier, such as a river or railway, with comparatively few crossing points. It should be straight to avoid vehicles crossing it more than once on the same trip; it should not pass through the central area where the complexity of vehicle trips is almost certain to involve vehicles crossing and recrossing it on the same trip; and it should not pass too close to the external cordon. An alternative to the use of a screen line is the use of two or three control points, preferably in different parts of the study area. Viaducts, bridges, underpasses or other well-known points through which large volumes of traffic pass are most suitable locations for these control points, and the objective is to compare the actual vehicle trips passing through the control point with the number of trips reported in the home and roadside interviews which should pass through the same control point.

The traffic counts carried out at both the screen line and the control points are similar, and include the use of automatic vehicle counters, recording total traffic flows in one hourly periods, supplemented by classified manual counts.

In addition to the checks provided by the screen line or control points, data collected at the external cordon roadside interviews can be used to assess the accuracy of the trips across the external cordon reported in the home-interview study by residents and commercial vehicle operators within the external cordon.

A comparison of the reported public transport trips with the total public transport movements for an average day, derived from the public transport operators, will reveal any discrepancies in this particular field.

The accuracy with which journeys to and from work have been reported can be assessed by comparing the number of persons employed in a particular zone, with the work trips into the zone as derived from the expanded-interview data. Allowance must be made for absenteeism and persons walking to work.

Analysis

Coding and punching

Before the data collected by the interviewers can be processed it must be coded into a predetermined series of number forms. This coded information is then punched on to paper tape or punched cards for mechanical sorting and processing. Occasionally the interview forms used in the field are so arranged that the results are entered on the form in the appropriate code, as the interview takes place. This process, however, places additional strain on the interviewer, and in practice it has been found that it is safer to use special staff to code the data in the office.

The coding operation is repetitive and tedious, and in an attempt to eliminate confusion and errors the process is usually broken down into a series of operations, each performed by an individual member of the coding staff, e.g. one person codes the origins and destinations only, another codes mode of travel and so on. Once the data has been coded it is transferred to punched cards or paper tape by specially trained operators, and is used in this form as the computer input.

Expansion factors

Data collected at the different types of field survey which utilize a sampling procedure, must be expanded to represent the whole population, and to account for missed interviews. This is achieved through the use of expansion factors and ordinarily they are calculated for each zone used in the survey:

1   The expansion factor used for the home-interview study is basically the total universe, i.e. the total number of households in the survey area divided by the total number of successful interviews. This is calculated from the following formula, for each traffic zone.

$$\text{Expansion factor} = \frac{A - \dfrac{A}{B}(C + \dfrac{C}{B} \times D)}{B - C - D}$$

where A = total number of addresses on original list

B = total number of addresses selected as original sample

C = number of sample addresses that are ineligible (e.g. demolished, non-residential)

D = number of sample addresses where no response is made (e.g. refusal to answer, no reply)

2   The external cordon survey expansion factor is usually derived for each class of vehicle, time interval and direction of flow used at the survey point. It is calculated from the following formula.

$$\text{Expansion factor} = \frac{A}{B}$$

where A = the number of vehicles of the specified class counted passing
through the survey point for the relevant time interval

B = the number of vehicles interviewed, of the same class and for
the same time interval

In addition '24-hour' factors are required to bring to a 24-hour basis the
information collected at the external cordon stations operated for a
16-hour period only. This is achieved from the following formula.

$$\text{24-hour expansion factor} = R \times \frac{A}{B}$$

where R = average expansion factor for time interval

A = average count for 'n' days for vehicles of appropriate class
passing through survey point in 24 hours

B = average count for 'n' days for vehicles of appropriate class
passing through survey point during the period of time interviews are made

3 The Commercial Vehicle Survey expansion factor is derived in the same
way as the home-interview survey expansion factor; from the formula

$$\text{Expansion factor} = \frac{A - \dfrac{A}{B}(C + \dfrac{C}{B} \times D)}{B - C - D}$$

where A = total number of registrations on the original list

B = number of registrations chosen as the sample

C = number of vehicles in the sample disposed of or unlicensed

D = number of vehicles for which refusals are recorded

A separate factor is usually calculated for each traffic zone.

'Through' trips
In theory 'through' trips will cross the external cordon twice, and will therefore be interviewed twice. The standard method of eliminating this dup-
lication is to punch a 0.5 expansion factor in all 'through' trip records.
Alternatively the processed tabulated values for through trips can be divided
by two.

Tabulations
Data collected in the various stages of a transportation study is comprehensive, and can be presented in many different forms. With the advantage

of hindsight it is frequently possible to say '. . . too many tabulations were certainly prepared, and some have never been used'.[20] To eliminate, as far as possible, the danger of such a situation arising, it is usual to prepare, in the initial stages, standard tabulations required for all transportation studies. At the same time care should be taken to ensure that the coded data in its punched state, or converted to magnetic tape, is so arranged as to facilitate the processing of any tabulations that may later be required.

Data for disaggregrate behavioural models

Disaggregate behavioural models rely on sampling and estimation theory in determining the data samples from which the model will be built. The characteristics of a 'good' sample depend on the specific model to be estimated and the costs involved. For this reason it is essential to carry out pilot surveys to establish potential sampling problems before commencing the main survey. Experience has shown that any broad class of stratified sample survey can be used to support model estimation. Thus '. . . aggregate data on a fraction of a population selecting various travel alternatives and having given characteristics can be of value in the estimation of individual choice models.'[21]

Although the observation of actual travel decisions made by a sample of decision makers is the predominant data source for the estimation of behavioural travel models, a number of studies have used hypothetical choice experiments to derive data. These have given results which are similar to those found with observation of actual travel decisions.[22] An advantage of this experimental approach is that it allows multiple choice observations to be obtained for each subject, in contrast with the one observation per respondent through the more traditional sample survey approach. However, the experimental approach is questioned on the basis that reported actions are likely to be more reliable than hypothetical choices.

Data for activity-based travel studies

Four data collection procedures have been identified as being of value in activity-based travel studies.[23] They are diary methods, unstructured interviews, gaming simulation, and participant observation. The diary method is the approach most commonly adopted.

Travel diaries[24]

These can be used to record the activity travel patterns of households over the same time period, for example a day, a week, a month. In simplistic terms respondents selected through structured or random samples are asked to complete a diary giving details of the household's travel patterns for the chosen time period, including, for example, timing and duration, location, travel mode, and sequencing. In the words of Jones they '. . . can be used to record what respondents are doing, with whom, where and why.'[25] Two general approaches to measuring activity patterns can be adopted – first to decompose the activity pattern into its component parts, the second attempts to treat the pattern as a whole. The majority of studies use the former approach. While diary studies are informative it should be acknowledged that they are often suspect quantitatively.

The following dimensions of activity patterns are important from a travel point of view.

Timing   This is frequently measured in terms of clock time, i.e. at what time did the activity take place? However it can also be measured in terms of its occurrence relative to other activities, such as work. For example, the day can be subdivided into five segments (prior to work, during the home–work trip, during work, during work to home trip, and after work) and the frequency with which people undertake different activities examined during each of these segments. Damm adopts such an approach and argues that separate modelling of trips within each time sequence should be undertaken.[26]

Duration   This is usually recorded as the amount of time individuals spend in particular activities.

Location   The location at which different activities take place, and the associated land-use category, are particularly important in transportation planning, especially the out-of-home activities. These should be coded to street addresses, rather than zones, and the land-use category at each location identified if the intricate relationship between land use and transport is to be understood.

Travel mode   The mode of travel used between activity locations is also an important factor to be recorded in the travel diary survey.

Sequencing and substitutability of activities   These are factors which have received little attention to date. However, the substitutability of one activity for another, or the capacity to re-order the sequence with which activities occur without incurring perceived disadvantages, inevitably affect the overall activity pattern. Thus they are important factors to be taken into account in any travel diary. However as Hanson and Burnett observe 'Given the range and complexity encompassed in these dimensions of activity travel patterns, it is not surprising that researchers have not managed to capture their full complexity in measurement devices.'[27]

Unstructured interviews
These allow respondents to describe their activities in their own terms and can also provide a degree of quantitative information. However the flexibility inherent in this approach precludes standardization across interviews. As a result this method of data collection is usually restricted to small samples as a cross check on diary procedures.

Gaming simulation

In general terms this approach uses probability theory to generate the expected relative frequencies of activities and then compares the results with the observed frequencies. Experience suggests that different gaming-simulation methodologies can be used in this respect, for example the HATS board simulation work carried out at the Transport Studies Unit, Oxford, which focuses on the constraints imposed on travel behaviour by societal roles. In this approach the roles of the household respondents are defined in terms of sex, age, marital status, and occupation. They are asked to plot a typical day's activity travel pattern on a map of their area, with an associated time scale, following which they are requested to simulate the alterations in their activity travel pattern which would occur if there was some change in a policy variable, such as the timing of bus services.[28]

Participant observation

This method has been used extensively in human activity studies but is largely untried in the context of travel. It allows the behaviour of individuals or groups to be observed over long periods in their social and environmental context, and provides unique information about specific population groups. However, as a method of data collection it is expensive in terms of both time and money.

References

1   Fischer, R. J. and Sosslau, A. B., 'Census data as a source for urban transportation planning', *Highway Research Board Record No. 141* (1966).
2   Sheath, R. and Lee, N. H., 'Zoning by National Grid References', *Traffic Engineering and Control* (1965).
3   Taylor, M. A., *Zoning for Urban Travel Studies*, Road Search Laboratory L N/415/M A T (1963) (unpublished).
4   Sheath, R. and Lee, N. H., *op. cit.*
5   Conducting a home-interview origin and destination survey, *Procedure Manual – National Committee on Urban Transportation*, Public Administration Service, Chicago (1954).
6   *Memorandum on Land Use/Transportation Studies for Medium Sized Towns*, Ministry of Transport (1966) (unpublished).
7   Buchanan Colin and Partners, *Bath: A Planning and Transport Study* (1965).
8   Ministry of Transport, Scottish Development Department, *Urban Traffic Engineering Techniques*, HMSO, London (1965).
9   Road Research Laboratory, *Research on Road Traffic*, Traffic Surveys (chapter 4), HMSO, London (1965).
10 Anderson, J. E. F., 'Transportation studies: a review of results to date from typical areas – Belfast', *Proceedings of the Transportation Engineering Conference* organized by the Institution of Civil Engineers, London (1968).
11 For example: 'The co-operation of British Rail, the Scottish Bus Group, and the Glasgow Corporation Transport Department' in the *Greater Glasgow Transportation Study* has facilitated the collection of data concerning fare structure, current passenger volumes, operating schedules and planned new routes.

12　See *Measuring Traffic Volumes – Procedure Manual*, National Committee on Urban Transportation, Public Administration Service, Chicago (1958).

13　See *Urban Traffic Engineering Techniques*, Para. 55–9, *op. cit.*

14　Wardrop, J. B. and Charlesworth, G., 'A method of estimating speed and flow of traffic from a moving vehicle', *Proceedings of the Institution of Civil Engineers*, Part II, Volume 3 (1954).

15　Buchanan, C. D., *Traffic in Towns – Reports of the Steering Group and Working Group*, Para. 452, HMSO, London (1963).

16　See (i) *Parking*, Eno Foundation, Saugatauk, Connecticut (1957). (ii) *Parking in Town Centres*, Ministry of Housing and Local Government, and the Ministry of Transport, HMSO (1965).

17　Buchanan, C. D., *Traffic in Towns, op. cit.*

18　See Central Statistical Office, *Standard Industrial Classification*, HMSO, London (1971).

19　Guy, C., 'The Estimation of Retail Turnover for Planning Purposes', *Journal of the Royal Town Planning Institute*, Vol. 70 No. 5 (May 1984) pp. 12–14. Wade, B., 'Retail Planning without Data, *Journal of the Royal Town Planning Institute*, Vol. 69, No. 1 (Jan–Feb 1983) pp. 26–8.

20　Martin, B. V., 'Transportation studies: a review of results from typical areas – 1. London' *Proceedings of the Transportation Engineering Conference* organized by the Institution of Civil Engineers, London (1968).

21　Manski, C. F., 'Recent Advances in and New Directions for Behaviour Travel Modelling', in Stopher, P. R., Meyburg, A. H. and Brog, W., *New Horizons in Travel Behaviour Research*, Lexington Books, Lexington, Mass, (1981) p. 78.

22　Thomas, K., 'A Re-interpretation of the Attitude Approach to Transport Mode Choice and an Explanatory Empirical Test', *Environment and Planning A 8, No. 7* (1976) pp. 793–810.

23　Jones, P. M., 'Activity Approaches to Understanding Travel Behaviour', in Stopher, Meyburg and Brog (1981) *op. cit.*, pp. 257–8.

24　See Guy, C., Wrigley, N., O'Brien, L., and Hiscocks, G., *The Cardiff Consumer Panel: A Report on the Methodology*, Papers in Planning Research No. 68, Department of Town Planning, UWIST, Cardiff (1983) for a detailed account of the methodology involved in producing a diary relating to shopping activity patterns.

25　Jones, P. M. (1981) *op. cit.*, p. 257.

26　As reported in Hanson, S. and Burnett, K. P., 'Understanding Complex Travel Behaviour Measurement Issues' in Stopher, Meyburg and Brog (1981) *op. cit.*, pp. 207–30. This chapter provides a good review of measurement issues in activity-based travel studies, especially pp. 213–25.

27　Hanson and Burnett (1981) *op. cit.*, p. 215.

28　Jones, P. M., *A Methodology for Assessing Transportation Policy Impacts*, paper presented at the 58th TRB Meeting, Washington, D. C. (1979).

Source (for Figures 6–8): Wycombe Area Transportation Study – Interview Manual, County Surveyor, County Planning Officer, Buckinghamshire County Council, Borough Engineer and Surveyor, High Wycombe.

4 Trip generation

Introduction

The trip generation stage of the transportation planning process is concerned with the prediction of future levels of person or vehicle travel, usually for traffic zones or combinations of traffic zones known as traffic districts. The techniques developed attempt to utilize the observed relationships between travel characteristics and the urban environment, and are based on the assumption that 'trip making is a function of three basic factors.

1 The land-use pattern and developments in the study area.
2 The socio-economic characteristics of the trip-making population of the study area.
3 The nature, extent and capabilities of the transportation system in the study area.'[1]

These basic factors can be represented by a variety of interdependent variables whose influence changes both with the geographic location of the study area, and with different time periods. Trip generation studies are a vital part of the transportation planning process – it is essential that the present-day determinants of trip production be understood before the nature of the future travel demand can be assessed. Once the significant land-use, population and transport characteristics influencing travel demand have been identified, they are projected to the target date to provide estimates of the total amount and kind of travel demand.

As part of the trip generation study, it is normal practice to estimate separately trips generated by residential zones (whether they be origins or destinations) and trips generated by activities at the non-home end of a trip, such as employment or shopping. The term *trip production* is used to describe the trips generated by residential zones; *trip attraction* is the term used to describe trips generated at the non-home end of a trip. Trips are estimated separately in this way to ensure that at the distribution stage of the process different combinations of trips which are not necessarily reversible can be adequately catered for, for example a typical combination of trips made by one person throughout the day might be from home to work; from work to recreation (cinema) and from recreation to home. The more commonly used synthetic distribution models incorporate both trip productions and trip attractions in their basic framework.

Depending on the design of the overall study process, trip generation models can be derived for person or vehicle movements, by trip purpose and time of day. For example, if the study is designed to incorporate a trip end modal split model (i.e. the allocation of the various movements to different modes of transport before the generated trips are distributed between the traffic zones), then the trip generation model could be designed to derive trips in terms of person movements by different modes of travel. If on the other hand a trip interchange modal split model is to be used, which allocates different portions of the total trip movements between zones to the various travel modes after the trip distribution stage, then the trip generation model could be designed to derive trips in terms of total person movements. Similarly, since person trips having different trip purposes present different trip distribution and modal split characteristics, it is often considered essential to stratify trips by purpose throughout the transportation planning processs. This in turn implies that trip generation analysis must be undertaken for different trip purposes. The number of different trip purposes used varies with the design of the individual study. A typical stratification of home-based trips could well take the following form.

1   From home to work
2   From home to shop
3   From home to other
4   From work to home
5   From shop to home
6   From other to home

The generation of non-home-based trips, such as delivery of goods from one industrial plant to another, is usually estimated in terms of vehicle movements. Depending on the design of the study this can be stratified into the different types of vehicle making these non-home-based movements, or can be estimated as total vehicle movements produced or attracted. A typical stratification could be into light, medium and heavy commercial vehicles.

Factors influencing trip generation

Land-use factors

Land use is a convenient way of classifying trip generating activities, because it is a factor which in Britain can be predicted with a reasonable degree of accuracy, and is readily measured. Different uses of land produce different trip generation characteristics. For example, land given over to shopping development or offices could be expected to generate more trips than open space.

Similarly the intensity with which different activities are pursued can produce different generation characteristics. For example, one acre of residential land developed at a high density would be likely to produce more total person movements than one acre of land developed for residential purposes at a low density. On the other hand, the low-density residential area occupied by fewer and probably more expensive dwellings could well produce more private motor vehicle trips than the high-density residential area.

Although the range of urban land uses is extensive, for the purposes of trip generation studies it is usual to consider only the most significant uses. Since between 80 and 90 per cent of all journeys have either a beginning or an end in the home, residential land use is of prime importance. The measure of residential development used in trip generation studies varies with the type of study being undertaken. It can for example be represented in terms of acres of residential land, number of dwelling units, number of dwelling units per acre, number of persons per acre, or total population.

Commercial and industrial land use, as employment centres, are the next most significant land uses in connection with trip generation, and as different types of commercial and industrial activities produce different generation rates it is usual to distinguish between manufacturing and service industry, retail and wholesale distribution, and office employment. A variety of measures of intensity of these activities can be used, but the most common tend to be the numbers employed per unit area of land; and the land area given over to, or the amount of floor space occupied by, such activities.

Other uses of land considered to be significant in terms of trip generation are educational and recreational developments. Educational establishments such as universities, technical colleges and comprehensive schools are large generators of movement and in many cases warrant particular attention. For example the *Guildford Study*, carried out by Buchanan and Partners, included a comprehensive study of the effect of the development of the University of Surrey on trip generation and distribution in Guildford.[2]

The most commonly used measure of the intensity of development at an educational institution tends to be the numbers in attendance. Small recreational facilities can by and large be ignored in the transportation planning process, but there are exceptional cases where careful consideration must be paid to these uses, e.g. large regional parks such as the Lea Valley Regional Park and the Central London area of concentrated theatre and entertainment developments.

The home[3]

Family size Travel is a function of human activity. Consequently a relationship should exist between the number and frequency of trips made from the home and family size. Schuldiner in his work on the Modesto area of California has shown that average trip frequency increases with increasing persons per household, at the rate of approximately 0.8 trips per day for each additional person. This increase in the number of trips with family size is, however, related mainly to non-work trips which tend to level off at the four person per dwelling unit family size.

Motor vehicle ownership   The ability to satisfy travel demands is affected by the availability of alternative means of transport and the adequacy of the highway system. Motor vehicle ownership, or the number of vehicles available for use by each household, has been found to have a significant influence on trip generation. Households with more than one motor vehicle tend to generate more trips per unit than households with only one motor vehicle, although the single-car households tend to utilize their vehicle more intensively.

Motor vehicle ownership and family size are to a certain extent related. Generally speaking it is the larger family which has the higher level of car ownership. It would appear that the greater trip generation inherent in larger families is only fully realized where sufficient motor vehicles are available for use by members of the family. Thus a large non-motor-vehicle-owning family can be expected to generate fewer trips than the same size family which has access to three motor vehicles. A variety of measures of car ownership can be used, the most common of which are the total number of cars per zone, car ownership per person, or car ownership per household.

Type of dwelling unit   It can be argued that the more permanent types of dwelling unit, such as a single family house, reflect a high degree of integration into the local community on the part of the household, and lead to a high rate of trip generation. Conversely the less permanent dwellings, e.g. a hotel room, result in a more limited integration with local affairs, with a lower resultant trip generation rate. Indeed Schuldiner found that this was the case although the difference was not as marked as was expected. Although the average number of 'from home' trips increased with the permanency of the dwelling type, when family size and car-ownership levels were taken into consideration, the difference in generation rates was not as great as appeared at first sight.

Occupied residents   The occupation of the head of the household is one of the major indicators of the standard of living enjoyed by the family and reflects to a certain extent the family income. In general terms it has been found that the proportion of work trips for the gainfully employed groups decreases as the occupational status increases, although the proportion of trips for non-work purposes varies little between the various groups with the exception of the unemployed. The number of residents in employment is of importance in trip generation studies because of its relationship with the work journey movement. It is closely related, however, to total resident population.

Family income   The ability to pay for a journey affects the number of trips generated by a household. Thus families with a high income can generally afford to satisfy more of their movement demands than low-income families. As one would expect, increasing family income leads to greater trip production. Family income tends to be related to levels of motor vehicle ownership.

Other factors influencing trip generation
A variety of other factors relating to the characteristics of the resident population are considered to be related to trip generation. The rateable value of a property is considered indicative of the occupiers' financial status. Thus the greater the annual outgoing in rent, or interest on invested capital, the more likely it is that the occupiers have resources available to spend on travel. Rateable value is related to family income, and because it is usually easier to obtain reliable information about rateable value than family income, rateable value is sometimes used in trip generation analysis instead of family income.

The age structure of the population is often taken into consideration in trip generation analysis on the basis that different age groups produce different movement demands and characteristics. The teenage population 15–20 years, for example, could be expected to produce more journeys of a social and recreational nature than older age groups.

Similarly, socio-economic characteristics of the population could be expected to produce different movement demands. Blue-collar workers, i.e. factory or manual workers, could be expected to produce quite different movement characteristics to white-collar workers, i.e. executive clerical workers. Again, preliminary work by Schuldiner has shown that trip generation analysis based on socio-economic characteristics held some promise for the future, especially in terms of a better understanding of trip length and trip interchange for the work and social trips. However, more recent work by Taylor has shown that for all modes of travel and a range of journey purposes there appears to be little relationship between the zonal socio-economic characteristics examined by him and trip generation.[4]

The degree of urbanization exhibited by an area can be used to represent the level of integration of the household in the local community. Schuldiner derived an index of urbanization based on fertility rate, female labour participation rate, and the incidence of single family dwellings, and found in his analysis of data relating to Chicago that it appeared to exert a significant effect on trip generation rates.[5]

Another measure of the degree of urbanization which is often used is distance from the central area. The argument for the use of this factor is that characteristics of the population and development, and hence the movement demand, change with distance from the central area. For example, within the central area the residential development may consist largely of 'temporary' hotel, flat and boarding-house accommodation occupied by young, single or transient persons, while the outer suburbs may consist largely of single family dwelling units occupied by married couples with families.

The quality of transportation facilities, and the resulting level of accessibility, must affect trip generation. However, apart from preliminary work done on Accessibility Indices in North America and Europe, little is known about any relationship which might exist. Further research in this field could well result in the improvement in techniques used to predict future trip generation.

A discussion of the many variables affecting trip generation does not, however, indicate their mutual interdependence and potential use through statistical techniques for estimating trip generation. This is usually derived through multiple linear regression analysis, although more recent techniques such as category analysis have been developed to estimate future levels of trip generation.

Methods of forecasting trip generation rates

Trip generation by expansion factors

Early transportation studies, such as the Detroit Metropolitan Area Traffic Study, used simple expansion (or growth) factors to estimate future trip ends for traffic zones or districts. In its simplest form, the method relates data collected in the movement studies to data collected in the land-use survey, to develop a trip generation rate for major land uses. Thus a hypothetical traffic zone consisting of 3000 acres of residential development, and giving rise to 6000 trip ends, would have a trip generation rate relating trip ends to land use of 2, i.e. 6000 divided by 3000. To derive an estimate of future trip ends for this zone the trip generation rate is then applied to the forecast land area. If one assumes for the hypothetical traffic zone that the area of land given over to residential development in the target year for the study will be 6000 acres, then the estimated trip ends will be 12,000, i.e. 6000 (acres) × 2 (trip generation rate). This simple approach, however, fails to take account of other factors influencing trip generation, such as car ownership, and density of development, and does not reflect the underlying causes of travel. Although the Chicago Area Transportation Study modified the approach to take account of car ownership and residential density, the method is of limited value and only tends to be used for short-term forecasting in rural areas, and to estimate trip ends for 'external–internal' and 'through' movements.

Trip generation by multiple linear regression analysis

Multiple linear regression analysis is the statistical technique most often used to derive estimates of future trip generation, where two or more independent factors are suspected of simultaneously affecting the amount of travel. This technique measures the separate influence of each factor acting in association with other factors, and the aim of the analysis is to produce from the traffic, land-use and socio-economic data an equation of the following form

$$y = k + b_1 X_1 + b_2 X_2 + \ldots \ldots + b_n X_n$$

where y is the dependent variable (i.e. the zonal measure of traffic in terms of person movements, or movements by mode and purpose).

X_1 to X_n are independent variables relating for example to zonal land-use, and socio-economic characteristics.

b_1 to b_n are the coefficients of the respective independent variable and k is a constant included to represent that portion of the value of *y* not explained by the independent variables.

In a typical regression analysis the given data relates to the present-day values of the dependent variable (*y*) and the independent variables (X_1 to X_n), for all the zones of the area under study. The statistical technique of 'Least Squares' fitting process is then applied to determine those values of the regression coefficients (b_1 to b_n) and the constant (k) which best fit the given data.[6,7]

The resulting regression equation is then solved using the estimated future values of the independent variables to derive the dependent variable (*y* – trips generated by each zone) for the appropriate target date for the study. For example assume that multiple linear regression analysis on present-day data derived a regression equation of the following form:

$$y = -0.59X_1 + 0.74X_2 + 0.88X_3 - 39.6X_4 + 112$$

where y = number of work trips by all modes
X_1 = number of dwelling units
X_2 = employed persons
X_3 = motor vehicle ownership
X_4 = distance to central area

To derive an estimate of *y* for the target date for the study, appropriate estimates of X_1 the number of dwelling units, X_2 number of employed persons, X_3 motor vehicle ownership and X_4 distance to the central area, are substituted and the equation solved using the already established coefficients. Thus

y = number of work trips by all modes for the zone
= 0.59 × the number of dwelling units in the zone
+ 0.74 × the number of employed persons in the zone
+ 0.88 × the number of motor vehicles in the zone
− 39.6 × distance to the central area
+ 112

The statistical validity of trip generation analysis derived through multiple linear regression can be assessed by considering the standard statistical tests.

1   The multiple correlation coefficient (R) indicates the degree of association between the independent variable (*y*) and the dependent variables
(X_1-X_n). This coefficient takes a value between 0 and 1, and the closer it

is to 1 the better the linear relationship between the variables. The closer R is to 0 the worse is the linear relationship, although it is possible that a non-linear relationship might exist. The significance of R is that its square (R^2) is approximately the decimal fraction of the variation in the dependent variable (y) which is accounted for by the independent variables (X_1 to X_n). Thus a multiple correlation coefficient of 0.9 indicates that approximately eight-tenths (or 80 per cent) of the variation of the independent variable y is explained by the independent variables included in the regression equation. In considering R it should be remembered that statistically reliable associations can be developed which have little to do with the underlying functional relationships.

2   The standard error of estimate (SEE) indicates the degree of variation of the data about the regression line established, and is used to assess the value of the regression equation for prediction purposes. This statistic is sometimes referred to as the root-mean-square error, or the residual standard deviation, and it is comparable statistically to the standard deviation of a group of values about their mean. It compares the quality of the values of y predicted for the present-day situation using the regression equation, with the observed values of y which were used to derive the regression equation, and is calculated as follows:

$$SEE = \frac{\sqrt{\Sigma (Y - Y_{est})^2}}{N}$$

where SEE = standard error of estimate
Y = observed data used to derive regression equation, e.g. total work journey movements from zone A by all modes.
Y_{est} = value of Y calculated from the regression equation, e.g. estimated total work journey movements from zone A by all modes.
N = total number of zones used in the study.

The standard error of estimate is most meaningful when it is expressed as a percentage of the mean observed value of the dependent variable y, i.e.

$$\frac{\text{Numerical } SEE}{\begin{array}{c}\text{Average number of}\\\text{trips generated}\\\text{per zone}\end{array}} \times 100$$

A good equation has a standard error of estimate which is a small percentage of the mean, and vice versa.

3   The mean observed value of y ($\bar{y}$) should be examined carefully. If it is too small then the development of statistically stable relationships is unlikely.

A small mean observed value generally results when the basic movement data has been overstratified in an attempt to obtain more meaningful explanations of the variations in trip making by purpose. If the equation constant in the regression set (k) is large in relation to the mean observed value of the dependent variable (y) then the relationship is suspect statistically.

4   The significance (or lack of significance) of the regression coefficient of each independent variable in a regression equation (b_1-b_n) is indicated by the 't' test statistic. The value of 't' is calculated by dividing the regression coefficient by its standard error, and must have a value of at least 2.0 for significance to be established. Independent variables which have a 't' value of less than 2.0 do not have a significant relationship with the dependent variable and therefore contribute nothing to the equation. Any such independent variable should be deleted from the equation.

   The 'F ratio statistic' may be used as an alternative measure of the significance of the regression coefficient of each independent variable, and is equal to the square of the 't' value, i.e. t^2.

5   The graphic plotting of observed and estimated trip ends by zone is a most useful method of evaluating the overall performance of a regression equation. Zones which are 'unique' in any way will generally tend to stand well away from a line drawn at 45° from the junction of the x and y axes, and should be examined carefully for 'unique' characteristics such as a large hospital, or hypermarket. In such cases these 'unique' traffic generators should be excluded from the regression analysis and analysed separately.

Problems associated with the development of linear regression models[8]
The selection and formulation of variables is critical in the design of the trip generation model. The dependent variable (y) should measure adequately what is to be predicted, while the independent variables should provide an adequate explanation of the dependent variable as well as retaining a separate identity.

   Two fundamental criteria should be adhered to in the formulation of variables.

1   All the variables should be capable of clear interpretation, i.e. they must be capable of being named and measured.
2   All variables should be of the same type, i.e. point and aggregate variables should not be mixed.

In theory in formulating zonal regression models there is an apparent choice between the use of aggregate and point variables, where aggregate variables express total zonal values such as population per zone, trips per zone, and point variables express mean zonal values such as trips per household per zone. However, experience has shown that when aggregate variables are used in the regression set, the size of the residual error is related to the size of zone, which is automatically reflected in the aggregate variables. Examination of a number of regression analyses for home-based trips indicates that there is a linear correlation between the number of households in a zone and the standard error of the residuals, which can be overcome by using point variables in regression analysis. It should be noted however that 'The residuals are . . . affected by other criteria such as sampling errors and mis-specification of the relationship. The application of least squares regression using rate variables will not therefore guarantee the condition of constant error variance. It is clear, however, that the condition is more likely to be satisfied when rate rather than aggregate variables are used.'[9]

Two assumptions are necessary before multiple linear regression can be applied in trip generation. They are:

1   That a linear relationship exists between the dependent and independent variables.
2   That the influence of the independent variables is additive, i.e. the inclusion of each variable contributes towards accounting for the value of the dependent variable.

It is normal practice to test for linearity of relationship between variables by plotting a sample of the relevant data on graph paper, and visually inspecting the results. If linearity does not exist then the original variables can be modified to produce a linear relationship by taking the log, square root or reciprocal of the variable; e.g. the *Cardiff Development and Transportation Study*[10] derived a regression equation to predict car ownership by using the log of income, and the log of residential density, to overcome problems associated with a non-linear relationship. The final equation took the form:

$$\text{Cars per household} = -1.976$$
$$+ 1.03 \times \log \text{income}$$
$$- 0.366 \times \log \text{residential density}$$

If two independent variables are highly interrelated they generally yield non-additive influences on the dependent variable. It is possible to test for this by carrying out tests for correlation between the independent variables suspected of having a high interrelationship. If the correlation coefficient(s) is high then it is assumed that the interrelationship between the independent variables tested is also high.

This problem can be overcome by either eliminating the least important variable in the model, or by combining the two variables, provided the new aggregate variable can be named and measured. If all the variables must be included in the model then the statistical technique of factor analysis can be adopted to aggregate variables into independent and therefore additive influences.

As a further check on the 'reasonableness' of results, the statistically valid regression sets should be considered closely. In particular the size of the regression constant (k) in relation to the mean observed value of the dependent variable (y) should be carefully examined – if it is 'large' then the regression set should be used with caution. An equation constant is considered to be large when it accounts for a significant proportion of the mean observed value of the dependent variable, e.g. if, in the following regression set

$$y = 0.59X_1 + 0.74X_2 + 0.88X_3 - 39.6X_2 + 112$$

the mean observed value of y (y) was 126 then the equation constant of 112 would be considered 'large'.

It is unsafe to make the generalization that large constants are always bad. However, in such cases, further examination of the relationships in the regression equation should be undertaken in an attempt to indicate any inconsistencies which could be eliminated or rectified.

Similarly the signing (either + or –) of the independent variables should be examined for logic, i.e. is it logical to expect an independent variable with a positive (+) sign to make a positive contribution to the value of the dependent variable? For example, in developing a regression set to estimate person trips by public transport it would be reasonable to have an independent variable representing car ownership with a negative (–) sign. In this instance it is logical to assume that as car ownership increases the use of public transport decreases.

Dissatisfaction with the results of trip generation studies based on zonal least squares regression has led to the logical extension of the method to develop disaggregated models which make no reference to zone boundaries.[11] In this situation the household is generally taken as the basic unit of trip making, largely because of the dominating influence of the head of household on the trip making activities of the household members.

To develop the least squares household model, data relating to the trip making and socio-economic characteristics of *each* household are input rather than the zonal values. The step-wise regression procedure is then used to produce the 'best-fit' regression set. The household least squares model developed in the *Glamorgan Land Use/Transportation Study* indicates the form of relationship between total home-based trips per household per day and other household characteristics.

$$y = 0.91 + 1.44X_1 + 1.07X_2$$
where y = trips per household
X_1 = employers per household
X_2 = cars per household

Other variables considered in this study were family size and household income.

To produce an estimate of total zonal trip ends (which is after all what is required of this stage of the process) the disaggregated least squares household model is then expanded to the zonal level, by multiplying the value of *y* (trips per household) by the number of households in the zone. The tests of significance and reasonableness are applied to the household model in the normal way. Usually the least-squares household model is developed for 'categories' of household rather than for all households collectively as in the above example.

The basic criticisms of multiple linear regression analysis in trip generation are that (1) because it is empirical in nature it fails to establish a causal relationship between the dependent and independent variables, and (2) to use the derived equation for prediction purposes it has to be assumed that the regression coefficients established at a given time will be relevant in the future.

An examination of the reports of the many transportation studies which have used multiple linear regression analysis to estimate future trip generation indicates that only on rare occasions is a full evaluation of the statistical validity and reasonableness of results included in the report. However, the trip generation analysis carried out as part of the Cardiff and Harlow transportation studies indicates some of the principles and problems associated with the application of multiple linear regression analysis in practice. The Cardiff study adopts a fairly traditional approach by producing regression sets on a zonal basis for a range of journey purposes. The Harlow study extends this approach by producing some regression sets for 'categories' of households, using the least-squares household method.

Cardiff[12]

1   The overall design of the study dictated that separate forecasts of person trips and commercial vehicle trips had to be made, and these were to be assigned to the network on a 24-hour basis.

2   To accommodate at the distribution stage trips which were not reversible it was necessary to forecast both trip productions and trip attractions for each zone. In addition, since person trips with different purposes display different distribution and modal split characteristics, trips were stratified by purpose throughout the forecasting stage, and separate trip generation analyses were undertaken for seven trip purposes:

> Home-based trips
> 1   from home to work
> 2   from home to shop
> 3   from home to other
> 4   from work to home
> 5   from shop to home
> 6   from other to home

Non-home-based trips
7   from non-home to non-home

3   Prior to regression analysis the multiplicity of land-use and socio-economic characteristics were rationalized, and only those which could be forecast with any degree of accuracy were selected – twenty in all. These were further reduced following statistical tests, so that only those variables which could be shown to be statistically significant were included in the final regression analysis.

4   In the analysis of trip production from home seven independent variables were included in the analysis. They were:

Population
Population three years of age and over
Number of households
Number of employed residents
Number of cars owned
Area of residential land
Distance from central area.

Using a step-wise regression analysis, whereby variables which do not accord with the required level of significance are successively deleted from the equation, the above seven variables were reduced to five – the eliminated variables being population of three years of age and over, and distance to the central area. All of the remaining five variables were used in the final analysis for trip generation by purpose. However, those not reaching the required level of significance were eliminated. The resultant trip production equations for the trips from home by purpose were:

1   Trips to work =   0.097 × zonal population
                 – 351   × number of households in zone
                 +   0.773 × number of employed residents
                 +   0.504 × number of cars owned
                 + 43.6
   R (multiple correlation coefficient) 0.99
2   Trips to shop = 0.266 × number of cars owned
                 + 1.19   × area of residential land
                 – 17.9
   R = 0.95
3   Trips to other = 0.086 × zonal population
                 + 1.5   × number of cars owned
                 – 10.1
   R = 0.99

5   Trip production at the non-home end. To take account of the different generation characteristics of the central area this part of the analysis considered central area and non-central area generation separately. The land-

use parameters used in the initial regression analysis were numbers in employment in

> Manufacturing industry
> Service industry
> Retail distribution
> Government offices
> Other offices
> Wholesale distribution
> Total zone employment
> Area of service industry land in acres
> Area of retail land (acres)
> Number of households

After the initial analysis five of the above variables were selected for the more detailed analysis. They were numbers in manufacturing industry, retail employment, and total employment; the area of retail land and numbers of households.

The final regression equations for trip productions at the non-home end were as follows:

Trips from work $= +$ $0.784 \times$ zonal population
$+$ 38.5

$R = 0.97$

Trips from shopping $= +$ $0.375 \times$ numbers in retail employment
$+$ $51.19 \times$ area of retail land
$+$ $0.032 \times$ number of households
$-$ 1.7

$R = 0.77$

Trips from other $= -$ $0.528 \times$ numbers in manufacturing industry
$+$ $0.358 \times$ total employment
$+$ $0.531 \times$ number of households
$+231.1$

$R = 0.77$

Similar equations were developed for central area trip productions, although the multiple correlation coefficient tended to be lower, ranging from 0.67 to 0.98, indicating that although the independent variables used provided the most appropriate regression equation, nevertheless they only accounted for approximately half of the value of the dependent variable.

6   The analysis of commercial vehicle trip generation was carried out in the same way as that for person trips, although only one equation was developed for productions and attractions for each of the two vehicle types, i.e. light

and heavy commercial vehicles. Five independent variables were found to be significant in determining the generation of commercial vehicle trips. They were total employment, office employment, retail employment, industrial employment, and numbers of households.

The two equations developed were:

Light commercial
vehicle trips = + 0.367 × number of households
+ 0.267 × total employment
– 0.339 × office employment
– 0.188 × industrial employment
+ 75.9

$R = 0.88$

Heavy commercial
vehicle trips = + 0.082 × numbers of households
+ 0.255 × total employment
– 0.321 × office employment
– 0.288 × retail employment
– 0.156 × industrial employment
– 22.2

$R = 0.84$

7 Similar regression procedures were adopted to determine appropriate equations for trip attractions to all zones. In all, thirty regression equations were used in the trip generation analysis stage of the Cardiff study, and the high correlation coefficients achieved in the analysis show quite clearly that a strong relationship exists between land use and trip generation.

Harlow[13]

The *Harlow Transportation Study* found that while an acceptable zonal regression set could be derived for home-based work trips, it was not possible to derive acceptable regression sets at the zonal level for non-work trips, since the household variables measured at this level did not adequately explain variations in these trips. It was found that the zonal aggregation of data tended to hide real variations within the data at household level. To overcome this problem data collected at household interview was categorized under particular combinations of household characteristics, viz. car ownership, household income, numbers in employment, number of residents. Trip generation rates were then determined for each category of household using the least-squares procedure.

The relationships derived in both the Cardiff and the Harlow studies are based on existing trends and characteristics, and it is tacitly assumed in the forecasting process that these relationships will not alter significantly with time. At best the application of trip generation equations to the projected future land-use situation gives only a broad estimate of future trips. They must therefore be applied carefully, and only in conjunction with considerable experience.

Cross classification and category analysis

Most traffic zones are not homogeneous in character in that they contain a range of social and economic activities. The use of regression equations based on the zonal aggregation of these different activities can obscure quite fundamental characteristics of travel demand. Indeed, work undertaken in North America suggests that the greatest variation in trip making exists within traffic zones rather than between zones, with much of this 'within zone' variation being lost through aggregation.[14] In an attempt to overcome this problem, an alternative method of trip generation known as *cross classification* or *category analysis* has been developed. This method uses the household rather than traffic zones as the basic trip-making unit.

Cross classification analysis originally developed in the *Puget Sound Regional Transportation Study*.[15] Basically it aims to cross-classify basic dwelling-unit data into relatively homogeneous sub-groups, and represent each sub-group by an average trip generation rate. The *Puget Sound Study* found that the three most significant determinants of trip production were family size, car ownership and median income of the head of household. Using these characteristics, in conjunction with a 'weighted average' representing population density, homogeneous sub-groups were identified and an appropriate trip generation rate by purpose and sub-group was established, e.g. a two-person household not owning a car produces 1.05 trips; a three-person household owning one car produces 8.2 trips by car per day. To forecast future trip productions for these particular sub-groups the estimated future number of such households in each zone is multiplied by the appropriate trip generation rate. Thus if zone x is expected to contain (a) 200, three-person, one car-owning households in 1990 then those households would produce $200 \times 8.2 = 1640$ trips, and (b) 40, one-person, non-car-owning households in 1990, then these households would produce 40×1.05 trips $= 42$ trips. This gives a total of 1682 trips produced in 1990 from zone x.

Home-based, trip attraction estimates were handled in the same way, using variables such as numbers in employment, and on school enrolments in place of car ownership, and median income.

This cross-classification technique was introduced to Britain and further developed as 'category analysis' in the second phase of the *London Traffic Survey*.[16]

This method is based on the assumption that trip generation rates for different categories of household will remain constant in the future. Thus by knowing the generation rate for each category of household, and the number of such households for some future date, estimates of future trip generation can be successfully derived. It places each household into one of 108 categories based on locational and household characteristics. From survey data relating to present-day trip generation an average trip generation rate is established. This average rate is then used in conjunction with future estimates of the number of households in each category, thus allowing future generation rates to be estimated, for three different modes of travel (drivers, passengers and public transport) and six journey purposes (work, business, education, shopping, social, non-home-based).

The underlying assumptions of category analysis are as follows.

1 The household as an independent unit, from which most journeys begin or end in response to the requirements of members of the family, is the fundamental unit in the trip generation process.
2 The journeys generated by the household depend on the characteristics of that household and its location relative to its required facilities such as work place and shops.
3 Households with one set of characteristics produce a different average trip generation rate from households with other characteristics.
4 Trip generation rates are stable over time so long as factors external to the household are the same as when the trip rates were first measured.

The 108 different categories of household were derived by considering those household characteristics most readily isolated and which are considered to be responsible for a systematic variation in trip generation. They are disposable income levels of car ownership and family size and structure. For each characteristic a number of categories was selected as follows:

Disposable income	1	Less than £500 p.a.
	2	£500 to £1000
	3	£1000 to £1500
	4	£1500 to £2000
	5	£2000 to £2500
	6	£2500 +
Car ownership	1	nil cars per household
	2	1 car per household
	3	2 + cars per household.

(At 1965–6 values).

Household structure
1 No employed residents and one non-employed adult.
2 No employed residents and two or more non-employed adults.
3 One employed resident and one or less non-employed adult.
4 One employed resident and two or more non-employed adults.
5 Two or more employed residents and one or less non-employed adult.
6 Tow or more employed residents and two or more non-employed adults.

In the original exercise consideration of the effect of the location of the household in relation to the required destination and to the existing transport facilities was attempted through the use of bus and rail accessibility indices, and the general conclusion was that such factors are of secondary importance in trip generation. However, the indices measured were crude in form, and it is possible that the use of more sophisticated indices might have revealed a stronger relationship between trip generation and locational qualities.

The number of observations within any category needed to generate mean trip ends within specified margins of error can be estimated from sampling theory.[17] Indeed, experience has shown that the sampling rate needed to produce reliable estimates may vary between 2 per cent and 20 per cent, depending on the frequency with which a particular household category occurs in the area under study.

Conclusions

Reliable short-term estimates of future trip generation rates have been derived by multiple linear regression analysis. Similarly it would seem that a comparable degree of accuracy will be achieved through category analysis. For the long term it is impossible to say at this stage if both, or either, will give acceptable predictions.

The fundamental weakness associated with multiple linear regression analysis is that it fails to establish a causal relationship between the dependent and independent variables, and assumes that regression coefficients established today will hold good for any future date. Both assumptions are questionable. An empirical examination of the current relationships between traffic and certain land-use/socio-economic factors may show a high degree of correlation which results from a peculiar set of present-day conditions rather than through any causal relationship. Thus given changing circumstances, with time the degree of correlation could be reduced to negligible proportions, with the result that predictions based on the original regression equation could be inaccurate. Similarly, changes in the land-use and socio-economic characteristics could result in a different relationship between the independent variables expressed in terms of completely different regression coefficients. Again, predictions based on the original regression equation could give wildly inaccurate results.

Category analysis, which bases its predictions on the assumption that the trip generation rates exhibited today by different classes of household will hold good in the future avoids these criticisms, and holds much promise for further research and development. However, the problems associated with predicting accurately on a zonal basis for some future date the number of households in each of the 108 categories are considerable, while the absence of any facility for testing the statistical significance of the variables thought to explain trip making is a serious deficiency in the technique.

References

1   Corradino, J. C., 'The effect of the highway system and land development on trip production', *Traffic Engineering* (1968).
2   Buchanan Colin and Partners, *Traffic in Guildford* (1965).
3   Schuldiner, P. W., 'Trip Generation and the Home', *Highway Research Board*, Bulletin No. 347 (1962).
4   Taylor, M. A., 'Studies of travel in Gloucester, Northampton and Reading', *Road Research Laboratory Report*, No. L R 141 (Tables 55 and 57).
5   Schuldiner, P. W., *op. cit.*
6   For an easily understood explanation of the statistical procedures involved in correlation and multiple linear regression analysis see: Spiegel, M. R., *Theory and Outline of Statistics*, Schaum Outline Series, McGraw-Hill (pp. 240–80), (1961).
7   For an explanation of the theory and application of correlation and multiple linear regression analysis see: Johnston, J., *Econometric Methods*, McGraw-Hill (1961).
8   Hill, D. M. and Brand, D., 'Methodology for developing activity distribution models by linear regression analysis', *Highway Research Board Record* No. 126 (1966).
9   Douglas, A. A. and Lewis, R. J., 'Trip Generation Techniques', *Traffic Engineering and Control* (Nov. 1970–Feb. 1971).
10   Buchanan Colin and Partners in association with Atkins, W. S., *Cardiff Development and Transportation Study, Main Study Report, Supplementary Technical Volume No. 5.*
11   Douglas, A. A. and Lewis, R. J., *op. cit.*
12   Buchanan Colin and Partners, *op. cit.*
13   Atkins, W. S. and Partners, *Harlow Transportation Study Vol. 2. Strategic Proposals* (1971).
14   Bureau of Public Roads, *Guidelines for Trip Generation Analysis*, US Department of Transportation, Washington D C, (1967).
15   *Puget Sound Regional Transportation Study* (Staff Report No. 16) (1964).
16   Wotton, A. J. and Pick, G. W., 'A model for trips generated by households', *Journal of Transport Economics and Policy* (1967).
17   Speigel, M. R., *op. cit.*, pp. 141–66.

5 Trip distribution

Introduction

Trip distribution, or in American terminology 'interzonal transfers', is that part of the transportation planning process which relates a given number of travel origins for every zone of the area under study, to a given number of travel destinations located within the other zones of the area. It is not necessarily concerned with the mode of travel used for a given trip, nor the routes which could be taken to complete this trip. Rather it is concerned with establishing the links between a number of zones for which trip generation calculations have previously been made.

During the past two decades various mathematical procedures have been developed and used for this purpose, and they tend to fall into two main groups.

1 *Analogous or growth factor methods* in which growth factors are applied to present-day interzonal movements.
2 *Synthetic or 'inter-area travel formulae'* in which an attempt is made to understand the causal relationship behind patterns of movement, by assuming them to be similar to certain laws of physical behaviour. Once understood, these causal relationships are projected into the future and the appropriate travel pattern is synthesized.

In addition, two other approaches have been applied.

1 *Multiple linear regression* in which attempts are made to establish the best predictors of trip distribution using origin and destination and land use and socio-economic variables.
2 *Linear programming* in which attempts are made to minimize for trip-makers the total amount of travel time spent in moving between origin and destination pairs.

Despite the diversity of formulation used in the various mathematical procedures developed, the underlying principle in all trip models is the same:

Travel between any two points will increase with increase of attraction for such travel, but decrease as the resistance to travel increases.[1]

Growth factor methods

Four different growth factor methods of trip distribution have been developed, each based on the assumption that present travel patterns can be projected into the future, using expected differential zonal rates of growth. This group of methods can be represented in general terms by the formula

$$T_{i\text{-}j} = t_{i\text{-}j} E$$

$T_{i\text{-}j}$ = future number of trips from zone i to zone j
$t_{i\text{-}j}$ = existing number of trips from zone i to zone j
E = growth Factor

Depending on the method used the growth factor (E) can be a single factor, or a combination of several factors, derived from land-use and trip generation projections. It can be calculated for the area as a whole, or for any number of zones within it, and is then applied to a complete origin and destination matrix for the study area.

The four growth factor methods in chronological order of their development are

1 Uniform factor
2 Average factor
3 Fratar
4 Detroit

Uniform factor

The uniform factor is the oldest and simplest method of projecting future trip distribution. A single growth factor is calculated for the entire area under study, and this is used to multiply all existing interzonal movements to produce estimates of future interzonal movements.

Mathematically this can be expressed as

$$T_{i\text{-}j} = t_{i\text{-}j} E$$

where $E = \dfrac{T}{t}$

$T_{i\text{-}j}$ = future number of trips from zone i to zone j
$t_{i\text{-}j}$ = present number of trips from zone i to zone j
T = total future number of trips in the area under study
t = total present number of trips in the area under study

The basic assumption behind the uniform factor method is that the expected growth in the area as a whole will exert the same influence on the growth of movements between any pair of zones located within it. However, this assumption is not strictly correct, for differential rates of urban development inevitably result in different rates of growth in movement. Thus in those zones where present-day development is limited, the potential changes in the pattern, density and type of land use are such that the application of a uniform growth factor to the existing volume of movements would lead to an underestimation of future movements. Similarly, it could lead to an over-estimation of movement volumes in those areas which are already intensively developed.

For this reason the method is now only used to update the results of recent origin and destination surveys in areas where the pattern and intensity of land uses are relatively stable.

Average factor

The average factor method was an early attempt to take some account of the differential rates of growth of movement which occur in urban areas. It utilizes a growth factor for each zone within the study area which, like the uniform factor method, is derived from land-use and trip generation predictions. Mathematically it can be expressed:

$$T_{i-j} = t_{i-j} \frac{(E_i + E_j)}{2}$$

where $E_i = \dfrac{T_i}{t_i}$ and $E_j = \dfrac{T_j}{t_j}$

T_{i-j} = future number of trips from zone i to zone j

t_{i-j} = present number of trips from zone i to zone j

E_i and E_j = growth factors for zones i and j

T_i, T_j = future movements originating in i or destined for j

t_i, t_j = present movements originating in i, or destined for j

In general, the calculated values will not give total flows originating or terminating in a zone which agree with future estimates derived from the trip generation analysis. That is

$$T_i \neq T_{i(G)}$$

where $T_i = \sum_{j=1}^{n} T_{i-j}$ = total calculated flows originating in zone i

and $T_{i(G)}$ = trip generation estimates for total flows originating in zone i.

This discrepancy can be reduced by an iterative process which uses the estimates of future traffic flows derived from the trip generation stage ($T_{i(G)}$) and those computed from the first application of the average factor (T_i) to calculate new growth factors, which are then applied to the estimated flows, as computed from the first application of the average factor method (T_{i-j}). Thus

$$E_i^1 = \frac{T_{i(G)}}{T_i}$$

$$E_j^1 = \frac{T_{j(G)}}{T_j}$$

and for the first iteration

$$T_{i-j}^1 = T_{i-j} \frac{(E_i^1 + E_j^1)}{2}$$

The process of iteration is continued until the new growth factors approximate to unity and T_i converges to $T_{i(G)}$.

Criticism levelled at the uniform factor method is also applicable to the average factor method. In addition, the residual discrepancies between forecasted and computed trips are not randomly distributed, but are inversely related to the growth factors. Thus for zones with lower than average growth factors, computed trip ends are greater than those originally predicted from the trip generation stage, while the reverse applies for those zones with higher than average growth factors.[2] This bias declines with each succeeding iteration, but if a large number of iterations is required to minimize this bias the accuracy of the results may be seriously affected. For this reason the average factor method is only rarely used today.

An interesting approach in the use of the growth factor technique in trip distribution is the method developed by W. S. Pollard Jr,[3] whereby human judgement is used in conjunction with the mechanical methods outlined above. Basically the method adopted by him involves the application of a growth factor to existing interzonal movements. This factor is an average of the growth factors of each pair of zones involved unless the circumstances relating to one or both of the zones require an adjustment to be made to the growth factor. The application of these adjustments to secure a balance in the trip distribution process requires time, and needs to be guided by 'sound judgement, intimate local planning and engineering knowledge'.[4] The fact that the adjustments can only be made after the movement concerned has been extensively studied would seem to rule it out as a practicable method of forecasting trip distribution in the urban transportation study, where many thousands of different movements must be catered for.

Fratar

T. J. Fratar, while working on travel forecasts for the Cleveland (Ohio) Metropolitan Region, used the process of iteration to develop a trip distribution method which overcomes the disadvantages associated with the uniform and average factor methods. The assumptions basic to his method are that (a) the distribution of future trips from a given zone of origin is proportional to the present trip distribution from that zone and (b) the distribution of these future trips is modified by the growth factor of the zone to which these trips are attracted.

This modification takes into account the effect of the location of a given zone with respect to all other zones, and is expressed as the reciprocal of the average attracting 'pull' of all these other zones. Broadly the method formulated involves the following.

1   The estimation of the total number of trips which are expected to originate and terminate in each traffic zone at the date for which trip distribution is required. (This is carried out at the trip generation stage.)

2   The distribution of future trip ends from each zone to all the other zones in the study area, in proportion to the present distribution of trips, modified by the growth factor of the zone to which the trips are attracted. This yields two values for each interzonal movement (i–j and j–i), and an average of these values is taken as the first approximation of the interzonal volumes.

3   For each zone the sum of the first approximation volumes is divided into the total volume desired for the zone, as estimated from the trip generation stage, to derive the new growth factor to be used in computing the second approximation.

4   The estimated interzonal trips for each zone in the first approximation are again distributed, in proportion to the present interzonal volumes and the new growth factor obtained in the first approximation. The pairs of values derived are again averaged and the process is repeated until the conformity between calculated and 'desired' trips is achieved.

Mathematically, the Fratar method can be expressed as

$$T_{i-j} = \frac{T_{i(G)}\, t_{i-j}\, E_j}{t_{i-j}\, E_j + t_{i-k}\, E_k + \ldots\ldots + t_{i-n}\, E_n}$$

where T_{i-j} = predicted number of trips zone i–j

$T_{i(G)}$ = expected future number of trips generated from zone i

$t_{i-j}\ldots\ldots t_{i-n}$ = present number of trips between zone i and all other zones $j\ldots\ldots n$

$E_i\ldots\ldots E_n$ = growth factors of individual zones $i\ldots\ldots n$

The process of iteration necessary to produce a balance between the number of predicted trips (T_{i-j}) and the number of expected trips $T_{i(G)}$ is fairly complicated and laborious. It is best illustrated by the example used by Fratar in explaining the method.[5]

The present-day interzonal movements shown in Table 9 are assumed.

Zones	A	B	C	D
A	—	10	12	18
B	10	—	14	14
C	12	14	—	6
D	18	14	6	—
Total	40	38	32	38
Future trips generated ($T_{i(G)}$) – estimated from trip generation analysis	80	114	48	38
First approximation growth factors	2	3	1.5	1

Table 9

Thus from zone A the future total trips (80) would be distributed between zones $A-B$, $A-C$, $A-D$ in proportion to the present-day interzonal movements, modified by the expected growth of the destination zones.

Thus $\quad T_{A-B} = \dfrac{80 \times 10 \times 3}{(10 \times 3) + (12 \times 1.5) + (18 \times 1)} = 36.4$

and $\quad T_{B-A} = \dfrac{114 \times 10 \times 2}{(10 \times 2) + (14 \times 1.5) + (14 \times 1)} = 41.5$

The average of these two values is then taken as the first approximation of future interzonal movements $A-B$, i.e. 39.

The same procedure is followed for all combinations of movements $A-B$, $A-C$, $A-D$, $B-C$, $B-D$, $C-D$, which produces a table for the first approximation of future interzonal trips, as shown in Table 10.

	$A-B$	$A-C$	$A-D$	$B-C$	$B-D$	$C-D$
	36.4	21.8	21.8	43.5	29.0	3.9
	41.5	16.0	15.8	28.0	18.3	4.0
Total	77.9	37.8	37.6	71.5	47.3	7.9
Average first approximation	39.0	18.9	18.8	35.7	23.6	4.0

Table 10

The averages for the trips generated from each zone are summarized, related to the expected volumes and the new growth factor is calculated (Table 11).

	A	B	C	D
	39.0	39.0	18.9	18.8
	18.9	35.7	35.7	23.6
	18.8	23.6	4.0	4.0
New totals	76.7	98.3	58.6	46.4
Expected volumes ($T_{i(G)}$)	80.0	114.0	48.0	38.0
New growth factor	1.04	1.16	0.82	0.82

Table 11

This process is repeated, using the new growth factor with the matrix formed with the values of the first approximation, until the required balance is achieved.

A modification of the Fratar method was suggested by the Urban Planning division of the United States Bureau of Public Roads, in 1962, to consider up to ten different trip purposes, and to apply growth factors by mode, time of day, or separately for trips entering or leaving a zone. This modification results in the method becoming much more sensitive to any land-use changes that might occur in a given zone. However, this advantage is offset by the fact that the modification complicates even further an already involved method.

Detroit

The Detroit method of trip distribution was developed in connection with the Detroit Metropolitan Area Traffic Study, in an attempt to overcome the shortcomings of the simpler growth factors, while at the same time reducing the computer operations necessary to bring the Fratar method to a satisfactory balance.[6] It is similar in approach to the average factor and Fratar methods, but introduces the assumption that although the number of trips generated in zone i will increase as predicted by the appropriate growth factor E_i, these will be distributed to zone j in proportion to the appropriate growth factor E_j divided by the growth factor for the area as a whole. Thus

$$T_{i-j} = t_{i-j} \frac{E_i \times E_j}{E}$$

where T_{i-j} = predicted future trips from zone i to zone j
t_{i-j} = existing number of trips from zone i to zone j
E_i, E_j = growth factors for zones i and j
E = growth factor for the area as a whole

As with the Fratar method the computed trip ends (T_{i-j}) for any zone will generally not equal the forecasted trip ends for that zone $T_{i-j(G)}$. Iteration is therefore necessary to bring the results into balance and the new growth factors E_i^1 and E_j^1 are computed using the ratio of the computed and forecasted trip ends. Thus

$$E_i^1 = \frac{T_{i(G)}}{T_i}$$

$T_{i(G)}$ = forecasted trip ends in zone i from trip generation stage
T_i = computed trip ends in zone i
The growth factors used in the Detroit method are much simpler to calculate than the complicated factors used in the Fratar method.

Conclusions

The main advantages associated with the growth factor method of trip distribution are

1   They are easily understood and applied, requiring only an inventory of

the present-day trip origins and destinations, and an estimation of simple growth factors.

2 The simple process of iteration quickly produces a balance between postulated ($T_{i(G)}$) and computed (T_i) trip ends.

3 They are flexible in application and can be used to distribute trips by different modes, for different purposes, at different times of the day, and can be applied to directional flows.

4 They have been well tested and have been found to be accurate when applied to areas where the pattern and density of development is stable.

These advantages are, however, outweighed by the problems associated with their application. Because they require as input data the results of a comprehensive Origin and Destination survey, they are expensive to apply. They cannot be used to predict travel patterns in areas where significant changes in land use are likely to occur, and the assumption that the present-day travel resistance factors will remain constant into the future is fundamentally weak.

Because the chances of statistical error are greater, the application of a growth factor to small present-day interzonal movements can result in extremely unreliable estimates of future movements. Zonal growth factors are derived after a process of crude approximation, yet the growth factor method of distribution relies on their accurate determination. Trips which have their destination in their zone of origin are automatically excluded from the growth factor method of distribution, and this results in errors, and increases the need for iteration which itself gives rise to the possibility of creating more errors.

For short-term predictions in stable areas, or for updating recent Origin and Destination survey data, these methods can be used with success. However, they cannot satisfy the requirements of modern urban transportation studies, which are usually designed to cater for conditions of continual and rapid change in the patterns of development, and the way of life of the population generally.

Synthetic methods

The fundamental shortcomings associated with the use of growth factor methods of trip distribution were identified in the early stages of their development, with the result that research work concentrated on the development of alternative methods, as well as the improvement of the growth factor techniques. The most successful alternatives – now generally referred to as the synthetic methods – were based on the assumption that (a) before future travel patterns can be predicted, the underlying causes of movement must first be understood; (b) the causal relationships giving rise to movement patterns can best be understood if they are considered to be similar to certain laws of physical behaviour.

Basically these synthetic methods include the gravity model, the 'opportunities' models, and the electrostatic model. In addition to these approaches to trip distribution, which attempt to understand the underlying causal relationships giving rise to movement, multiple regression analysis and linear programming techniques can also be used to estimate 'interzonal transfers'.

Gravity model method

The gravity model is perhaps the most widely used synthetic method of trip distribution, because it is simple to understand and apply, and is well documented. It adapts the concept of gravity as advanced by Newton in 1686 and is based on the assumption that trip interchange between zones is directly proportional to the relative attraction of each zone and inversely proportional to some function of the spatial separation between zones. In mathematical terms the gravity model is expressed

$$T_{i-j} = P_i \dfrac{\dfrac{A_j}{(D_{i-j})^b}}{\dfrac{A_j}{(D_{i-j})^b} + \dfrac{A_k}{(D_{i-k})^b} + \ldots\ldots + \dfrac{A_n}{(D_{i-n})^b}}$$

where T_{i-j} = number of trips produced in zone i with a destination in zone j

P_i = total number of trips produced in zone i

A_j = total number of trips attracted to zone j

$D_{i-j} \ldots D_{i-n}$ = measure of spatial separation between zones $i-j \ldots\ldots i-n$

b = empirically determined exponent which expresses the average area-wide effect of spatial separation between zones on trip interchange.

Development of the gravity model

The early gravity model had its origins in sociological studies. In 1929, W. J. Reilly developed a simple gravity model in an attempt to analyse and understand the pattern of retail trade areas associated with different towns. His 'law' stated that

Two cities attract retail trade, primarily shopping goods, from an intermediate city or town . . . approximately in direct proportion to the population of the two cities, and in inverse proportion to the square of the distances from these two cities to the intermediate town.[7]

The first real application of the gravity model technique to transportation planning came when Reilly's Law was adapted by H. J. Casey Jr to allocate to any number of 'towns' the purchases of any number of 'intermediate' towns.[8] Basically this adaptation states 'the purchases of the residents of a neighbourhood . . . are attracted to the retail centres in direct proportion to the size of the centres and inversely as the squares of the driving time distances from the neighbourhood to the retail centre.' Mathematically this is expressed

$$B_{i-a} = \left[\frac{\dfrac{F_a}{(D_{i-a})^2}}{\dfrac{F_a}{(D_{i-a})^2} + \dfrac{F_b}{(D_{i-b})^2} + \ldots \ldots + \dfrac{F_n}{(D_{i-n})^2}} \right] \times B_i$$

where B_{i-a} = purchases made by residents of neighbourhood i in shopping centre a

B_t = 'buying power' of neighbourhood i

$F_a, F_b, F_c, \ldots F_n$ = amount of retail floor space in shopping centres $a, b, c, \ldots n$

$D_{i-a} \ldots D_{i-n}$ = driving time distances between neighbourhood i and competing shopping centres $a, b, c \ldots n$

Further research by Voorhees showed that although the principle of the law of gravity could be used with advantage in trip distribution the measure of attractiveness of a zone of attraction, and the exponent of the distance factor, varied with the purpose of the journey being undertaken. Thus the basic formula, derived by Casey, was re-written to distribute work journey trips

$$W_{i-a} = \left[\frac{\dfrac{E_a}{\sqrt{D_{i-a}}}}{\dfrac{E_a}{\sqrt{D_{i-a}}} + \dfrac{E_b}{\sqrt{D_{i-b}}} + \ldots \ldots + \dfrac{E_n}{\sqrt{D_{i-n}}}} \right] \times W_i$$

where W_{i-a} = number of work journeys from neighbourhood i to work zone a

W_i = total number of workers resident in neighbourhood i

$E_a, E_b \ldots E_n$ = total number of jobs in work zones $a, b \ldots n$

$D_{i-a} \ldots D_{i-n}$ = driving time distance between neighbourhood i and work zones $a, b \ldots n$

Voorhees found that the most satisfactory measure of attractiveness of the work zones was the total number of persons employed; and that the most appropriate exponent of the distance factor was $\frac{1}{2}$. Similarly, Voorhees found that when distributing social trips the exponent of the distance factor was 3 (D^3), and when distributing shopping trips the exponent was 2 (D^2).

This relatively simple gravity model was a major breakthrough in the field of trip distribution. It stressed the importance of specific values of trip attraction and resistance, and recognized the influence of trip purpose on travel patterns. It could be used with advantage over the growth factor methods in that changes in the future land-use pattern could now be accounted for, and that improvements to existing transportation facilities could be taken into consideration in the travel-resistance factor.

Despite these advantages two major shortcomings were associated with this simple gravity model: (a) the inverse power of distance was an unsatisfactory resistance function because it could not cover the full range of trip possibilities and failed to give valid estimates when the distance factor was very small or very large; (b) the comprehensive iteration process required to calibrate the model, allied to the number of trip purposes used as input and the variations in travel with zonal location that had to be accounted for, gave rise to serious computational problems.

In an attempt to overcome these difficulties considerable research has been undertaken in North America and Great Britain, primarily aimed at developing a measure of the effect of spatial separation on zonal trip interchange which more accurately reflects the complex nature of this relationship than the single exponent of either distance or time. In North America this work has led to the development of a gravity model formulation which incorporates empirically derived travel time factors to express the effect of spatial separation on zonal trip interchanges. In Great Britain a generalized measure of the 'cost' of the various aspects of trip making, e.g. cost, time, has been developed to represent travel impedance.

The gravity model today
Travel time factors   To take account of these travel time factors, the basic gravity model formula is modified. Thus

$$T_{i-j} = \frac{P_i A_j F_{i-j} K_{i-j}}{\sum_{j=1}^{n} A_j F_{i-j} K_{i-j}}$$

where T_{i-j} = number of trips from zone i–j
P_i = total number of trips produced in zone i
A_j = total number of trips attracted to zone j
F_{i-j} = empirically derived travel-time factor expressing the average area-wide effect of spatial separation
K_{i-j} = specific zone to zone adjustment factor to account for other social and economic factors influencing travel pattern but not accounted for in the model.

In effect the travel time factors are a measure of the probability of trip making at each chosen increment of travel time. They are empirically derived through a 'trial and error' process, and the usual procedure is to start with the adoption of a set of travel time factors already calculated for a similar town (an alternative is to assume that travel time has no effect on trip distribution and adopt 1 as the first travel-time factor). The next step involves the calculation of zonal interchanges using the gravity model (T_{i-j}), which are then compared with the present-day zonal interchanges derived from the O–D survey (t_{i-j}). An iterative process is adopted until there is close agreement between the two sets of zonal interchanges. Generally it is accepted that satisfactory agreement is reached when the difference between average trip lengths is ± 3 per cent, and trip length frequency curves are 'close' when compared visually.

Mathematically, iteration is achieved by

$$F_{i-j}^{1} = F_{i-j} \times \frac{t_{i-j}}{T_{i-j}}$$

where F_{i-j}^{1} = travel time factor to be used in the next step of the procedure
$\quad\quad F_{i-j}$ = travel time factor adopted from similar town, (or assumed 1)
$\quad\quad T_{i-j}$ = trips $i-j$ as a percentage of total trips calculated from gravity model
$\quad\quad t_{i-j}$ = trips $i-j$ as a percentage of total present-day trips derived from O–D survey

In addition to the travel-time factors incorporated in the gravity model used today, provision is also made for the inclusion of zone to zone socio-economic adjustment factors (K_{i-j}), should they prove necessary for the successful calibration of the model. Experience has shown that these factors are not usually necessary in smaller towns of less than 100,000 population. However, there are occasions when they have to be used in the larger urban areas to produce satisfactory trip distribution results, and eliminate any systematic errors which might occur.

The procedure adopted to calculate the socio-economic adjustment factor is to compare the estimated trip interchanges between large generators of movement, using the gravity model (T_{i-j}) with the observed present-day interchanges (t_{i-j}). Both sets of movements are manually assigned to a transport network, to reveal any systematic discrepancies.[9] Mathematically the adjustment factor (K_{i-j}) is derived from

$$K_{i-j} = R_{i-j} \frac{I - X_i}{I - X_i R_{i-j}}$$

where R_{t-j} = ratio of O–D trip interchanges t_{i-j}, to gravity model trip interchanges T_{i-j}
$\quad\quad X_i$ = ratio of O–D trips $i-j$ to total O–D trips leaving zone i

Generalized cost Work completed by A. G. Wilson and the Mathematical Advisory Unit (MAU) of the Ministry of Transport, on the application of the concept of entropy in system modelling, has led to the development of a gravity model using a 'generalized' cost function of the various elements that are likely to influence travel impedance.[10] The measure of 'generalized cost' developed is a linear function of the following elements: time associated with travel; distance; excess travel time (i.e. time spent waiting or gaining access to a mode of travel); terminal costs at the destination end of the journey, such as parking charges; and the value the travelling public associates with time, distance, and excess travel time.

In general terms this linear function can be expressed as:

$$C_{i-j} = A_1 T_{i-j} + A_2 E_{i-j} + A_3 D_{i-j} + P_j + \delta$$

where　　C_{i-j} = the generalized cost of travel from zone i to zone j by a particular mode of travel

T_{i-j} = time of travel between zone i and zone j by a particular mode

E_{i-j} = excess travel time, i.e. access and waiting time

D_{i-j} = distance between zone i and zone j

A_1, A_2 and A_3 = constants representing the value the travelling public associates with time, excess time, and distance respectively

P_i = terminal cost at the end of the trip

δ = a calibrating statistic representing factors such as comfort and convenience which are not represented elsewhere. (This value is usually referred to as the 'inherent modal handicap'.)

In addition to the more straightforward elements involved in the estimation of the generalized cost, such as time (T), distance (D), excess time (E) and terminal cost (P), the values that the travelling public associates with time spent travelling (A_1), excess time spent on 'access' roads and/or waiting (A_2), the perceived cost per mile of travel by each mode (A_3) and the inherent modal handicap (δ), must also be estimated and input to the model. These latter elements are generally referred to as 'behavioural' elements and their perceived values will differ from person to person and situation to situation. Consequently they cannot be precisely determined. Similarly these components of 'generalized cost' are unlikely to remain stable over time. For example, as *real* income grows it is likely that the public will place a higher value on time than it does at present (A_1). Consequently in developing generalized cost functions, it is important that plausible assumptions be made about the future variation in the weightings (A_1 and A_3) of these components.

The general formulation for the calculation of 'generalized cost' is made operational by expressing this cost in 'units of time'. This is achieved by dividing the assessment of the value for excess time (A_2) and perceived cost per mile of travel (A_3) by cost of travel (A_1). Thus as the value of A_1 changes over time so the relative importance of the direct cost term (D_{i-j}) decreases. This approach hypothesizes that perception of the impedance to travel in time units remains stable with time.

The recommended measure of generalized cost expressed in 'time units' is thus

$$C_{i-j} = T_{i-j} + \frac{A_2 E_{i-j}}{A_1} + \frac{A_3 D_{i-j}}{A_1} + \frac{P_j}{A_1} + \frac{\delta}{A_1}$$

It should be further pointed out that all journey purposes do not have the same value of time, e.g. the travel time spent in the course of work is invariably valued more highly than time spent travelling on leisure journeys. Thus in applying 'generalized cost', different values of time should be used for different journey purposes. In the interests of computational efficiency this is sometimes achieved by incorporating different values of time for off-peak and peak period, the assumption being that these time periods reasonably reflect the breakdown of journey purposes.

In general terms the gravity formulation incorporating 'generalized cost', takes the following form.

$$T_{i-j} = A_i\, O_i\, B_j\, D_j \exp(-\lambda\, cij)$$

where T_{ij} = trips from zone i to zone j

$A_i = \dfrac{\text{I}}{\underset{j}{\Sigma}\, B_j\, D_j \exp(-\lambda cij)}$ = balancing factor or competition term which ensures that total number of trips leaving zone is equal to the number of trips generated by that zone.

O_i = trips generated in zone i

$B_j = \dfrac{\text{I}}{\underset{i}{\Sigma}\, A_i\, O_i \exp(-\lambda cij)}$ = balancing factor or competition term which ensures that the number of trips entering a zone is equal to the number of trips absorbed by that zone.

D_j = trips attracted to zone j

$\exp(-\lambda cij)$ = generalized cost of travel between i and j, expressed as a negative exponential value

It should be noted that A_i and B_j are 'balancing factors' incorporated in the model to ensure that the model is doubly constrained, i.e. the number of trips leaving each zone is equal to the number of trips generated by that zone ($\underset{j}{\Sigma}T_{ij} = O_i$) and the number of trips entering any zone is equal to the number of trips absorbed by that zone ($\underset{j}{\Sigma}T_{ij} = D_j$). By contrast a singly constrained gravity model ensures that while the 'origin' constraint is met (i.e. the total number of trips leaving a zone is equal to the number of trips generated by that zone) the destination constraint is not imposed. This singly constrained version of the gravity model is used to distribute trips to a destination (such as a shopping centre) where the number of trips attracted to that destination could change with changes in accessibility.

In the above formulation of a gravity model incorporating generalized cost, the negative exponential value of that cost has been used, rather than the inverse power of distance function, which is used in the earlier versions of the gravity model. Experience has shown that the negative exponential function more accurately reflects the complex nature of the deterrence function than does the simple inverse power function.

Gravity models incorporating generalized cost, and using negative exponential values to represent the deterrence function, have been used extensively to model trip distribution in transport studies. Perhaps the best-known example of their application is provided by the SELNEC Study (South East Lancs and North East Cheshire), where Wilson's model, disaggregated by income, car ownership and household structure has been applied and tested.

The gravity model is easy to understand and use. It recognizes that trip purpose is a major influence in determining travel patterns, and accounts for the competition which exists between different land uses. Any changes in travel time between zones can be readily taken into account, while the use of an adjustment factor ensures that socio-economic factors can be accommodated if necessary.

The basic operational difficulty associated with the use of the gravity model is that it requires a considerable amount of adjustment and manipulation to achieve satisfactory results. This can be taken as an indication that the gravity model procedure allows a sufficient number of adjustments to be made to the model so that the existing travel pattern is accurately reproduced, without adequately representing the relationships underlying these movements. There is no guarantee that present-day travel time and socio-economic factors will remain constant up to the design year.

The 'opportunities' methods

There are two basic 'opportunities' methods of distributing future movements (*a*) the intervening opportunities model and (*b*) the competing opportunities model. Both methods introduce the theory of probability as the theoretical foundation on which the trip distribution is based, and were developed as the result of research undertaken in connection with the Chicago, Pittsburgh and Penn–Jersey transportation studies.

In essence both the opportunities models can be represented by a general formula

$$T_{i-j} = T_{i(G)} \times P_j$$

where T_{i-j} = predicted number of trips from zone i to zone j
$T_{i(G)}$ = total number of trips originating in zone i
P_j = calculated probability of a trip stopping in zone j

The difference between the two opportunities methods is the way in which the probability function P_j is calculated.

Intervening opportunities

The intervening opportunities model was developed for the *Chicago Area Transportation Study* and was the first method to use the probability function to describe trip distribution in an urban area. The assumption basic to the model is that within an urban area all trips will want to remain as short as possible, lengthening only as they fail to find an acceptable destination at a shorter distance.

. . . a trip prefers to remain as short as possible, but its behaviour is governed by a probability of stopping at any destination it encounters – it cannot always go to the nearest destination and stop; it must consider the nearest destination, and if that is unacceptable, consider the next nearest and so on.[11]

It is of interest to note that this idea is similar to the physical law concerning the principles governing the distribution of lengths of path of molecules in a gas, and was first developed by S. A. Stouffer in a study of migration patterns of families in Cleveland, Ohio, in the 1930s.[12] Stouffer found that the number of people migrating a given distance was proportional to the opportunities for satisfaction at that distance and inversely proportional to the number of intervening opportunities.

A simple example, taken from the *Report of the Chicago Area Transportation Study*[13] illustrates the principles involved in the application of this idea to the distribution of movements. Assume that

1 Within an urban area, one destination in every one hundred destinations sells milk.
2 Of those destinations which sell milk, only every second one sells 'brand *X*'.

In the above situation the probability that a randomly chosen destination within this area will satisfy a hypothetical movement wishing to obtain brand *X* is

$$\frac{1}{100} \times \frac{1}{2} = \frac{1}{200}$$

In other words, the person has a 1 to 200 chance of obtaining brand *X* at his first destination, and therefore a 199 in 200 chance of going on to the next destination. The chances of this person stopping at the second destination are the chances of his having got there (199 in 200), multiplied by the chance of stopping there (1 in 200).

i.e. $\frac{199}{200} \times \frac{1}{200}$ = the chance of stopping at the second destination.

Similarly for the third destination the chances of obtaining brand *X* are

$$\frac{199}{200} \times \frac{199}{200} \times \frac{1}{200} = \frac{199^2}{200} \times \frac{1}{200}$$

From the above example it is possible to derive the intervening opportunities model, by assessing the probability that a given trip will stop in a given zone of destination *j*.

Let L = probability of a particular trip origin stopping at any randomly chosen destination (i.e. $\dfrac{1}{200}$ in the above example)

v = number of destinations found closer to the point of origin i, than zone j

v_j = number of destinations in zone j

The probability that a given trip will get to j is given by $(1-L)^v$ (i.e. $(1 - \dfrac{1}{200})^2$ in the above example) and the chance that the trip will not find a satisfactory destination in j and go on to the next zone after j is $(1 - L)^{v + v_j}$. Therefore the chance that the given trip will have stopped in j is the difference between the two values, i.e. $(1 - L)^v - (1 - L)^{v + v_j}$.

In practice all the journeys starting from a particular zone will not have the same value for L, i.e. some trips will be more selective than others. To sum the infinitely large number of probabilities, which would vary from point to point, involved the use of calculus, but because of the difficulties associated with this integration the basic model was simplified for practical use to

$$T_{i-j} = \sum_{L \; min}^{L \; max} T_{i(G)} L \left((1 - L)^v - (1 - L)^{v + v_j} \right)$$

where T_{i-j} = number of trips from zone i to j

$T_{i(G)} L$ = total number of trips generated from zone i, with a particular L value

$(1 - L)^v$ = probability that a given trip will get to a given destination

$(1 - L)^{v + v_j}$ = probability that a given trip will not find a satisfactory destination in j and go on to the next zone.

NB the term $((1 - L)^v - (1 - L)^{v + v_j})$ = Probability function P_j.

To synthesize existing and future travel patterns using this model it is necessary to provide an operational definition of V, i.e. all trip destinations closer to the zone of origin than the zone j. Distance and cost of travel were considered in Chicago but were eventually rejected because cost is difficult to measure, and distance takes no account of varying travel speeds. Travel time was eventually chosen as the most appropriate method of determining the order of search likely to be adopted in deciding on the destination for a particular journey from a particular zone of origin.

The probability of a particular trip origin stopping at any randomly chosen destination (L) must also be given an operational definition. To reduce the amount of computational work in the Chicago study trip, origins for every zone were classified into long trips and short trips, L_{max} and L_{min}, and the two values for L were determined by fitting empirically values which satisfied for the short trips, the observed proportion of journeys taking place within the zone of origin, and for the long trips the observed total of vehicle miles of travel in the system.

Two basic assumptions were essential to fit this model to the existing travel patterns.

1   '. . . all trips in all zones falling in either one of the two groups could be represented by a single value of *L*.'

2   '. . . the larger and more specialized journeys would be restricted so that trips from residential origins could only connect with non-residential destinations, and *vice versa*.'[14]

To utilize the model in the projection of future travel patterns and to derive values for *L* and *V* it is necessary to assume that
(*a*) the present-day proportion of trips satisfied without leaving their zone of origin will hold good to the design year, and
(*b*) the future transportation network of the area under consideration is known.

In Chicago these two assumptions were made, although the future values for *L* were modified by yet another assumption, that the volume of destinations in each zone would increase, thereby producing lower values for *L*. To simulate the procedure likely to be adopted by a future traveller in choosing his destination it was assumed that the existing comprehensive transport network would be improved rather than materially altered, with the result that the relative closeness of present-day zones would be altered in the future.

Competing opportunities

The competing opportunities model, which was developed from an analysis of 1947 origin and destination data, was used to analyse the data collected in the *Penn–Jersey Transportation Study*. The method involves the direct application of probability theory in conjunction with certain aspects of the gravity model and the Fratar technique of successive approximations.

The basic formula is

$$T_{i-j} = T_{i(G)} \times P'_j$$

where T_{i-j} = number of one-way trips from zone i to zone j
$T_{i(G)}$ = total number of trips originating in zone i
P'_j = adjusted probability of stopping at destination j

The adjusted probability of stopping is defined as the product of two independent probabilities – the probability of attraction and the probability of satisfaction.

The theoretical derivation of this model and its application to trip distribution is fully explained in an article by A. R. Tomazinis,[15] but in outline is as follows.

Theoretical derivation   Assume a universe with total population N, and two sub-populations H and S (see Figure 19). Part of sub-population H forms

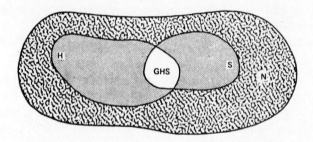

Figure 19 *Diagrammatic representation of theoretical universe* (N) *and sub-population* (H *and* S) – *theoretical derivation of intervening opportunities*

Source: Tomazinis, A. R., 'A new method of trip distribution in an urban area', *Highway Research Board, Bulletin No. 347* (1962)

part of sub-population *S* which is *GHS*. The probability of randomly selecting a member of the universe population *N*, which is also a member of the sub-populations *S* and *H*, is determined.

The probability that the chosen member is a member of sub-population *H*, ($P_{(H)}$) is

$$P_{(H)} = \frac{H}{N}$$

The probability that it is a member of sub-population *S* is

$$P_{(S)} = \frac{S}{N}$$

and the probability that it is a member of both *H* and *S* is

$$P_{(HS)} = \frac{GHS}{N}$$

To obtain the probability that $P_{(H)}$ will take place given that $P_{(S)}$ has already taken place, it is necessary to define the conditional probability of $P_{(H)}$ given $P_{(S)}$, $P_{(H/S)}$: In terms of formal probability theory this is given by

$$P_{(H/S)} = \frac{P_{(HS)}}{P_{(S)}} = \frac{\dfrac{GHS}{N}}{\dfrac{S}{N}} = \frac{GHS}{S}$$

Application to trip distribution The study region is divided into a series of 'time districts' each having a certain time distance separating it from the zone of origin. If it is assumed that the population of the universe (*N*) (see Figure

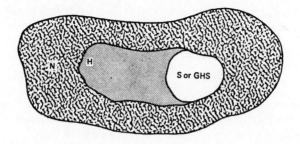

Figure 20 *Diagrammatic representation of study area and travel time districts – application of intervening opportunities to trip distribution*

Source: Tomazinis, A. R., 'A new method of trip distribution in an urban area', *Highway Research Board, Bulletin No. 347* (1962)

20) is the equivalent to the total trip opportunities in the study area; that the number of trip opportunities within one travel time district from one zone of origin is H; and that the total number of trip opportunities within the district of destination is S, then by applying the conditional probability equation already defined, it is possible to determine $P_{(S/H)}$ – the probability of attraction.

Application to trip distribution

$$P_{(H)} = \frac{H}{N}; \quad P_{(S)} = \frac{S}{N}; \quad P_{(SH)} = \frac{S}{N} = P_{(S)}$$

which gives

$$P_{(S/H)} = \frac{P_{(SH)}}{P_{(H)}} = \frac{\dfrac{S}{N}}{\dfrac{H}{N}} = \frac{S}{H}$$

In simple terms this implies that the probability that a trip will go to a district depends on the ratio between the trip opportunities in the district and its competing opportunities.

The total number of trip opportunities in the study area is used indirectly to define the pertinent (adjusted) probability. The summation of the probability of each district within the area should be unity because the total trips distributed should equal the trips available in the district of origin.

Hence $\qquad \Sigma P'_i = 1$

where i represents 1, 2, . . . n i.e. all the districts into which trips are distributed.

To obtain $\Sigma P'_i = 1$, the $P_{(S/H)}$ of each district is divided by the summation of all the conditional probabilities. Thus

$$\frac{P_{i(S/H)}}{\Sigma P_{i(S/H)}} = P'_i$$

The new adjusted probability of each district is then multiplied by the trip origins of each district of origin to obtain the trip interchange, e.g. the one-way trips from district x to district y are given by

$$T_{xy} = P'_y \times T_x$$

where P'_y = the adjusted probability of district y
T_x = the trip origins in district x
T_{xy} = one-way trips from district x to y

Once the above process has been repeated for each district, and the total number of trips into each district from all other districts estimated, then the use of a balancing technique may be required to bring the estimated and actual trips into equilibrium.

The opportunity methods have been successfully used by three of the most comprehensive transportation studies made to date, and as a result have been thoroughly researched and tested. They are based on a concept which seems logical, i.e. that trips lengthen only because they fail to find an acceptable destination closer to their origin. The formulae evolved are computationally convenient and well behaved mathematically, and there is a possibility that once existing data has been used to calibrate and obtain values for their parameters, and the models have been shown to be reliable, the future need for comprehensive origin and destination studies will be eliminated.

However, there are certain problems associated with their use. The simplicity of the earlier methods has been lost and the introduction of more complex relationships as a basis for these methods has resulted in the need for more experienced staff and large computer facilities. An iterative process is necessary to ensure that the number of trips arriving at a particular zone of destination agrees with the number of trips established at the trip generation stage. To date, extensive and expensive surveys have been necessary to calibrate these models but the most serious disadvantage associated with their use is that the methods can account only for a relative change in the time-distance relationship between all the zones in a given urban area. Consequently their use like the growth factor methods is restricted to those areas where no major changes in land use or the transportation network are expected.

The 'electrostatic field' method
In an attempt to overcome the need for expensive *O–D* surveys R. T. Howe

developed a model to distribute person movements, based on Coulomb's Law of Electrostatic Force. His model

. . . considers human beings as electronics. Given the initial distribution of these unit negative charges corresponding to centres of residence, and the distribution of centres of positive charge, representing places of employment, with magnitudes equalling the number of persons employed, the probability of movements between places of residence and places of employment can be predicted on the basis of the electrostatic field theory.[16]

The first stage in the development of the model involved the consideration of work journey movements only, and made the following assumptions.

1   The area under examination is a closed system, i.e. every worker lives and works within the same area, and every job within the area is filled by a worker resident in the area.
2   The work journey movement pattern is stable, i.e. every worker travels to work every day.
3   The employment structure is balanced throughout the area, i.e. no unusual concentrations of a particular type of employee exist.
4   All income levels are evenly distributed throughout all the residential zones in the area.
5   The spatial separation between zones of residence and employment is measured by the straight line distance.
6   Movement occurs within the system because of the initial imbalance between positive charges (jobs) and negative charges (people).

From the original hypothesis, and using the assumptions outlined above, Howe, in a study of the work trips in the Minneapolis–St Paul area, developed two equations to distribute person movements.

1
$$V_{P_iQ_j} = \frac{\dfrac{Q_j}{R_{ij}} P_i}{\displaystyle\sum_{j=1}^{m} \dfrac{Q_j}{R_{ij}}} \quad (i = 1, 2, \ldots \ldots n)$$

2
$$V_{Q_jP_i} = \frac{\dfrac{P_i}{R_{ij}} Q_j}{\displaystyle\sum_{j=1}^{n} \dfrac{P_i}{R_{ij}}} \quad (j = 1, 2, \ldots \ldots n)$$

where $V_{P_iQ_j}$ = probability of movement from zone i to zone j
P_i = number of workers living in zone j
Q_j = number of jobs available in zone j
R_{ij} = straight line distance from zone i to zone j
$V_{Q_jP_i}$ = probability of movement from zone j to zone i

Equation 1 ensures that the correct number of workers is drawn from each zone of residence. Equation 2 ensures that the correct number of workers is assigned to each employment zone. However, the two equations yield different sets of movements, with the result that to avoid under or over assignment of person movements to the different traffic zones, a balancing process using correction factors must be undertaken.

Following his analysis of the work/journey movements, Howe extended his theory to include shopping trips. Based on similar assumptions, the whole theory was again extensively tested against 1957 *O–D* data from the Cedar Rapids–Mario area, Iowa, and similar equations were derived.

The electrostatic field method by Howe is similar in form to the early gravity models. The advantages claimed for it are that the method is simple and inexpensive to apply. The future pattern of movements can be predicted without analysing the existing movements. Information relating to the numbers and locations of workers and jobs, and the straight line distance between zones is all that is required for the process to be set in motion.

The disadvantages associated with the method are that it can only deal with a closed system. It cannot simulate movements across an external cordon. In addition the similarity of the model to the early gravity models implies that it has the same shortcomings as those models although no attempt is made to overcome these shortcomings by the introduction of adjusting factors.

Multiple linear regression analysis

The multiple regression method is an empirical approach to determine from origin and destination and land-use/planning data the socio-economic variables that are the best predictors of trip distribution. It was first developed by Sam Osofsky in California, in connection with a research project to find 'a reliable, logical and practical method of developing data to be used in designing and locating freeways of the future'.[17]

The project utilized data collected in the *San Diego Home Interview Study*, and as a first stage plotted as the dependent variable the number of trips from a specified zone to all other zones, against four independent variables known to be significantly related to trips between zones – the distance between zone centroids in miles, population, employed persons and vehicle ownership in the zone.

As a result of this exercise it was found that the number of trips between zones tends to increase with an increase in zonal populations, employed persons and car ownership, and decrease with increasing distance between zone centroids. However, no clear-cut relationship which related to all the zones within the study area was established.

The next stage in the research project was the consideration of a multiple regression approach, which was based on the assumption that trip distribution is inversely proportional to the distance between zones, and is directly proportional to the population, employment, car ownership and land use of each zone. A number of trial regression equations were developed for the Modesto and Sacramento area, and the method adopted involved the following.

1   The selection of an appropriate equation form, determined from experience and theory.
2   The calculation of a set of coefficients relating a specific zone to all other zones. These coefficients were derived from origin and destination and land-use/planning data, and the process was repeated treating each zone in turn as a specific zone, until a set of coefficients was derived for each zone and cordon station.
3   The estimation of the 'theoretical' trips at the survey period, using the same independent variables, and the coefficients derived above.
4   The comparison of existing interzonal movements and theoretical trip distribution to check that the original equation form was sound.
5   The projection of the independent variables to the design year.
6   The calculation of future trip distribution in the design year using the projected independent variables from 5 above and the coefficients calculated in 2 above.

Mathematically an equation of the form

$$t_{i-j} = a_0 + a_1 x_1 + a_2 x_2 + \ldots\ldots + a_n x_n$$

is determined for each zone, to explain the present-day movements, using the method of least squares.

To forecast future movements a similar equation is developed of the form

$$T_{i-j} = a_0 + a_1 X_1 + a_2 x_2 + \ldots\ldots + a_n X_n$$

where t_{i-j} = present-day movements from zone $i-j$
a_0 = constant
a_1-a_n = coefficients determined by method of least squares
x_1-x_n = present-day values for independent variables, e.g. population, car ownership
and T_{i-j} = predicted trips $i-j$ for the design year
X_1-X_n = predicted values for design year of same independent variables, i.e. population, car ownership

The final equation developed by Osofsky took the form

$$T_{i-j} = a_1 \frac{P^2}{D^{1.5}} + a_2 \frac{E_2}{D^{1.5}} + a_3 \frac{V}{D^{1.5}} + a_4 \frac{L}{D^{1.5}} + a_0$$

where P = population in each destination zone
E = employed persons in each destination zone
V = vehicle ownership in each destination zone

L = land-use index for each destination zone

D = distance

As part of the project the multiple regression method of trip distribution was compared with a gravity model method, and it was found that the root-mean-square error* was considerably less for the multiple regression model.

As a method of forecasting future trip distribution the multiple regression model has several distinct advantages. Unlike the gravity model it can include in the equation any variable thought to have an influence on trip distribution. It is easy to understand and it can be applied to any area for any trip purpose. One underlying weakness, however, is the assumption that the relationship between trip volumes and the independent variables (i.e. the coefficients a_0, $a_1 \ldots a_n$) remains constant from the present time to the design year.

Linear programming

In recent years linear programming has been put forward as an appropriate method of trip distribution. It is an optimizing technique, originally developed to deal with problems of military logistics, and is concerned to achieve the optimum allocation of limited resources to meet specified or desired objectives. Basically the technique aims to find non-negative values of variables ($X_1 - X_n$) which minimize (or maximize) some linear function of these variables (the objective function) and satisfy a set of linear inequalities in the variables (the constraints).

The general formulation of the model to 'solve' trip distribution problems with 'm' origins and 'n' destinations is

Minimize $\qquad Z = \sum\limits_{i=1,m} \sum\limits_{j=1,n} X_{ij} C_{ij}$

Subject to, **a** $\qquad X_{ij} \geq O\,(i = 1, m; j = 1, n)$

and **b** $\qquad \sum\limits_{j=1,n} X_{ij} = O_i\,(i = 1, m)$

and **c** $\qquad \sum\limits_{i=1,m} X_{ij} = D_j\,(j = 1, n)$

Where X_{ij} = interzonal transfer values (to be determined by the model)

$\quad\;\; C_{ij}$ = 'cost' of making the trip, e.g. distance between zone centroid – (input to model)

$\quad\;\; Z$ = minimized value of the linear function of the variables (calculated by the model)

$\quad\;\; O_i$ = total trip productions (input to the model)

$\quad\;\; D_j$ = total trip attractions (input to the model)

The following simple example illustrates the basic characteristics of linear programming in a trip distribution context. For a situation where there are

* Root-mean-square error – see p. 112 of Chapter 4, Trip Generation for explanation.

three origin zones (m) and four destination zones (n), assume that the total work trip productions (O_i) and trip attractions (D_j) have been derived from the trip generation stage of the process, and that the 'cost' of making a trip between each pair of zones (C_{ij}) is measured in distance in miles between zone centroids.

Origin	Dest. 1	2	3	4	(O_i) Total
1	X_{11}	X_{12}	X_{13}	X_{14}	7
2	X_{21}	X_{22}	X_{23}	X_{24}	5
3	X_{31}	X_{32}	X_{33}	X_{34}	8
(D_j) Total	5	6	7	2	20

Table 12 *Total trip productions and attractions (O_is and D_js)*

The O_is and D_js are given in Table 12, while the interzonal transfers (X_{11}–X_{34}) are the values to be determined by the model. Similarly the 'cost' of trip making between zones is shown in Table 13.

Origin	Dest. 1	2	3	4
1	5	3	1	2
2	2	1	10	4
3	7	5	3	9

Table 13 *'Cost' of trip making in miles*

The linear programming model in minimizing

$$Z = \sum_{i=1,m} \sum_{j=1,n} X_{ij} C_{ij}$$

would calculate the minimum (or optimum) value of Z, and values for X_{11}, $Z_{12} \ldots Z_{34}$ from

$Z = (X_{11} \times 5\,\text{miles}) + (X_{12} \times 3\,\text{miles}) + (X_{13} \times 1\,\text{miles}) + (X_{14} \times 2\,\text{miles})$
$+ \ldots + (X_{34} \times 9\,\text{miles})$

The calculated values for $X_{11} \ldots X_{34}$ must meet the non-negative constraint (i.e. have a positive value or be set to zero) while the combined values of these variables must equal the row (O_i) and column totals (D_j), i.e.

$$X_{11} + X_{12} + X_{13} + X_{14} = 7\,(O_i) \text{ and}$$
$$X_{11} + X_{21} + X_{31} \qquad\quad = 6\,(D_j) \text{ and so on}$$

The optimum value of Z in this situation would be the minimum number of miles of work journey travel to accommodate the interzonal transfers, and is calculated by producing a first basic but sub-optimal solution. This first basic solution is subsequently 'developed' to a solution which is closer to the optimum solution, and the process repeated until the value of Z is minimized. To illustrate the method of proceeding, using the situation outlined in Tables 12 and 13, the first basic solution could be calculated by using the 'north-west corner rule' as follows:

Commence in the north-west corner (i.e. with the cell to be occupied by value X_{11}) and set this value equal to the minimum value of either O_1 or D_1. This will satisfy either an origin or destination constraint in the first step. If O_1 is less than D_1 then X_{11} is set equal to O_1 and X_{12}, X_{13} and X_{14} are set to zero to meet the O_i constraint. The next move in this situation is to the cell to be occupied by X_{21} and this value is set to the minimum value of O_2 or $D_1 - O_1$. If, however, O_1 is greater than D_1 then X_{11} is set equal to D_1, and X_{21} and X_{31} are set to zero to meet the D_j constraint. The next move is then to the cell to be occupied by X_{12}, and this variable is set to the minimum value of $O_1 - D_1$ or D_2. Thus at the second stage either a second origin or destination constraint is satisfied. The procedure continues in this way, satisfying at each step an origin or destination constraint until the total number of trips has been distributed. Because at each stage either an origin or destination constraint is satisfied, only $m + n - 1$ of the cell values will be greater than zero.

In the simple situation illustrated in Tables 12 and 13, O_1 is greater than D_1. Therefore the value of X_{11} is set equal to D_1, and the values for X_{21} and X_{31} are set to zero. The next move is to cell X_{12} which is set to the minimum value of $O_1 - D_1$ ($7 - 5 = 2$) or D_2 (6). Thus X_{12} is set to 2 and the values for X_{13} and X_{14} must be set to zero to satisfy the O_i constraint. The value for X_{22} is then set equal to the minimum value of O_2 (5) or $D_2 - X_{12}$ ($6 - 2 = 4$). Thus X_{22} is set to 4 and X_{23} to zero to satisfy the D_j constraint.

The next move is to cell X_{23} which is set equal to the minimum of D_3 (7) or $O_2 - X_{22}$ ($5 - 4 = 1$) and so on until all origin and destination constraints are satisfied (see Table 14.)

Dest. Origin	1	2	3	4	(O_i) Totals
1	5	2	0	0	7
2	0	4	1	0	5
3	0	0	6	2	8
(D_j) Totals	5	6	7	2	20

Table 14   *First basic feasible solution*

If this first basic feasible solution is not optimal, then a second feasible solution is derived through the use of parameters known as 'Lagrange Multipliers', and the procedure repeated until an optimal solution is derived.

The technique is comparatively simple to apply and requires similar input to the gravity model. The assumptions underlying its use are similar to those underlying the 'opportunities' models and seem logical. Yet the method has one major drawback – it will only produce $m + n - 1$ cell values and not the $m \times n$ values required for a complete origin and destination matrix, i.e. in the above situation it would produce six positive cell values only whereas the complete matrix would require twelve.

This difficulty can be partially overcome by stratifying journey purpose in some detail. For example, rather than consider the work journey movement as one type of movement it could be stratified by types of job such as mining; manufacturing; office, etc. Thus a series of incomplete O and D matrices would be built up relating to different sections of the work journey movement. When amalgamated these matrices would give a more complete O and D matrix relating to the work journey movement as a whole. Perhaps because of this problem the technique has been applied to trip distribution in research situations only.

Evaluation of trip distribution models and future developments

The growth factor methods of trip distribution have been thoroughly used and tested. The advantages and problems associated with their use are well known and have been outlined already. The synthetic models are still in the process of being developed, tested and compared, and although their individual disadvantages are known their comparative efficiency is still in question. Work by Witheford[19] in connection with the *Pittsburgh Area Transportation Study* led him to the conclusion that the intervening opportunities model was better than the gravity model in simulating trip distribution, because the gravity model required extensive adjustments to achieve adequate results. However, the gravity model tested by him was not stratified by trip purpose, and did not include the socio-economic adjustment factors.

K. E. Heanue and C. E. Pyers[20] on the other hand have tested a stratified gravity model, including socio-economic adjustment factors, against the Fratar and opportunity methods and concluded that as a technique it is perfectly adequate in most respects.

More recent work carried out by H. Lanson and J. Dearinger[21] compared and tested four methods of forecasting the zone to zone interchange of industrial work trips. The four models tested included the gravity model, the electrostatic model, the competing opportunities model and the multiple regression model, and the work journey movement was chosen because of its position as the most significant, repetitive and easily forecasted movement.

The basis of the comparison was the existing origin and destination data for the Lexington/Lafayette area of Kentucky, and the predictive accuracies of the four models were evaluated by computing the root-mean-square error (RMS).

The conclusions reached by Lanson and Dearinger were that

1 The multiple regression model gave the most accurate distribution results both numerically and by RMS.
2 The gravity model – which included socio-economic adjustment factors – gave the most accurate distribution pattern by RMS for the theoretical models.
3 The competing opportunities model was the most accurate theoretical model in terms of the total number of trips distributed to a zone, but the patterns of distribution were divergent.
4 The electrostatic model produced varied results overall.

In general terms Lanson and Dearinger concluded that the gravity model when used with only one purpose is simple and easy to use, and is sensitive to changes in travel time. The multiple regression model is flexible in that any variable thought to have an influence on trip distribution can be included. It is easy to understand and can be applied to any urban area for any trip purpose. The electrostatic model is relatively inexpensive to apply as it operates independently of existing movement patterns, while the competing opportunities model requires less origin and destination data for calibration than the gravity model. In terms of accuracy, however, the multiple linear regression and the gravity models are favoured by Lanson and Dearinger.

Future development
Of the trip distribution models discussed the gravity and opportunity models show the greatest promise for future development. The growth factor methods, although simple to apply and useful in stable conditions, have little relevance in a situation which is changing rapidly. The development of a 'purpose' Fratar method offset some of the limitations associated with growth factors, but the problem of zero flows in the base year remains.

The gravity model, although well documented and tested, could be improved by developing more sophisticated attraction and resistance parameters for use in the formulae. Attraction parameters based as they now are on a single factor such as zonal employment, or population, could well be developed so that one factor is produced combining aspects of all these single factors.

While the development of a more sophisticated 'generalized cost' resistance parameter has improved the gravity model as it is generally applied in Great Britain, further work is necessary to establish the relationship between socio-economic variables and the K adjustment factor.

The opportunity methods have two major disadvantages which must be overcome before they can be considered universally applicable.

1 The '*L*' values, as determined for the Chicago study, change with time, and to overcome this difficulty research is needed into trip length trends.

2 The methods cannot easily account for an absolute change which might take place to alter the 'separation' between a given pair of zones. For example, the construction of a bridge such as the Severn or Forth road-bridges would make it extremely difficult for an opportunity model developed before the opening of these bridges to be used to distribute movements for a design year after their opening. Again further research is needed to overcome this difficulty.

The multiple regression model would appear to have the advantage over the other methods described. It is extremely flexible in that any variable thought to have an influence on travel patterns can be included in the basic equation. However, there is a danger that although a satisfactory relationship between independent variables can be derived for the present movement patterns, the variables represented in the equation may not all be 'explanatory' variables, with the result that the projection of non-explanatory variables to the base year could produce erroneous trip distribution patterns. Research is therefore necessary to derive a more satisfactory understanding of the motivations giving rise to movements before the multiple regression model can be used with confidence. In addition, the application of a separate equation to each pair of zones in the study area involves an enormous amount of data collection and computational procedures. The work carried out by F. R. Wilson in his analysis of journey to work movements[22] indicates that some of this time-consuming basic work can be eliminated by stratifying zones, but again more work on these matters is required.

More recently, linear programming has been put forward as an appropriate method of distributing traffic movements. Despite the fact that this technique will produce an incomplete matrix of *O* and *D* movements, it does hold out some promise for further development, especially in those situations where a quick, cheap and comparatively crude assessment of the future pattern of movements is required.

Should all the above problems associated with trip distribution be eliminated by further research, then great improvements in the overall accuracy of this part of the transportation planning process would be achieved. Whether these improvements would transform the whole process from a highly suspect estimating procedure to a precise working tool is another matter.

References

1   Davinroy, T. R., Ridley, T. M., Wootton, H. J., 'Predicting future travel', *Traffic Engineering and Control* (1963).

2   Oi, W. Y. and Schuldiner, P. W., *An Analysis of Urban Travel Demands*, North-Western University Press, Chicago (1962).
3   Pollard Jr, W. S., 'Forecasting traffic with a modified growth factor procedure', *Highway Research Board*, Bulletin No. 297 (1961).
4   Pollard Jr, W. S., *op. cit.*
5   Fratar, T. J., 'Vehicle trip distribution by successive approximations', *Traffic Quarterly*, Eno Foundation (1954).
6   Bevis, H., 'Forecasting zonal traffic volumes', *Traffic Quarterly*, Eno Foundation (1956).
7   Reilly, W. J., *The Law of Retail Gravitation* (2nd edition), Pilbury, New York (1953).
8   Casey Jr, H. J., 'Applications to traffic engineering of the law of retail gravitation', *Traffic Quarterly*, Eno Foundation (1955).
9   *Calibrating and testing a gravity model for any size urban area*, US Department of Commerce, Bureau of Public Roads, Washington (1965).
10   Wilson, A. G., 'The use of entropy maximizing models in the theory of trip distribution, mode split, and route split', *Journal of Transport Economics and Policy*, Vol. 3 (1969).
11   *Chicago Area Transportation Study, Final Report Volume II* (1960).
12   Stouffer, S. A., 'Intervening opportunities: a theory relating to mobility and distance', *American Sociology Review*, 4 (1940).
13   *Chicago Area Transportation Study, op. cit.*
14   *Chicago Area Transportation Study, op. cit.*
15   Tomazinis, A. R., 'A new method of trip distribution in an urban area', *Highway Research Board*, Bulletin No. 347 (1962).
16   Howe, R. T., 'A theoretical prediction of work trip patterns in the Minneapolis–St Paul area', *Highway Research Board*, Bulletin No. 347 (1962).
     See also: Howe, R. T., 'A theoretical prediction of work trip patterns', *Highway Research Board*, Bulletin No. 253 (1960).
17   Osofsky, S., 'A multiple regression approach to forecasting urban area traffic volumes', *Proceedings of the American Association of State Highway Officials*, Washington (1958).
18   Blunden, W. R., *The Land-Use/Transportation System – analysis and synthesis*, Pergamon Press (1971).
19   Witheford, D. K., 'A comparison of trip distribution by opportunity model and gravity model', *Pittsburgh Area Transportation Study* (1961).
20   Heanue, K. E. and Pyers, C. E., 'A comparative evaluation of trip distribution procedures', *Highway Research Board*, Record No. 114 (1966).
21   Lanson, H. and Dearinger, J., 'A comparison of four work journey distribution models', *Proceedings of the American Society of Civil Engineers*, Highway Division, Volume 93, No. H. W. 2 (1967).
22   Wilson, F. R., *The Journey to Work – Modal Split*, Maclaren (1967).

6 Network planning and traffic assignment

Introduction

The network planning stage of the transportation planning process aims to develop alternative highway and public transport networks for the selected land-use plan(s). These alternative networks should ideally reflect different policies and take the form of complete systems serving the area as a whole.

Traffic assignment is that part of the process which allocates a given set of trip interchanges to a specific transport network or system. It can be used to estimate the volume of traffic on various links of the system for any future year, or to simulate present conditions. The traffic assignment process requires as input a complete description of either the proposed or existing transportation system, and a matrix of interzonal trip movements. The output of the process is an estimate of the traffic volumes on each link of the transportation system, although the more sophisticated assignment techniques also include directional turning movements at intersections.

The purposes of traffic assignment are, broadly

1   To assess the deficiencies in the existing transportation system by assigning estimated future trips to the existing system.
2   To evaluate the effects of limited improvements and extensions to the existing transportation system by assigning estimated future trips to the network which includes these improvements.
3   To develop construction priorities by assigning estimated future trips for intermediate years to the transportation system proposed for those years.
4   To test alternative transportation system proposals by systematic and readily repeatable procedures.
5   To provide design hour volumes and turning movements.

Broadly speaking three major alternative procedures have been developed to assign estimated future trips to a transportation system. They are
(a) All or nothing assignments
(b) Diversion curve assignments
(c) Capacity restraint assignments
The choice of assignment procedure to be adopted in any particular transportation study depends largely on the purpose of that study, and the degree of sophistication required in the output.

Assignment techniques have developed in conjunction with origin and destination studies, to determine the route likely to be taken by interzonal trips traditionally illustrated by some form of desire line diagram. In the early 1950s considerable difficulty was experienced in assessing the driver's choice of route to complete his or her interzonal trip, and route choice decisions were often arbitrarily based on personal knowledge and an assessment of travel time, distance and user cost.

Empirical studies were undertaken in the United States, in an attempt to relate choice of route to time and distance factors, and as a result the American Association of State Highway Officials developed a standard traffic diversion curve as recommended policy for determining the future use of urban highways. However, this technique was only capable of dealing with a single motorway with existing parallel routes.

In 1957 a major breakthrough in traffic assignment occurred. The Armour Research Foundation working on the problem of traffic assignment in *The Chicago Area Transportation Study* developed a computer program capable of finding the minimum time or distance path through a network. This program was only capable of handling a very small network, but provided a basis for further research, which resulted in the development of a program for a large high-speed computer capable of assigning traffic to the existing and proposed street system for the entire Chicago area. Today this 'minimum path' technique of assignment is known as the 'all or nothing' assignment procedure.

Further research led, in 1960, to the development by the General Electric Computer Department in co-operation with the District of Columbia, of an assignment program capable of prohibiting selected turns in the calculation of the minimum path. This latest modification has been developed into the capacity restraining technique of traffic assignment.

Network planning

In developing alternative transport networks, factors such as the generation rate of trips, trip length, land-use characteristics, cost and transport design and operational criteria, need to be carefully considered. However, the approach adopted towards network planning varies from study to study, and in many instances involves little more than the determination of which elements of the existing highway network will be used in conjunction with long-standing commitments to major highway improvements to form the future highway network. Public transport networks are invariably developed to accommodate those movements which the preferred highway network cannot cope with.

Highway networks
In the United States, a generalized but fairly typical example of the procedure

which tends to be adopted in the development of alternative highway networks as part of the traffic functional transport planning process could take the following form. For the selected land-use plan and the estimated demand for movement associated with it, carry out the following steps.

1 Determine the optimum number and spacing of major links in the highway network. Here 'optimum' tends to be equated with cost, and thus the 'optimum spacing' generally attempts to minimize the sum of both travel costs and network construction costs. A variety of approaches can be adopted at this stage. *The Chicago Area Transportation Study*, for example, developed both a graphical approach and a simple mathematical model took the following form

$$Z = 2.24 \frac{\sqrt{C}}{DK \left(\frac{1}{V_y} - \frac{1}{V_z} \right) P_s}$$

Where Z = optimum network spacing in miles
   C = average network construction costs
   K = constant, capitalizing the value of time
   D = average vehicular trip density per square mile
V_y, V_z = average speed on motorway and non-motorway links in the networks
   P_s = proportion of trips with the opportunity to use motorway links in the network

As a check on this simple model, a graphical array of both travel and construction costs at various network spacings was also produced. This allowed a least-cost solution to be determined by inspection.[1] Other studies have used more intuitive assessments of the optimum network spacing.

The determination of the optimum network spacing is important in that it enables the planner to make preliminary estimates of the likely extent of the 'optimum' transport network and plan by successively applying the approach to those parts of the urban area exhibiting different trip and residential densities. However, it should be stressed that the results of this type of exercise are not applied rigidly. Rather they are used as an aid to decision making, and are modified in the light of local conditions.

2 Consider the fundamental design principles to be applied at the network design stage, such as continuity of movement throughout the system (i.e. no unnecessary stop, or changes of direction) lane balance (i.e. the same number of traffic lanes leaving an intersection as entering it) and the avoidance of confusing situations for the motorist.

3 In the light of the general design principles determined above, produce design standards and criteria, for example design speed, capacity and

hence scale, width and number of roads to be constructed.
4   Assess the constraints likely to influence the design of alternative network proposals, e.g. committed proposals to improve or extend the existing highway network (these usually have to be incorporated in any new network proposals), while topographical and other physical features, environmental considerations and cost invariably influence the form of any networks produced.
5   Produce layout plans of alternative networks. These are examined closely to determine the impact of the proposals on the areas through which the networks pass; to estimate the land area and earth movements required for each alternative; to assess the problems likely to arise from the relocation of people and business; to determine the scale of the costs involved, and to examine the problem of incorporating any new links into the existing highway network.

In Britain a variety of approaches have been adopted towards network planning, all incorporating to a greater or lesser extent the steps, if not the procedure, outlined above. At one extreme there is the approach adopted in the *London Traffic Survey* which defined twenty-three alternative road networks and several possible combinations of improvements to public transport, without making public the methods by which any of alternative network plans were prepared. Of the alternative proposals three road networks and two public transport networks were tested, and even then the choice of road plans for testing left a great deal to be desired as the minimum network tested formed an integral part of the middle-range network which in turn formed part of the maximum network.[2] Work carried out by Oxford City Corporation, in conjunction with transportation planning consultants, indicates that the problems of route location in network planning can be approached systematically.[3] Briefly the method adopted involves an examination for the whole of the study area of those factors which could influence the location of any new links in the highway network, for example engineering factors (such as land liable to flood, geology) or environmental factors (such as quality and use of open space, and the quality, use, age and condition of buildings). Each of these factors is given a weighting which reflects the importance of the particular factor. The study area is examined on a zonal basis and a 'score' given to each of the factors considered to influence route location. An aggregate score is derived for each zone and this is taken as a reflection of the resistance to route location of each zone. By then, plotting the zone totals on a map of the study area 'contours of hardness' with respect to route location are derived. From an analysis of this map the majority of alternative routes can generally be eliminated as being unsuitable, on engineering or environmental grounds, leaving a reduced number of alternatives to be examined in greater detail.

The procedure is open to criticism on the grounds that

1   It is based on a purely subjective assessment of the factors influencing route location
2   It approaches network planning from a negative point of view, i.e. it highlights those areas where new network links should not be inserted, and then goes on to examine the remaining alternatives.

However, in its favour, it does attempt to consider systematically all the factors which could influence route location, before drawing up network plans for testing.

Perhaps the most interesting, positive and systematic approach adopted towards network planning in Great Britain, is that applied by Colin Buchanan and Partners in their work on Guildford.[4] The alternative highway networks for Guildford were developed from the estimated 1981 travel patterns, and based on the morning peak hour flows. Data relating to this basic travel pattern was presented in the form of a desire volume diagram, and analysed by a series of screen lines. The volume of traffic crossing these screen lines was accumulated to determine in a general way the ideal number, location and orientation of traffic lanes and highways required in various parts of the town. This analysis resulted in a crude network which should in theory give optimum service to movement desires.

The next stage in the exercise involved the adaptation of this theoretical network to Guildford taking account of physical, environmental, traffic and other constraints. Two alternative networks evolved, and these were tested in preliminary feasibility studies and subsequently modified to produce the first practical and alternative networks which were thoroughly tested and compared, and from which the final 'preferred network' was selected.

Public transport networks
The design of alternative public transport networks involves the same general procedure as that adopted for the development of highway networks, although the factors which need to be considered are completely different. In addition, the way in which these factors are considered will also differ according to whether public transport is seen as only one component in the overall transport system, or whether it should be looked at in relation to other aspects of urban and social planning, for example by supporting the existing central area.

Two basic alternative modes of public transport are generally examined in the development of alternative public transport networks. Firstly, rapid mass transit (e.g. underground or suburban railways) and secondly the motor bus. The establishment of firm criteria for the development of complete public transport systems is complex in the extreme, especially as experience of recent developments in this field is limited to such ventures as the Bay Area Rapid Transit District in San Francisco. Indeed, most existing public transport systems were developed prior to the widespread ownership and usage of the motor vehicle, and frequently in areas of high population density, and central area congestion.

Conclusions
In general terms the procedure followed in developing alternative network plans is one of gradually identifying the constraints within which alternative solutions must be found. Indeed the report of *The Chicago Area Transportation Study* summarizes the approach generally adopted.

The actual planning of new transportation facilities is not done on a clean slate; the process, rather, is one of successively imposing limits within which the solution must be found. Existing expressways, boulevards, and transit lines are one set of limits. Land uses (such as housing developments, industrial districts and commercial centres) impose other limits. The forecasts of future traffic demands fix the magnitude of the improvements which must be made. Finally, objectives and standards control the solutions greatly.[5]

Traffic assignment

General procedure
The traffic assignment procedure is based on the selection of a minimum time path over an actual route between zones. Although the process is invariably carried out by computer, it can be done manually. For the task to be accomplished by computer it is necessary to describe the highway network, code and store it in the computer's memory. The computer then chooses the minimum path between zones, assigns estimated trips to this path and accumulates traffic volumes for each section of the route.

For coding purposes the highway network is broken down into links and nodes (see Figure 21). A link is defined as the one-way part of the route

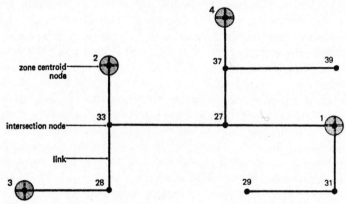

Figure 21   *Highway network description – links and nodes*

between two intersections and, depending on the assignment technique to be used, detailed information concerning the length, speed and/or travel time of vehicles, capacity and existing volumes on each link is coded and stored in the computer. Nodes are of two types – zone centroid, and intersection nodes where two or more links meet. Nodes are identified by a numeric code which is applied systematically while links are identified by the node number at each end of the link.

Once the coding is completed the data is punched, checked and stored in the computer, which then chooses the minimum time path between zones after a systematic search and accumulation of travel times stored in the memory.

The minimum time path is the shortest route from one zone centroid to another, and this route is known as a 'tree'. It is selected after the computer, moving outwards from the starting node, has compared travel times between adjacent nodes to derive the quickest path between all nodes. At each node in the network the travel time back to the starting centroid and the immediate previous node are recorded systematically to derive the travel time and route between the starting node and all other nodes.

The next stage in the process is to assign the zone to zone trips to the links on the minimum path routes (or trees) between the various zones. Trips generated by each zone are dealt with successively, and the process is repeated until all trips from all centroids have been loaded on to the links of the network.

At this stage traffic loads on individual links of the network may be in excess of the capacity of the proposed facilities, and a new set of minimum time paths between zones must be derived, using a set of adjusted travel times. If this is done automatically the programme is known as a capacity restraint programme, and adjustments are made to the network after the computer has checked the ratio of the assigned traffic volume to the capacity for each link, and in accordance with a predetermined relationship. This relationship is based on the assumption that as the volume of traffic on a link increases so the travel time on that link increases. Thus the speed necessary to travel that link is reduced just as increased congestion causes speeds to be lowered in real situations.

Traffic assignments can be produced for total daily traffic, or any sub-division of the 24-hour period, such as the morning or evening peak periods; for directional or non-directional flows; and for any particular purpose or mode. However, it is more usual to first make an average daily traffic assignment (ADT) and from this obtain traffic assignments for other periods of the day by using conversion factors determined during the survey stage of the process.

Number and types of assignment
Generally speaking three basic categories of assignment should be

undertaken in the transportation planning process although the number and type of assignments made will depend on the size of the area under examination, the purpose of the study and the financial resources available.

1   The assignment of existing trips to the existing network to check the adequacy of the assignment procedure by testing its ability mechanically to reproduce the existing travel patterns.
2   The assignment of estimated future trips to the existing network plus the committed extensions and improvements. This type of assignment is undertaken to determine the deficiencies in the existing network and to provide a framework for the development of future additions and improvements to this network.
3   The assignment of estimated future trips to the future network. At this stage the effect of land-use distribution and the proposed transportation system must be carefully analysed and it is usual practice to assign the estimated future trips to several alternative land-use plans with their accompanying transport systems.

Optimum programming of the network construction can be determined by partial network assignments, while assignments made by five yearly incremental periods will allow the evaluation of the procedures adopted and provide for future adjustments in forecasting and assignment, if necessary, instead of waiting for the forecast year to arrive.

Diversion curves in traffic assignment

For any trip from one zone to another there are usually several alternative routes, which can be chosen by the person making the trip. Each route has its own 'travel resistance' derived from its characteristics of distance, travel time, speed and level of service. These characteristics are evaluated either consciously or subconsciously by the driver before a particular route is chosen. Thus a route with a high travel resistance, e.g. a busy urban street with bus stops, parked cars, numerous intersections, and pedestrians, will not be used by as many drivers as a comparable route with low travel resistance. This concept of travel resistance is used in traffic assignment by deriving a quantified measure of the resistance and examining empirically the relationship between this measure and the usage of two alternative routes. Diversion curves are then derived from these empirical studies to show what proportion of drivers are likely to transfer to a new urban motorway, should one be constructed.

Numerous diversion curves have been constructed using different measures of travel resistance, some of which are illustrated in Figure 22. The principal ones are: travel time saved (derived from $A-B$); distance saved ($C-D$); travel-time ratio (B/A); distance ratio (D/C); cost ratio (F/E); travel

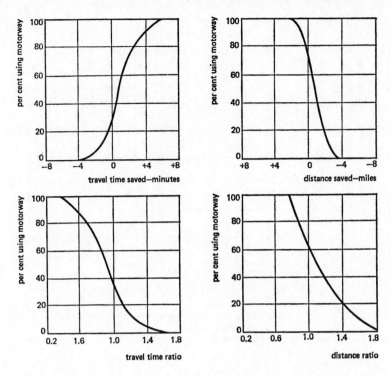

Figure 22   *Typical diversion curves (based on North American data)*

time/distance saved (known as Californian curves) and distance/speed ratio (known as Detroit curves), where

A = travel time via quickest non-motorway route
B = travel time via motorway
C = distance via shortest non-motorway route
D = distance via motorway
E = cost on alternative non-motorway route
F = cost on motorway

Three diversion curves are in current use today – the time ratio curve, the travel time and distance saved curve, and the distance speed ratio curve.

Of the remaining curves the travel time saved diversion curve tends to separate trips by length, as the longer trips usually have a large travel-time saving.

The distance saved diversion curve is sensitive to small charges in distance, and because distance alone cannot account for as many 'travel resistance' factors as travel time does these curves are generally unreliable and are infrequently used today.

The distance ratio diversion curve is again based on an inadequate measure

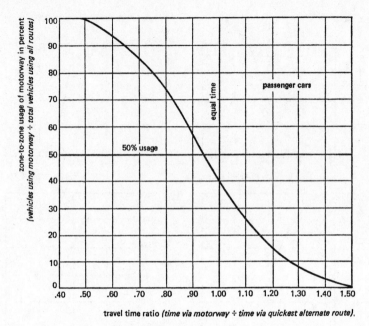

Figure 23   *Bureau of Public Roads diversion curves*

of travel resistance and has the added disadvantage that for trips with the same distance ratio, the same diversion curve is used, regardless of trip length.

The cost ratio diversion curve is not used extensively, mainly because of the problems associated with placing a money value on time.

Travel-time ratio curve

The travel-time ratio curve bases the percentage of trips to be assigned to a motorway or new facility on the ratio of the travel time via the motorway to the travel time via the quickest alternative route. The curve as an S-shaped curve, and using the Bureau of Public Roads curve as an example (Figure 23) it is seen that the percentage of trips using the motorway varies from 100 per cent at a time ratio of 0.5 or less, to zero per cent at a time ratio of 1.5 or more. If travel time by both the motorway and the alternative route is equal, then 42 per cent (approximately) of the trips are assigned to the motorway, because such trips with their faster speeds require a larger travel distance.

One difficulty associated with the use of the travel-time ratio curve is that, regardless of length, trips with the same travel-time ratio are given the same diversion rate.

Travel time and distance saved diversion curves

This set of diversion curves (Figure 24), developed by the California Division

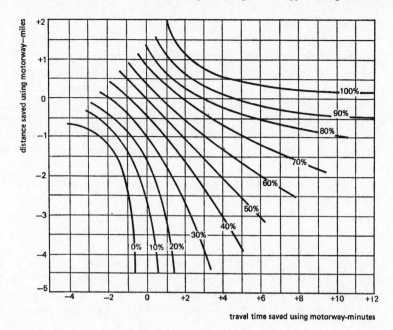

Figure 24 *Travel time and distance saved diversion curve*

Source: Moskowitz, K., 'California method of assigning diverted traffic to proposed freeways', *Highways Research Board, Bulletin No. 130* (1956)

of Highways,[6] consists of a family of hyperbolas, constructed on a mathematical basis, using the results of observations on freeways in California. The assumptions basic to the derivation of these curves are

1 Factors other than time and distance cannot be measured explicitly, nor forecasted, and can therefore be ignored.
2 The greater travel time and distance saved the greater the usage.
3 When only small savings in time and distance occur some drivers will transfer to the motorway, others will not.
4 Some drivers will drive any distance to save travel time; few drivers will select the shortest route in terms of distance at the expense of travel time.

These curves are expressed in the equation

$$P = 50 + 50 (d + \tfrac{1}{2}t) [(d - \tfrac{1}{2}t)^2 + 4.5] - \tfrac{1}{2}$$

where P = percentage of motorway usage
$\quad\quad d$ = distance saved in miles via the motorway
$\quad\quad t$ = time saved in minutes via the motorway

Speed distance ratio curve

This family of curves (Figure 25), developed for the Detroit Area Traffic Study,[7] relates the percentage of motorway use to speed and distance ratios, using the assumption that although time, distance and speed are the principal factors affecting a driver's choice of route, because they are interrelated it is only necessary to define two of them.

Distance ratio and speed ratio were adopted with the result that if this set of curves is used, then the need for a travel time study is eliminated as a ratio between speeds on a motorway or new route and on existing city streets can be assumed.

The speed ratio used in this method is the average trip speed via the new route divided by the average trip speed on the existing city street route.

It can be seen from Figure 25 that with a speed ratio of 1 and a distance ratio of 1, approximately 45 per cent of the trips are assigned to the new route.

Diversion curves are constructed to enable assignments to be made to proposed transport facilities. However, they have their limitations. Although present-day travel resistance characteristics are reflected in the curves themselves, the extent to which these will remain constant in the future depends on

Network planning and traffic assignment

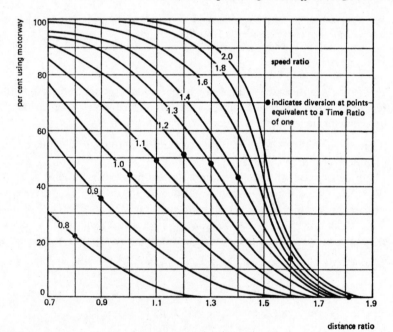

Figure 25   *Distance and speed ratio diversion curve*

Source: *Detroit Metropolitan Area Traffic Study* (1956)

the extent and nature of proposed changes in the transport system. For example, if the highway network is completely changed and the level of service improved, the characteristics of the old network are also likely to change. At the same time the attitude of drivers towards factors such as time, distance, comfort and convenience can also change. In general terms diversion curve assignments are not ideally suited to large area transportation studies where far-reaching changes are proposed for the transport system. However, for small towns where minor extensions and improvements are contemplated they can be used effectively and economically.

All or nothing assignments

All or nothing assignments are based on the assumption that the path taken by vehicles travelling from zone of origin to zone of destination will be the one with least travel resistance. Although travel resistance can be measured in terms of distance, cost, time, or some combination of these factors, the measure normally used is that of time.

The basic procedure in all or nothing assignments involves

1   The description and coding of the network into links and nodes.
2   The determination of minimum path time from each zone with originating traffic to all other zones. (This stage is often referred to as 'build trees'.)
3   The assignment of all traffic flows from each zone to every other zone by the appropriate minimum path, and the aggregation of total flows on each link in the defined network.

Description and coding of network: This process is similar for all traffic assignment techniques and has been outlined on page 160.
Determination of minimum paths: If done manually the determination of minimum paths between zone centroids is a laborious and time-consuming task, as the following example illustrates.

The object of this example (Figure 26) is to determine the minimum path from Zone Centroid 1 to all other nodes on the network.

1   Start at Zone Centroid 1 and proceed outwards to all connecting nodes. At each node record the travel time to it.
From Node 1 to Node 16 (T_{16}) = 2.0 minutes
From Node 1 to Node 22 (T_{22}) = 3.0 minutes

2   The Node closest to Zone Centroid 1 is considered next, i.e. 16, thus
From Node 16 to Node 15   = 3.0 minutes
∴ From Node 1–16–15 (T_{15}) = 5.0 minutes
From Node 16 to Node 17   = 3.0 minutes
∴ From Node 1–16–17 (T_{17}) = 5.0 minutes

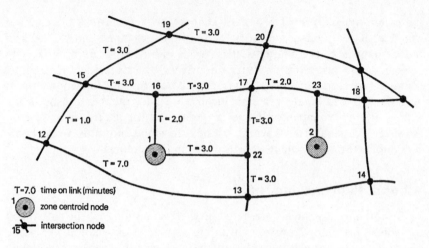

Figure 26   *Network for calculation of minimum path*

3   The next closest node to Zone Centroid 1 is then considered, i.e. Node 22. Thus

From Node 22–13   = 3.0 minutes
∴ From Node 1–22–13 (T_{13})   = 6.0 minutes
From Node 22–17   = 3.0 minutes
∴ From Node 1–22–17 (T_{17})   = 6.0 minutes

At this stage there are two routes from Node 1–17 (i.e 1–16–17 and 1–22–17) taking 5 and 6 minutes respectively. As the assignment technique requires that only the shortest route is used, the longer route 1–22–17 of 6 minutes is eliminated.

4   This process is repeated until all nodes have been reached via the minimum path time from Zone Centroid 1. The same procedure is used to 'build trees' for all the zones in the network. Fortunately it is possible to build minimum path trees by using a computer to select the minimum path on the basis of the information concerning journey time or other travel resistance factors that have been fed into it.

All traffic flows from zone centroids to all other zone centroids are now assigned to the minimum path trees already calculated. A simple example illustrates the procedure adopted, which can be carried out manually or by computer.

In Figure 27 only the minimum paths from Zone Centroid 1 to Nodes 2, 3 and 4 are given. The minimum paths in the reverse direction from Nodes 2, 3 and 4 to Node 1 may well be different, as the links may not have the same travel time in the reverse direction.

Assume that for the above example the traffic flows to be assigned from

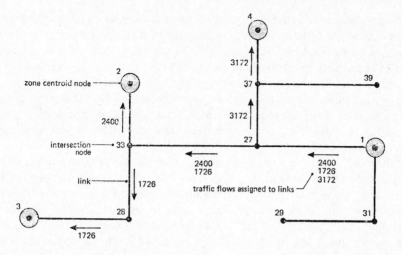

Figure 27 *Minimum path tree calculated from Node 1 in sample network*

Home Node 1 are 1–2   2400 vehicles
              1–3   1726 vehicles
              1–4   3172 vehicles
The minimum path from 1–2 is 1–27–33–2 and consequently 2400 vehicles are assigned to each link of the network between 1 and 2. Similarly, the minimum paths between 1–3 and 1–4 are 1–27–33–28–3 and 1–27–37–4 respectively, and the appropriate vehicles are assigned to each link.

This process is repeated for each zone in relation to every other zone and the total number of vehicles on each link of the network is then aggregated.

In the limited example above it can be seen that link 1–27 carries 7298 vehicles, link 27–33 4126 vehicles, link 27–37 3172 vehicles, and so on.

In addition to the traffic volumes on each link of the network, the turning movements at each junction are also derived through the same procedure.

To complete this stage of the process a check must be carried out to ensure that no link in the network has been overloaded. (An overloaded link is one on which the total of the trips assigned to it is in excess of the capacity of that link.) If the assignment has been carried out by computer then a tabulation is printed out giving the traffic flows on all the links in the route of minimum time paths, thus enabling a manual check to be made for overloading. If overloading is found to occur then the journey time on the overloaded links is amended, and the assignment re-run until it is found to be in balance. Because of the amount of checking and rechecking involved in bringing an assignment into balance it is usual to 'check and correct if necessary sample trees for about 20 or 30 home centroids on the assumption than others will be acceptable'.[8]

Although the all or nothing method of assignment is simple to understand

and apply there are disadvantages associated with its use. One major draw-back is that the technique takes no account of increasing congestion associated with increased volumes and assigns too many vehicles to the better routes as travel time on these routes will be better than on the multi-purpose streets. In real-life situations, however, it has been found that vehicle drivers use both routes. Another problem arises from the fact that for longer journeys in terms of distance more people tend to transfer to motorways, yet the all or nothing assignment technique based on shortest journey times ignores this factor.

Some differences in journey times by different routes between the same origin and destination can bring about unrealistic journey paths when the all or nothing assignment is used. Indeed Buchanan and Partners found that in the all or nothing assignment procedure used to support the development of the inner relief road across Christchurch Meadow, Oxford, 'the differences (in journey time) are so small that drivers could hardly be expected to be aware of them'.[9]

Capacity restraint assignment

A capacity restraint assignment is an alternative method of dealing with over-loaded links in the network. It is carried out entirely by the computer and is completely automatic. The input required by capacity restraint assignments is similar in many ways to that required by 'all or nothing' assignments. In addition the practical capacity of each link of the network is fed into the computer as well as journey time. The first stage of the capacity restraint assignment involves the building of minimum path trees in exactly the same way as they are built for the all or nothing technique. Traffic is then assigned to these minimum paths but as the assigned volume on each link approaches the practical capacity the computer, through an iterative procedure in which loaded link information is used as a feedback to the tree-building process, automatically lowers the assumed speeds on the affected links thereby making these links less attractive to traffic.

The procedure for the description and coding of the network required for the capacity restraint assignment is identical to that carried out for the all or nothing technique.

This first set of minimum paths between zone centroids is also determined in a similar manner, using the practical capacity of each link and the speed at which traffic would flow on each link when loaded to capacity. Traffic from each zone of origin to each zone of destination is then assigned to the network and the loads on each link are compared with the practical capacity of that link. If a link is found to be overloaded then a new journey time which makes allowance for the effect of congestion or excessive traffic flows on speed, is calculated for that link. It is assumed that the relationship between journey time (or speed) and volume on each link in a highway network can be expressed by the equation[10]

$$T = T_0 \left[1 + 0.15 \left(\frac{\text{assigned volume}}{\text{practical capacity}} \right)^4 \right]$$

where T = journey time at which assigned volume can travel on the appropriate link

T_0 = base journey time at zero volume which = journey time at practical capacity × 0.87

Using this equation it is possible to determine the speed at which the assigned volume could theoretically be carried. For example, assume that a link 27–32 is one mile long, and has a practical capacity of 40,000 vehicles per day, and a speed at that capacity of 40 m.p.h. The travel time on that link is therefore $1\frac{1}{2}$ minutes. Travel time at zero volume (T_0) is 1.5 × 0.87 minutes = 1.31 minutes. After the network has been loaded it is found that link 27–32 has 60,000 vehicles per day assigned to it. Using the above formula, the travel time for the assigned volume is estimated.

$$T = 1.31 \left[1 + 0.5 \left(\frac{60,000}{40,000} \right)^4 \right]$$
$$1.31[1 + .76]$$

2.3 minutes (or 26 m.p.h. at which 60,000 vehicles per day can travel on link 27–32)

The new speed, based on an adjustment of the balance travel time is used in the next iteration to minimize the imbalance of volume on the link. However, experience has shown that by changing the travel time on a link an inverse change in the loading occurs. Consequently the full effect of this change is moderated by using a speed for the next iteration which is only one quarter of the way from the last assignment speed to the new balance speed. Thus in the above example a speed of 40 m.p.h. corresponds to a travel time 1.5 minutes, while the travel time at the first assigned volume is 2.3 minutes. To find the speed to use in the next iteration one quarter of the difference between 2.3 and 1.5 minutes (or 0.8 minutes) is added to the previous travel time. This results in a value of 1.7 minutes or a speed of 35 m.p.h.

It has been found that this method of adjustment eliminates large oscillations of loads on the links from one iteration to the next. The next step in the procedure involves the building of a new set of trees by using the adjusted speeds on each link. Traffic is assigned to the modified network; the volume to capacity ratio is examined again and if necessary further adjustments are made to overloaded links. The process is continued for as many iterations as desired although experience has shown that after four iterations the accuracy of the assignments does not improve appreciably.

Modified capacity restraint[11]
Interesting work carried out by the traffic branch of the Department of Highways Transportation of the Greater London Council has shown that capacity restraint assignments tend to produce unrealistic results by assigning local traffic movements to the primary road network rather than to equally convenient secondary routes. In theory this problem can be overcome by a 100 per cent inspection and subsequent modification of the trip paths, between pairs of traffic zones. However, such a solution is time-consuming and because of the shunting around of overloads by the capacity restraint programme, well-nigh impossible.

In an attempt to overcome this problem the GLC have strengthened the assignment procedure by interrupting the computer assignment program at certain stages and substituting manual techniques which enable a comprehensive check of all minimum time paths to be made, and to control the type of trips to be asigned to the primary network.

Basically, the new improved alternative assignment procedure rests on the assumption that only the longer distance trips will use the primary network. Trips between adjacent zones will generally use the existing secondary network.

Using the assumption that only longer distance trips will use the primary network it is argued that the path taken between one group of zones to another group of zones some distance apart will for much of the distance follow a common route, diverging only at the beginning and end of the journey.

Therefore after the first assignment of the longer distance trips has been carried out, a visual inspection of the middle distance part of the route between groups of zones is all that is necessary. If this is satisfactory, then the inspection is extended to those routes linking zone centroids to the start and end of the middle distance part of the route. Using this concept of the middle distance, a comprehensive inspection of all minimum paths can be carried out quite rapidly.

To ensure that the assignment procedure assigns the longer distance movements only to the primary network, the origin and destination trip matrix is inspected visually. Using predetermined criteria about the constitution of long distance trips, a Trip Classification Table is produced, differentiating between long and short distance trips. The short distance trips are then cancelled from the matrix, and the computer program assigns the primary trips to the network. After the first assignment the link loadings are checked manually for overloadings and/or underloadings, and the Trip Classification Table is reassessed. To cope with overloadings the more local trips between pairs of zones which were previously assigned to the primary network are cancelled, or transferred to another route if a suitable alternative exists. Any spare capacity on the primary network revealed by underloadings and which might reasonably be used by local trips is taken up by reclassifying such trips as primary. Successive iterations are carried out until the primary network is in balance. Secondary (local) trips must be assigned to the secondary network, and this can be accomplished manually. The secondary network must be capable of carrying the secondary load, in addition to the primary trips assigned to the primary network and which have trip ends in the area under consideration. If there are excessive loadings on the secondary network then theoretically additional links are necessary on the primary and/or secondary network. If for environmental or financial reasons this is not possible, then some restraining influence must be incorporated into the procedure to select primary or secondary trips.

Linear programming and traffic assignment

Linear programming can be used in traffic assignment.[12, 13] It is assumed that motorists choose their routes as if they are aware of the way in which that choice influences the travel times of all drivers using the road network. Trip interchanges are assigned to the different paths in the network in such a way that the aggregate travel time on the network is minimized. The assignment is constrained by two conditions

1 The capacity of each link in the network is not exceeded
2 All journeys leaving an origin must arrive at a destination

The general formulation of the model to 'solve' the assignment problem is

$$z = \sum_{k,j,i} l(i)a(i,j,k)v(j,k)$$

Subject to (a) $\sum_{k,j,} a(i,j,k)v(j,k) < c(i)$

and (b) $\sum_{j} v(j,k) = t(k)$

where $l(i)$ = travel time on link i

$a(i,j,k)$ = 1 if link i is in path (j,k), (0 otherwise)

$v(j,k)$ = flow on path (j,k) between k^{th} 0–D pair

$t(k)$ = trip interchange between k^{th} 0–D pair

$c(i)$ = capacity of link i

The objective function of the above equation is the minimization of the product of all volumes and travel times over all paths between every pair of zone centroids.

Assignment to public transport systems

The basic principles of road traffic assignment are directly applicable to the assignment of movements by public transport systems – the concept of travel resistance still holds good. Indeed in most cases the same basic road traffic assignments are used to assign public transport movements, although additional artificial links have to be inserted into the network to take account of factors such as the time taken to transfer from one type of public transport to another, for example change from tube to railway, or from car to public transport; and waiting and walking time at origin and destination.

Conclusions

Few comparative studies of the various methods of traffic assignment have been undertaken, for two reasons

1　The cost of collecting sufficient data to allow such comparisons to be made would be extremely expensive
2　The all-or-nothing assignment is generally felt to provide an adequate basis for strategic transport planning decisions for a period some twenty years or so ahead

However, the use of the more sophisticated methods of assignment can be justified for short-term traffic engineering problems, when greater detail concerning flows and turning movements is required.

References

1　*Chicago Area Transportation Study Final Report* III (1962).
2　*The London Transportation Study* (or Phase III of the London Traffic Survey), Greater London Council (1969).
3　Whittle, R. J., 'Route Location in Oxford', *Journal of the Institution of Municipal Engineers* (1968).
4　Buchanan and Partners, *Traffic in Guildford* (1963).
5　*Chicago Area Transportation Study, op. cit.*
6　Moskowitz, K., 'California: method of assigning diverted traffic to proposed freeways', *Highway Research Board*, Bulletin No. 130 (1965).
7　*Detroit Metropolitan Area Traffic Study*, Part II, 'Future Traffic and Long Range Expressway Plan' (1956).
8　Reid, A. U. and Cottee, J. G., *A procedure for the design of a road network*, Report HT/T.1, Greater London Council (1967).
9　Buchanan, C. D., Unpublished proof of evidence at Public Enquiry for Oxford Development Plan, Quinquennial Review (1965).
10　*Traffic Assignment Manual*, US Department of Commerce, Bureau of Public Roads, Washington (1964).
11　Reid, A. U. and Cottee, J. G., *op. cit.*
12　Mosher, W. W., 'A Capacity Restraint Algorithm for Assigning Flow to a Transportation Network', *Highway Research Record No. 6*; Highway Research Board, Washington DC (1963).
13　Tomlin, J. A., *A Linear Programming Model for the Assignment of Traffic*, Australian Road Research Board, Melbourne (1966) pp. 263-9.

7 Modal split

Introduction

Modal split can be defined as the proportionate division of the total number of person trips between different methods or modes of travel. It can be expressed numerically as a fraction, ratio or percentage of the total number of trips.

Many different procedures have been developed to derive this split in the transportation planning process, all based on the assumption that of a given total travel demand the proportion carried by bus, tube, surface railway or private motor car will depend on the standing of each mode of transport in relation to its competitors. The measure of competitiveness is usually derived from an analysis of three sets of factors

1　Characteristics of the journey to be made, e.g. length, time of day the journey is made, purpose of the journey
2　Characteristics of the person making the journey, e.g. car ownership, income, social standing
3　Characteristics of the transportation system, e.g. travel time involved, cost, accessibility, comfort

Early modal split models fall into two categories

1　Models which are applied prior to the trip distribution stage of the process, and allocate a portion of the total travel demand to the different modes available. These are known as *trip end modal split models*.
2　Models which allocate portions of given trip movements resulting from trip distribution to the competing modes of transport. These are referred to as *trip interchange modal split models*.

A failing of these early models was their inability to identify and handle separately those persons who have no choice but to use public transport (captive users) and those who have a choice between using public transport and the motor vehicle (choice users). In an attempt to overcome this problem, modal split models have been developed which are based on an analysis of individual behaviour (behavioural modal split models). More recently, models have been produced which explicitly address the problem of choice and captive users through the application of a two stage approach to modal split.

Factors influencing modal choice

The choice of a particular mode of travel in urban areas is neither a static nor a random process. It is influenced either singly or collectively by many factors such as speed, journey length, comfort, convenience, cost, reliability of alternative modes, the availability of specific travel modes, town size, age, and composition, and the socio-economic status of the persons making the journeys.[1] Of all these potential factors influencing modal choice many are incapable of being quantified accurately and reliably. Consequently such factors tend to be omitted or discarded from analyses of modal split on the grounds that their influence is minimal, or can be represented by some other more easily quantified variable. However, those variables which appear to be most significant have been examined in some depth and attempts have been made to derive a reliable measure of their effect on the choice of mode.

Characteristics of the journey

The two most significant factors in this category are journey length and journey purpose.

Journey length   The length of a journey has been found to influence the modal choice of those persons making that journey.[2] It can be measured in a variety of ways. The airline distance in miles between zone centroids is possibly the simplest measure of journey length. A more accurate measure of distance can be derived from measuring the route distance most likely to be taken between zone centroids, for both public and private means of transport. The time taken to complete a door-to-door journey is another measure of journey length and is often preferred to the measure of distance because it can incorporate the excess travel time associated with journeys.*

The travel-time ratio between competing modes (i.e. the relative travel time by public transport compared with the time for the same journey by private motor vehicle) can be used as a measure of journey length. However, its use in isolation can obscure large absolute differences in journey time by competing modes and must be used with caution, or in conjunction with some other measure of distance. For example if the travel-time ratio for a journey by private car and public transport is 0.5 and the respective average speeds are 20 m.p.h. and 10 m.p.h., then for a 1-mile journey the time difference between modes is small (three minutes). But for a 5-mile journey the time difference is fifteen minutes, which could well have a greater relative effect on choice of mode than three minutes. Thus fewer people can be expected to use public transport as the length of journey increases.

---

* Excess travel time is the time spent on that part of a journey which does not involve the use of a vehicle, and includes time spent walking to or from a vehicle, waiting for a vehicle and changing from one vehicle to another.

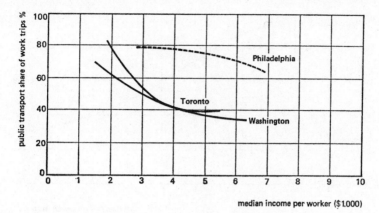

Figure 28 *Income diversion curve for work trips in peak periods*

Source: Hill, D. M., Von Cube, H. C., 'Development of a model for forecasting travel mode choice in urban areas', *Highways Research Board, Record No. 38* (1963)

Journey purpose Experience has shown that there is a relationship between the numbers using public transport and the purpose of the journey being undertaken. Home-based journeys generally given rise to more public transport journeys than non-home-based journeys, while home-based school and work journeys have a higher rate of public transport usage than home-based shopping journeys. This can be explained by the fact that the motor vehicle is essential for some journeys, while for others there is open choice.

Characteristics of the traveller

The most significant factors in this category which affect modal split are concerned with the socio-economic characteristics of the households making the journeys and include variables such as income, car ownership, family size and structure, density of residential development, the type of job undertaken, and the location of workplace. Although these factors can be discussed in isolation, in practice they are highly interrelated in the influence they have on modal choice.

Income The use of a motor car for any journey depends on one's ability to purchase and maintain it. Car ownership is therefore a function of income – and income must therefore influence modal choice. Figure 28 illustrates a typical relationship between income and public transport usage. Indeed, F. R. Wilson in his work in the Coventry area found that virtually no one with an annual salary in excess of £1500 p.a. (1965–6 prices) used the Corporation bus system for the work trip.[3]

Various measures of income can be used, e.g. income of head of household, total family income. However, it is often difficult, if not impossible, to derive at a zonal level reliable statistics concerning income for use in such a way. As a substitute other factors such as car ownership, density of residential development, or type of dwelling are used as 'indicators' of income.

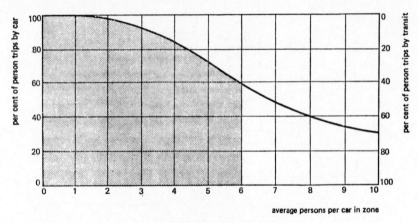

Figure 29   *Effect of car ownership on travel mode*

Source: Wilbur Smith and Associates, *Transportation and Parking for Tomorrow's Cities*, New Haven, Connecticut (1966)

Car ownership   Car ownership, or the availability of a car, is possibly the most significant factor affecting modal choice (see Figure 29). Households without a motor car have a much lower overall trip generation rate than car-owning households, and in urban areas of all sizes, have the heaviest demand for public transport journeys, as a result of having no other available mode of transport.

In contrast with income, it is considered easier to make reliable estimates of future car ownership at a zonal level than to attempt to predict income for the same future date at the same level. Although multi-car ownership substantially increases the total trips performed by members of households, it only marginally reduces the number of journeys made by public transport in the largest urban areas.

Density of residential development   It has been found that as net residential density increases, so the use made of public transport decreases. The *Pittsburgh Area Transportation Study*[4] found that school journeys by public transport are inversely related to net residential density, while other journeys by public transport are directly related to it. The inverse relationship between school journeys by public transport and net residential density was attributed to the greater numbers walking to school in the more densely developed areas.

This relationship can be explained by the fact that it is difficult to provide an adequate and economic public transport service for low density areas. In addition, low density areas tend to be occupied by the middle and higher income groups with the result that levels of car ownership are higher, and consequently the demand for public transport lower.

Conversely, high density areas can be economically and adequately served by public transport. Indeed, such areas usually developed in conjunction with the public transport system and are oriented towards the use of that system. In addition, today, lower income residents tend to occupy the high density residential areas vacated by the higher economic classes of a previous age. Thus car ownership tends to be lower in high density areas.

Other socio-economic factors Family size, the age-sex structure of the family, the proportion of married females in the labour force, the type of property occupied and the type of employment of the head of household are all factors influencing modal choice.

Table 15 indicates in general terms the relationship between certain socio-economic variables and the use of public transport, and it is apparent that indicators of high socio-economic status are negatively associated with public transport use.

Item	Correlation Negative	Coefficient Positive
Percent of units with two or more automobiles	– .74	
Percent of units with no automobiles		0.71
Percent of units – owner occupied	– .66	
Median school years completed	– .65	
Percent of divorced females		0.63
Median gross rent	– .62	
Percent civilian labour force unemployed		0.60
Median value of each dwelling unit	– .58	
Median income of families	– .55	
Percent married women, husband present in labour force	– .55	
Percent housing units deteriorated and dilapidated		0.52
Percent of males in high status occupations	– .47	
Percent of separated males		0.46
Number of black people		0.38
Percent of total labour force – female		0.33

Table 15 *Correlation of public transport use with selected socio-economic variables (Milwaukee, Wisconsin).*

Source: J. K. Hadden, 'The use of public transportation in Milwaukee, Wisconsin', The Eno Foundation for Highway Traffic Control, *Traffic Quarterly*, XVIII, No. 2, Table VI, 230 (1964).

Characteristics of the transportation system

The level of service offered by competing modes of transport is a critical factor influencing modal split, while comparative journey times and out of pocket expenses for public and private transport facilities also influence the choice of travel mode.

Relative travel time   In the more recently developed modal split models relative travel time between competing modes has been found to influence modal choice. This travel-time ratio can be expressed as a time ratio of door-to-door travel time by public transport divided by the door-to-door travel time by private motor vehicle. The travel-time ratio developed by the National Capital Transportation Agency is a typical travel-time ratio.[5]

$$\text{(Travel-time ratio) TTR} = \frac{X_1 + X_2 + X_3 + X_4 + X_5}{X_6 + X_7 + X_8}$$

where X_1 = time spent in public transport vehicle
X_2 = time spent changing between public transport vehicles
X_3 = time spent waiting for public transport vehicle
X_4 = time spent walking to public transport vehicle at origin
X_5 = time spent walking from public transport vehicle at destination
X_6 = time spent driving car
X_7 = time spent parking vehicle at destination
X_8 = time spent walking from parked vehicle to destination

An alternative measure of relative travel time is the absolute difference between travel time by public transport and private motor vehicle and in Leeds this has been shown to be the more reliable measure.[6] However, a basic objection to the widespread use of the absolute difference in travel times is that it has a greater relative effect on the shorter trips. Figure 30 illustrates the effect of travel-time ratio on the public transport share of work trips in the peak hour.

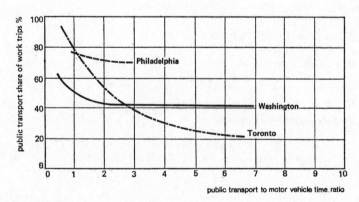

Figure 30   *Travel-time ratio diversion curve for work trips in peak periods*

Source: Hill, D. M., Von Cube, H. G., 'Development of a model for forecasting travel mode choice in urban areas', *Highway Research Board, Record No. 38* (1963)

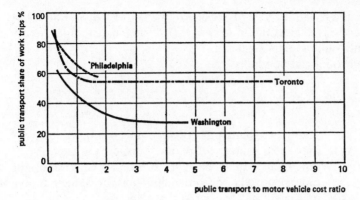

Figure 31   *Cost ratio diversion curve for work trips in peak periods*

Source: Hill, D. M., Von Cube, H. G., 'Development of a model for forecasting travel mode by choice in urban areas', *Highway Research Board, Record No. 38* (1963)

Relative travel cost   The relative cost of travel between competing modes has been found to influence modal choice and this relative cost ratio can be expressed as the out-of-pocket travel cost by public transport, divided by the out-of-pocket cost by private motor vehicle (see Figure 31). The relative travel-cost ratio developed by the National Capital Transportation Agency is a typical example,[7] where

$$\text{(Travel-cost ratio) TCR} = \frac{X_9}{(X_{10} + X_{11} + 0.5X_{12})/X_{13}}$$

where X_9 = fare by public transport
X_{10} = cost of petrol
X_{11} = cost of oil
X_{12} = cost of parking
X_{13} = average car occupancy

The other costs of running a motor vehicle, such as road tax and insurance, are ignored as it has been found that drivers do not consider these costs when considering a particular journey.

In the above example, the modal split model referred to the morning peak period only. To take account of the fact that it related to the one-way cost of the journey, only half of the parking costs have been included.

Relative level of service   The relative level of service offered by public and private transport is affected by a variety of factors, the majority of which are subjective and difficult to quantify, for example, comfort, convenience, ease of changing from one mode to another. The measure of the relative level of service derived by the National Capital Transportation Agency is again fairly typical and is defined by a factor called excess travel time, that is time spent outside the vehicle (public or private) during a particular journey, for example walking, parking delay.

As a ratio it can be expressed

$$\text{(Travel-service ratio) TSR} = \frac{X_2 + X_3 + X_4 + X_5}{X_7 + X_8}$$

where X_2 = time spent changing between public transport vehicles
X_3 = time spent waiting for public transport vehicle
X_4 = time spent walking to public transport vehicle at origin
X_5 = time spent walking from public transport vehicle at destination
X_7 = time spent parking car at destination
X_8 = time spent walking from parked vehicle to destination

Accessibility indices   In the trip-end modal split models developed in the early 1960s, such as the *Puget Sound* and the *South-eastern Wisconsin Regional Land Use Transportation Study*, accessibility indices have been used as a measure of the quality of service provided by the alternative modes of transport. These indices measure the ease with which activity in one area can be reached from a particular zone on a specific transportation system. For example, the accessibility from zone i to zone j is defined as the product of trip attractions in zone j multiplied by the friction factor for the zonal interchange. These products are then summed from zone i to all other zones in the area to obtain the accessibility index for zone i. The accessibility index used by the *South-eastern Wisconsin Regional Land Use Transportation Study* is typical and illustrates these points.[8]

Thus

$$Q_i = \sum_{j=1}^{n} A_j (F_{ij})$$

where Q_i = accessibility index for zone i to all other zones (by public transport or motor vehicle)
A_j = attractions in zone j (by public transport or private motor vehicle)
F_{ij} = travel-time friction factor for travel from zone i to zone j on the particular transportation system being considered
n = total number of zones

The friction factor (F_{ij}) is equal to one divided by the door-to-door travel time, raised to some power b which varies with the travel time.

$$F_{ij} = \frac{1}{(\text{door-to-door travel time})^b}$$

Door-to-door travel time for motor vehicles includes walking at origin and destination, 'unparking' and parking time, and driving time, while door-to-door travel for public transport includes walking and waiting time at origin; time spent travelling on the vehicle; changing time between vehicles where applicable, walking time at destination. Relative travel service provided by two modes is measured by the ratio of the private motor vehicle accessibility index divided by the public transport accessibility index. This is referred to as the accessibility ratio.

Other transportation studies have used different indices of accessibility. *The London Traffic Survey* accessibility index for example reflects the number of routes serving a zone, the frequency of service and the area of zone.[9] Thus the bus accessibility index was defined as

$$AI = \frac{\sum_i \sqrt{N_{ij}}}{A_j}$$

where N_{ij} = off-peak frequency of buses on route i and passing through zone j

A_j = area of the zone in square miles

Similarly, the rail accessibility index was defined as

$$AI = \frac{\sum_i \sqrt{N_{ij}}}{A_j}$$

where N_{ij} = number of trains during off-peak period stopping at station i in zone j

The advantages claimed for these indices are that they are simple, rational and easy to calculate. However, it can be argued that they do not provide a completely satisfactory measure of the relationship between one zone and another. For example a zone of origin may have a very comprehensive and frequent bus service within the zone, but may be linked only to the central area, and, say, one other zone *en route*. Thus the accessibility of the origin zone to all other zones may be poor despite a high level of service within the zone.

Modal split in the transportation planning process

Early modal split models

The procedure adopted for estimating modal split in the transportation planning process varies with the type of model used. A trip-end model allocates total person movements to alternate modes of travel before the trip distribution stage of the process, while trip interchange models allocate movements to the alternate modes after the total movements have been distributed between zones of origin and destination.

Early trip end models, for example that used in the *Chicago Area Transportation Study*,[10] utilized only characteristics of the journey to be made and the person making the journey in assessing modal split. More recently, however, trip end modal split models have been derived which combine the characteristics of the journey, the person making the journey and the transportation system, for example the *South-eastern Wisconsin Regional Land Use Transportation Study*.[11]

The earliest and simplest form of trip interchange modal split model is the public transport diversion curve, which attempted to relate the use of public transport to some measure of the relative travel times by competing models.

However, a fundamental drawback with the simple diversion curve is that it ignores completely the characteristics of the person making the journey, and is incapable of dealing with a complete transportation system at one time. More recently the diversion curve approach to modal split has been refined to take account of journey purpose, time of day, relative travel time and cost, relative travel service and the economic status of the person making the journey. An example is the *National Capital Transportation Agency, Washington*.[12]

Trip-end modal split model   The general procedure adopted in trip-end modal split models is similar, although the journey purposes and variables used to determine the modal split often vary with the design and characteristics of different transportation studies. A typical trip-end modal split model might use for journey purposes, e.g. home-based work, shopping, social/recreational, and miscellaneous, and base its modal choice on a range of variables.

Using forecasted land-use and socio-economic data, total person trip productions and attractions are estimated for each zone for the base year, in the trip generation stage of the process.

The next stage in the process involves the allocation of total person trip productions to public transport for each journey purpose, by considering the attractiveness of the public transport system as measured by the variables considered to influence modal split in the area under examination (see Figure 32). This allocation is usually achieved through the application of diversion curves of the type described earlier (Figures 28 to 31) or the use of multiple linear regression techniques. A typical multiple linear regression equation might take the following form.

$$Y = a_0 + a_1 \log x_1 + a_2 \log x_2 + a_3 x_3 + a_4 x_4 + a_5 x_5 + a_6 x_6 + a_7 x_7$$

where Y = percentage of all journeys to work by public transport
  x_1 = travel-time ratio
  x_2 = travel-cost ratio

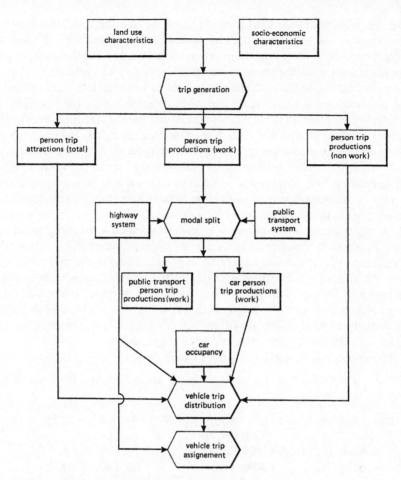

Figure 32 *Generalized trip-end modal split diagram*

Source: Modal Split, Bureau of Public Roads, Washington (1966)

x_3 = car ownership
x_4 = family-size index
x_5 = economic-class index
x_6 = length of journey
x_7 = percentage of females in employed population.[13]

Journeys made by motor vehicle are derived by subtracting the estimated public transport trip productions from the total person trip production estimate.

Future trip attractions by public transport are then estimated, again using diversion curves or by multiple linear regression techniques, using, for example, variables such as the location of the destination zone, the employment level in the zone, and the characteristics associated with the use of public transport in that zone. Subtraction of this figure from the total person trip attractions gives the journeys made by private motor vehicles.

The estimated public transport and private motor vehicle trip productions and attractions are then distributed and assigned using, for example, a gravity model, and the appropriate highway and public transport networks. Motor vehicle person productions and attractions must first be converted to vehicle productions and attractions to obtain a motor vehicle origin and destination matrix, and this is achieved by introducing vehicle occupancy rates.

The *London Traffic Survey* used a trip-end modal split model based on an analysis of household parameters rather than traffic zone characteristics to project the modal distribution of trip generation. This process forms part of the 'category analysis' technique described in Chapter 4 on trip generation and 'places each household into one of a large number of categories according to the location and characteristics of the household, and expresses from the information on trip generation for the sampled households in each category, an average trip generation rate for each travel mode and trip purpose, and for central area, non-central area, peak and off-peak trips. Knowing the number of households in each category for future years allows a modal distribution of trips in these years to be made.'[14]

The variables included in the analysis were

1   *Car ownership*   Three categories were distinguished – 0,1, and 2 or more cars owned

2   *Household income*   Three income categories were determined
  Low   £1000 p.a.
  Medium   £1000–2000 p.a.
  High   £2000 p.a.   (at 1965–6 values)

3   *Employed residents*   Three categories of household were distinguished based on the number of employed residents – 0, 1, and 2 or more employed residents

4   *Rail accessibility*   Three ranges of rail accessibility index were distinguished
  Low   (0–10)
  Medium   (10–25)
  High   (25)

5   *Bus accessibility*   Three ranges of bus accessibility index were distinguished
  Low   (0–8)
  Medium   (8–25)
  High   (25)

Future values of bus and rail accessibility were estimated by examining past trends in the extension or retraction of bus routes, and in the case of rail by determining the amount of new rail construction likely under present transport policies.

Trip-interchange modal split models Trip-interchange modal split models allocate journey movements to different modes after total person movements between pairs of zones have been distributed. The procedure adopted by different trip-interchange modal split models is similar, although they may be designed to operate with a particular type of distribution model, and use different variables to determine the modal choice (see Figure 33).

A typical trip-interchange model designed, for example, to operate in conjunction with a gravity distribution model, would accept as input a zone to zone gravity model distribution of home-based person trips. From this input, the model determines zone to zone public transport travellers, and motor

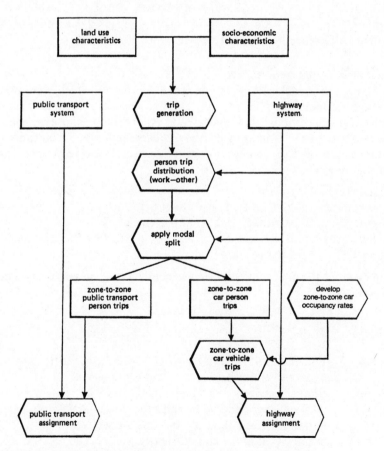

Figure 33 *Generalized trip-interchange modal split diagram*

Source: Modal Split, Bureau of Public Roads, Washington (1966)

vehicle trips using variables representing characteristics of persons making the journey; characteristics of the destination end of the journey, and characteristics of the transport system, all measured on a zone to zone basis. These include relative travel time from door to door; income; net residential density and employment density at destination end. Again diversion curves or possibly multiple linear regression analysis are used for this purpose.

By subtracting the public transport trips between pairs of zones from the total person trips between the same zones the person trips made by motor vehicle are derived. By dividing this total by appropriate car occupancy factors the vehicle interchanges between zones are determined, which can then be assigned to the highway network.

Two criticisms can be levelled at these early models of modal choice. First, they cannot identify and handle separately captive and choice public transport users. As a result the models do not reflect the way in which the choice users react to changes in the transport system. Second, as explained in Chapter 4, Trip Generation, the use of zonally aggregated data tends to hide important differences in trip-making behaviour.

Behavioural modal split models

A number of modal split models have been developed which focus on the behaviour of individuals in choosing their mode of travel rather than on zonally aggregated modal choice behaviour. All these models use the concept of *generalized cost* in estimating the use of different modes of transport (see Chapter 5, pp. 136–8 for an outline of generalized cost). This concept is based on the assumptions

1 That trip making has a number of features which are unpleasant for the person making the trip, such as waiting time for public transport, congestion and delay for the private motor vehicle
2 That the deterrent effect of these features will influence choice of mode of travel

It will be recalled from Chapter 5 that in general terms generalized cost can be expressed as:

$$C_{ij} = A_1 T_{ij} + A_2 E_{ij} + A_3 D_{ij} + P_j + \delta$$

where C_{ij} = the generalized cost of travel from zone i to zone j by a particular mode of travel

T_{ij} = time of travel between zone i and zone j by a particular mode

E_{ij} = excess travel time, i.e. access and waiting time

D_{ij} = distance between zone i and zone j

$A_1, A_2\, A_3$ = constants representing the value the travelling public associates with time, excess time and distance respectively

P_j = terminal cost at the end of the trip

δ = a calibrating factor representing, for example, comfort and convenience (this value is referred to as the 'inherent modal handicap')

In applying generalized cost in modal split non-car owners are assumed to be captive public transport travellers, and for each pair of origin and destination zones the ratio of trips by car to trips by public transport is estimated from

$$\frac{T_{ij}^1}{T_{ij}^2} = \frac{f(C_{ij}^1)}{f(C_{ij}^2 + \delta)}$$

where $f(C_{ij})$ has the same functional form as the deterrence function in the 'generalized cost' distribution model, although it may have a different exponent and

$$T_{ij}^1 = \text{trips from zone } i \text{ to zone } j \text{ by car}$$
$$T_{ij}^2 = \text{trips from zone } i \text{ to zone } j \text{ by public transport}$$
$$f(C_{ij}^1) = \text{generalized cost of trip from zone } i \text{ to zone } j \text{ by car}$$
$$f(C_{ij}^2 + \delta) = \text{generalized cost of trip from zone } i \text{ to zone } j \text{ by public transport, including an empirically derived value representing public transport handicap}$$

This type of model has been justified theoretically by Wilson[15] and empirically by Quarmby[16].

Discriminant analysis and modal split

More recently, the Local Government Operational Research Unit has been examining the use of the technique known as discriminant analysis to explain and predict modal split.[17] The assumptions implicit in the use of this technique are that (a) individuals choose a mode of travel, and (b) in making a choice the advantages and disadvantages of alternative modes of travel are evaluated, consciously or subconsciously. The factors which are used in this evaluation are considered to relate to such aspects as journey time, cost, comfort, and reliability. Inevitably, in a real-life situation, in evaluating these sorts of factors in relation to alternative modes of travel, individuals apply a 'weighting' to represent the importance of each of the individual factors. The statistical technique of discriminant analysis is used to derive an estimate of the weightings which are most likely to explain the observed modal split (or more appropriately 'modal choice').

By applying discriminant analysis to survey data relating to Liverpool, Manchester, Leicester and Great Yarmouth, the Local Government Operational Research Unit developed a 'global' equation* which it is considered can be used to estimate the proportion of those who have access to a car, and who use that car for the work journey movement. The data from which this equation was developed related to characteristics of the journey made (e.g. journey time, length, cost); the individual's attitude to travel by different modes, and the socio-economic characteristics of the individual making the journey (e.g. income, age, sex). In addition composite variables derived from the survey data were also used in the analysis, for example travel-time difference for the same journey by different modes.

* A 'global' equation is one which is considered to have relevance to all towns in Britain, as a basis for estimating modal choice.

Data relating to the variables surveyed was then grouped into 'mode of travel' pairs for comparison, to estimate the probability that certain individuals would travel by either of the modes in the pair using a probability function of the form

$$P(z) = \frac{e^z}{1 + e^z}$$

The grouped pairs were bus/car, bus/train, and car/train.

From the pooled data relating to the four towns a general set of equations was developed for each mode pair; for a public/private transport pair, and each pair classified by income, age, employment and travel time. The equation took the form

$$Z_j = a_{0m} + \sum_i a_{im} X_{ij} \qquad m = 1, 4$$

where a_0 is a constant

a_i is a coefficient measuring the importance of the ith variable in determining travel choice

X_{ij} is the value of the ith variable for the jth individual and

Z_j is a measure of the individual's preference for travel by a particular mode

However, the set of general equations did not satisfactorily explain modal choice, primarily due to differences in scale of the four towns which was unexplained by the variables. To overcome this problem the raw data was 'normalized', i.e. it was transformed to a normal distribution with a unit standard deviation and a zero mean. From the normalized data a global equation of the following form was derived for the bus/car mode pair.

$$Z = 0.2 + 0.804X_1 + 0.571X_2 + 0.337X_3 + 0.526X_4$$

where X_1 is the difference in walking time at origin and destination ends between bus and car

X_2 is the difference in waiting time between bus and car

X_3 is the difference in 'in-vehicle' time between bus and car

X_4 is the difference in cost between bus and car

+ 0.2 is the constant (a_0)

Z is a measure of the individual's preference for travel by bus or car.

Using this global equation as a basis it is then possible to develop a specific equation for the town or area where the model is to be used for predicting modal split. This is achieved by

1 Estimating coefficients b'_i for each of the variables X_1–X_4, and which relate to the specific town or area from

$$b'_i = \frac{a_i}{\sigma_i}$$

where b'_i = the derived coefficient applicable to the town under consideration

a_i = the coefficient relating to the variables X_1 in the global equation (i.e. 0.804; 0.571; 0.337 and 0.526)

σ_i = the standard deviation of the variables X_1–X_4 relating to the town under consideration. *NB* these values are absolute – they are not 'normalized'.

2 estimating a scaling factor (b'_0) for the specific town which is derived from

$$b'_0 = - \sum_i b'_i X_i + \log_e \frac{(n^2)}{(n^1)}$$

where b'_i are the coefficients for variables X_1–X_4 derived for the town under consideration

X_i are the variables X_1–X_4 for the town under consideration

$\dfrac{(n^2)}{(n^1)}$ is the ratio of bus users to car users

If the present modal split is unknown (i.e. values of n^2 and n^1) then it is recommended that the value of $\log_e \dfrac{(n^2)}{(n^1)}$ is estimated from the regression set

$$\log_e \frac{(n_2)}{(n_1)} = 0.727 + 0.028X_1 + 0.177X_2$$

where X_1 = the mean value of total travel time difference

X_2 = the mean value of total cost difference

The multiple correlation coefficient for this regression set was 0.98, which is only just significant as there were only four sets of data input to derive the regression set.

A hypothetical example illustrates the way in which the global model is applied to estimate the probability of a car owner using public transport for the work journey movement.

1 Take the global equation.
2 Assume the following mean values (μ) and standard deviations (σ) for walking time difference (X_1), waiting time difference (X_2), in-vehicle time difference (X_3) and cost difference (X_4) for a hypothetical town.

	σX_j	μX_j	units
X_1	9.0	9.6	minutes
X_1	8.4	22.0	minutes
X_3	18.6	28.0	minutes
X_4	8.0	– 23.0	old pence

3   Derive the appropriate equation coefficients for the hypothetical town from

$$b'_i = \frac{a_i}{\sigma X_i}$$

viz., $b'_1 = \dfrac{0.804}{9.0} = 0.089$ $b'_3 = \dfrac{0.337}{18.6} = 0.018$

$b'_2 = \dfrac{0.571}{8.4} = 0.68$ $b'_4 = \dfrac{0.526}{8.0} = 0.066$

Thus $Z = 0.089X_1 + 0.068X_2 + 0.018X_3 + 0.066X_4$

Now the mean values for the variables $X_1 - X_4$ are 9.6, 22.0, 28.0 and -23.0, and by inserting these into the above derived equations a value for Z can be calculated thus

$$\begin{aligned} Z &= (0.089 \times 9.6) + (0.068 \times 22.0) + (0.018 \times 28.0) + \\ &\quad (0.66 \times -23.0) \\ &= 1.34 \end{aligned}$$

Taking the existing modal split for the town (i.e. the existing $\dfrac{n^2}{n^1}$) b'_0 the scaling factor is calculated to be 0.88.

Using the probability function

$$P_{(b)} \% \ \frac{\exp(x + b'_0)}{1 + \exp(z + b'_0)}$$

the probability of a car owner using a bus to travel to work, assuming base data conditions (e.g. free parking; existing fare structure) is estimated as

$$\frac{e^{1.34 + 0.88}}{1 + e^{1.34 + 0.88}} = 0.62$$

That is, 62 per cent of the car owners will use the bus for the work journey given base data conditions.

In developing the derived equation for the specified town, the constant in the global equation is dropped, as it has no relevance in the specified town. Calibration is achieved through the scaling factor b'_0. Also it should be noted that the variables for the specified town are not normalized.

The method goes some way towards improving our knowledge and understanding of modal split. It is comparatively easy to apply, and more recent work by the Local Government Operational Research Unit has concentrated on developing a multi-modal model (i.e. four competing modes rather than the two mode example outlined above).

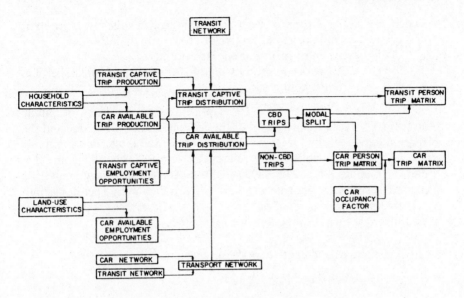

Figure 34   *Flow diagram for two-stage modal split model*

Source: Hutchinson, B. G., *Principles of Urban Transport Systems Planning*, McGraw Hill, London (1974)

Two stage approach to modal choice[18]

A number of two stage modal choice models have been developed which separately take account of choice and captive users of public transport.[19, 20] Figure 34 illustrates the broad structure of this type of model which in general terms

1   Establishes trip productions and attractions of captive and choice users of public transport
2   Distributes the two groups of person movements from origin to destination
3   Allocates the choice for public transport users to either car or public transport using a model which reflects the relative characteristics of the trip by car and public transport

The two stage model developed by Vandertol, Hutchinson and Shortreed[21] is typical and illustrates the approach adopted in such models admirably. The main stages are as follows.

1   Estimate work trip productions on a zonal basis for captive and choice users of transport from

$$P_i^q = h_i tp^q$$

where p_{iq} = the number of work trips produced in zone i by q group of trip maker, i.e. captive or choice trip makers

h_i = the number of households in zone i

t_p^q = the work trip production rate for q group of trip maker, i.e. captive and choice

This work trip production rate for captive and choice users of public transport (t_p^2) is seen as a function of the economic status of a zone and the average number of employees per household. In the model the economic status of zones is established by reference to three levels of income distribution of males ($<$ \$3000; \$3000–6000; $>$ \$6000). Category analysis is then used to derive the appropriate work trip production rate per household for captive and choice users of public transport. These rates are then applied to establish work trip productions for each zone.

2   Estimate choice and captive work trip attractions to zones from

$$a_j^q = [pr_c^q] \ [r_{ct}] \ [e_{tj}]$$

where a_j^q = the number of work trips allocated to zone j by q group of trip maker, i.e. captive or choice

$[pr_c^q]$ = a row vector of the probability of q group of trip maker being in occupation type c

$[r_{ct}]$ = $c \times t$ matrix of the probabilities of an occupation category c being within an industry type t

$[e_{tj}]$ = $t \times j$ matrix of the number of jobs within each industry type t in each zone j

Four occupation categories (c above) and five industry types (t above) are used. They are

Occupation categories (c)	primary, professional-managerial, clerical-sales; labour-service
Industry types (t)	primary; manufacturing, service, commercial and other

The assumption underlying the use of these occupation categories and industry types is that the type of employment at the attraction end of the work trip will determine whether a trip is choice or captive.

The probability of a person in each of the employment categories (c) being a captive or choice user of public transport is estimated from

$$[pr_q] = [pr_1^q, pr_2^q, \ldots, pr_c^q]$$

where pr_c^q = the probability of a person with a job in category c being a choice or captive trip maker type q, q = 1 = public transport captive, q = 2 = choice, c = 1 = primary occupation . . . . c = 4 = labour-service occupation.

3 Simulate the origin and destination linkages

The numbers of choice users of public transport whose destination is the central area are allocated between public transport and the motor car using diversion curves or generalized cost. Choice users whose destination is somewhere other than the central area are assumed to use the car for their journey. Matrices for public transport and car trips are then assembled as input for the trip distribution stage of the process.

Multiple linear regression analysis can also be used to estimate captive users of public transport as part of a two stage approach to modal split analysis. Morall and Morasch[22] in work on Calgary produced the following captive work trip production and attraction equations for the morning peak period.

Captive public
transport work $\quad = \; - \; 45.3 \; + \; 0.097$ number of households; $R^2 \; = \; 0.77$
trip productions

captive public
transport work
trip productions $\quad = \; - \; 39.0 \; + \; 0.082$ number of households; $R^2 \; = 0.64$
to central area

captive public
transport work $\quad = \; - \; 99.2 \; + \; 0.115$ numbers in employment; $R^2 \; = 0.94$
trip attractions

Conclusions

In estimating modal choice, trip makers should be treated as two separate groups (a) captive public transport users who do not have access to a car for the particular trip under study, and (b) choice public transport users who are in a position to choose whether to use car or public transport for a particular journey. Income, sex, and age are the three main factors in determining 'captive' or 'choice' status.

Early modal split models fall into two broad categories – trip end models and trip interchange models. There are advantages and disadvantages associated with the use of both approaches. The trip-end approach to modal split, unlike trip-interchange, is capable of making separate public transport and private motor vehicle distributions between pairs of zones, and this is considered desirable because of the frequently differing lengths of journey by car and public transport. Thus the distribution of total person trips is often considered a basic weakness of trip-interchange models.

Another disadvantage associated with trip-interchange models is that with an increase in the number of zones used in the transportation study, the number of 'splits' required to determine modal choice for the area under study increases with the square of the number of zones used. There are disadvantages associated with the trip-end models, the most significant of which is that characteristics of the transportation system are fed into these models as average area-wide values. Thus the trip-end model is unable to reflect a particular zone to zone combination as precisely as trip-interchange models.

General criticisms of both types of models are based on the fact that present-day levels of service are used, which have a built-in bias in favour of the motor car. Thus the situation could arise where future estimates of public transport usage could be on the low side if a substantially improved public transport system is developed by the base year, or if the road pricing and parking policies affect the use of the motor vehicle. More fundamentally, these models cannot identify and handle separately captive and choice public transport users, while the use of zonally aggregated data tends to obscure important differences in trip making.

The application of a generalized cost approach provides an improved basis for modal choice estimation especially when used in combination with a binary choice stochastic model such as discriminant analysis. A more sensitive modal split analysis is provided by the application of the two-stage model which recognizes explicitly the captive and choice public transport users.

Despite the uncertainty associated with the determination of future modal choice, great advances have been made in the past ten years. However, little systematic knowledge exists on these matters, and considerable research, especially in the field of motivation studies, is required before it can be said that acceptable and reliable estimates of future modal split can be made.

References

1   See Wilson, F. R., *The Journey to Work – Modal Split*, pp. 119–70 Maclaren (1967).
2   National Capital Transportation Agency, 'A model for estimating travel mode usage', *Traffic Forecasting*, Vols. I, IV and V, Washington (1962).
3   Wilson, F. R., *op. cit.*
4   Schwarz, A., 'Forecasting transit use', *Highway Research Board*, Bulletin No. 297 (1961).
5   National Capital Transportation Agency, *op. cit.*
6   Quarmby, D. A., 'Choice of travel mode for the journey to work', *Journal of Transport Economics and Policy* (1967).
7   National Capital Transportation Agency, *op. cit.*
8   Weiner, E., *A modal split model for Southeastern Wisconsin*, Technical Records (Vol. II, No. 6) Southeastern Wisconsin Regional Planning Commission (1966).
9   Freeman, Fox, Wilbur Smith and Associates, *London Traffic Survey*, Vol. II (1966).
10 *Chicago Area Transportation Study, Final Report*, Volumes 1 and 2 (1960).
11 Weiner, E., *op. cit.*
12 National Capital Transportation Agency, *op. cit.*
13 Wilson, F. R., *op. cit.*
14 Freeman, Fox, Wilbur Smith and Associates, *op. cit.*
15 Wilson, A. G., 'The use of entropy maximising models in the theory of trip distribution, mode split, and route split', *Journal of Transport Economics and Policy*, Vol. 1 (1967).

16 Quarmby, D. A., 'Choice of travel mode for the journey to work: some findings', *Journal of Transport Economics and Policy*, Vol. 1 (1967).

17 Rogers, K. G., Townsend, Gillian, and Metcalf, A. E., *Planning for the Work Journey - a generalized explanation of Modal Choice*, Local Government Operational Research Unit Report No. C67, revised edition, February 1971.

18 For a fuller discussion of two stage modal split models, see: Hutchinson, B. G., *Principles of Urban Transport Systems Planning*, McGraw Hill, London (1974) pp. 68-78.

19 Ferreri, M. G., and Cherwony, W., *Choice and Captive Modal Split Models*, Highway Research Record No. 392, Highway Research Board, Washington DC (1972).

20 Morall, J. F. and Morasch, L. H., 'Transit Planning Models for Calgary', Paper presented at Canadian Transportation Research Forum (April 1973).

21 Hutchinson, *op. cit.*

22 Morall and Morasch, *op. cit.*

8 Computers in transportation planning

Introduction

Computers are an integral part of the transportation planning process, and advances in this field have invariably been paralleled by the evolution of digital computer technology. Without the aid of the computer, analysis of the large quantities of data collected would be so laborious and time-consuming, that it would not be attempted, while the solution of the different models and simulation processes can often only be satisfactorily completed by computer.

The first application of computers to the transportation planning process was concerned primarily with the tabulation of the extensive survey information collected, although, as the size of core store increased and the difficulties of programming were reduced, the computer was used to solve the early trip distribution models such as the Fratar and Detroit growth factor models.

The most significant development in the field of traffic assignment by computer occurred in 1957 with the work of E. F. Moore[1] on the theory of switching. Further work by the Armor Research Foundation led to the development of a limited traffic assignment by computer, which was refined and ultimately applied by the staff of the Chicago metropolitan area. By 1962, the transportation planning process was served by a complete package of computer programs for mainframe computers covering distribution and assignment models, and complex data analysis. These programs are well recorded and documented and are readily available to potential users.[2,3,4]

The development of larger computers, capable of carrying out calculations and data manipulation at very high speeds, had a marked effect in the field of transportation planning. The development of simple programming languages such as Cobol and Fortran allowed the transportation planner to write his or her own programs for specific jobs. Larger core storage facilities ensured that extensive and complex transportation networks could be studied relatively easily. Faster and larger machines and easier programming encouraged the development of different approaches to the same problems with the result that alternative models and procedures can be used for the different steps of the process. More recently, microcomputers have increasingly been used in transport systems analysis and forecasting – for the reasons that they are cheap, flexible, compact and can be used in an interactive way to achieve in most situations the same end product as the larger mainframe machines. The use of such machines; their rapid reduction in price, and their capacity for interaction with mainframe machines are likely to further transform the transportation planning process in practice.

Computers

It is not the intention of this work to describe in detail computing techniques and languages. These are fully documented elsewhere.[5] However, to understand the relationship between computing technology and transportation planning, it is necessary to outline the basic elements of a digital computer, and the method of giving instructions to the machine. The basic elements of the digital computer system are the central processing unit, which carries out the calculation required by a particular program – and the peripherals – which are devices to put data into the computer and record the results. These peripheral devices are known as input and output devices. Because the central processing unit carries out the required calculations extremely rapidly – in millionths of a second – it is vital that both input and output devices should also operate as quickly as possible to achieve the fastest possible overall rate of working.

Generally speaking, input and output media are divided into two categories (a) slow-speed media which can be created and read manually, and (b) high-speed media which can only be created and read by the computer.

Input and output devices
Punched cards are perhaps the simplest form of computer input. They are straightforward to use and are long established, although compared with other forms of input they are relatively slow. Despite this shortcoming, they are still in use with some standard transport planning packages. The standard card in use is the eighty-column card, which has twelve rows each with its numerical significance. Alphabetical characters are represented by a simple extension of the numeric code. They can be created and read manually. Basic information is punched on to the cards in accordance with a predetermined coding system, and this information is transferred to and held by the central processor, by means of a card reader. Punched cards can also be used to record output data.

A cheaper and more easily stored form of input record is punched paper tape, although it has the slight drawback of being more difficult to read manually. Data is punched on to 5, 6, 7 or 8 track paper tape and read into the computer by a paper tape reader. A character is represented by holes marked off across the tape in a 'set' or 'frame'. Paper tape can also be used to record output data in the same way as punched cards, although its speed of use in this connection is very slow.

Both punched cards and paper tape can be used initially as input to create a magnetic tape or disk file which, once created, is used on subsequent occasions as the principal high speed peripheral device. It can be used as a means of input and for recording output. Data is recorded by magnetized spots in 'sets' or 'frames' across the magnetic tape, in much the same way as data is recorded on paper tape. A typical magnetic tape reader is capable of reading input data, or writing output data at a rate which is considerably faster than using either cards or paper tape as direct input to the central processing unit. Magnetic disks consist of a surface with a number of bands. Each band is capable of holding characters in a code of magnetized dots. The reading of data from, or the recording of data to such disks is extremely fast. Disks are convenient and simple to handle and store, and have the great advantage of providing random access to any data stored, rather than the next sequentially stored data.

By far the most frequently used input device is a terminal linked directly to the computer. Such terminals can be situated in work stations which are remote from the computer. They consist of an alpha-numeric keyboard and monitor screen. Data and/or program instructions can be entered through the terminal to create a file on magnetic tape or disk. Information entered in this way is presented on the monitor screen so that it can be checked for error and corrected immediately by the individual creating the file. The use of terminals allows the user to interact directly with the computer, both when creating a data file and running a program.

Terminals can also be used as output devices with the output displayed on the monitor screen. However, since the bulk of a computer's output must eventually take a form which can be read by people, the line printer, another 'peripheral', is an extremely important output device. This peripheral, in response to a program instruction, normally prints a horizontal line of characters on stationery which is fed continuously through the machine. This stationery is 'spaced', i.e. the paper moves up one line before that line is printed. The number of printing positions in a line varies with the type of computing system and machine specification.

To avoid delaying the next calculation to be carried out by the central processing unit line printers, rather than transferring the print line direct from the central processing unit to the print barrel, have an intermediate station incorporated. This stores the next line to be printed, while the line printer is printing the previous line, and the central processing unit continues with the assembly of the next line.

The central processor
The central processing unit of any computing system comprises a storage medium in which data can be held and manipulated. It also holds the program of instructions to be followed by the processing unit. A range of names has been used to describe the central processing unit's storage, but perhaps the most meaningful are core storage, magnetic core storage, and

magnetic ferrite core storage. All three terms are based on the fact that the storage medium is composed of magnetic ferrite. Purely numeric data can be held in the core storage by use of the binary number system, which takes the base 2. The numbers 1 or 0 are held in each position, and in excess of 1 a 'carry' forms to increase the next highest position. Thus instead of units, tens, hundreds, thousands, numbers are represented in the following way, for example:

32s	16s	8s	4s	2s	Units	
1	1	0	0	1	1	= 51

Pure binary is simple and economic requiring that each unit of ferrite core store is in one of two positions 'on' or 'off'. Some digital computers are pure binary machines throughout, and such machines are designed for scientific work which requires only numeric answers. However, most problems requiring computer analysis also require alphabetic and decimal character data to pass through the computer unchanged. A simple method has been devised to allow this to take place by using a character code known as binary-coded decimal. For each decimal digit four indicator positions are used, and each position may be either 'off' or 'on'. By utilizing the different permutations of 'on' and 'off' it is possible to represent decimal characters, and alphabetic characters.

To utilize to the full the core storage available in the central processing unit, most computer systems are designed so that arithmetic operations are carried out using pure binary, while for non-arithmetic purposes binary-coded decimal is accepted by the computer.

Program instructions

As well as the data to be manipulated, core storage holds the program of instructions to be followed by the processing units. These instructions are made up of characters or binary numbers just like the data to be manipulated, and each instruction has a pattern known as the instruction format. A typical instruction format could consist of an operation code (e.g. add, subtract) and give the address of both items of data to be operated on. The computer operates by continuously alternating between analysing the next instruction and obeying that instruction. A specially prepared 'master' program is held in core storage, to carry out many functions which would otherwise require detailed programming. This master program, which is known as the Executive, is a series of subroutines (or elements of a program) using the instructions to which the computer is designed to respond, and among other functions it is responsible for the allocation of core storage. Before program instructions can be understood by the central processing unit, they must be in the form of pure binary or binary-coded decimal. Programs written in this way are said to be in machine language. This type of programming language is difficult for the average person to use. To overcome this, languages such as Fortran or Cobol which are more compatible with verbal and mathematical statements have been developed, and the central processing unit is supplied with a special program called an assembler which can translate these high-level languages into machine language. Thus, to write a computer program, a knowledge of a high-level language such as Fortran, is all that is required. Once written it is fed into the processing unit, compiled, and checked for errors by the assembler. When all program errors have been eliminated, the program is run using test data to check the logic of the program of instructions.

Before preparing program instructions for the computer analysis of a particular problem, it is usual to set out the problem and its solution in the form of a flow chart, which follows certain diagramming conventions. The object is to define and represent the problem as a series of logical steps capable of solution. Once this is completed it is a comparatively simple matter to convert the flow chart into a language which the computer can understand.

Mini and microcomputers

The last eight years has seen the most significant and rapid development of mini and microcomputers. Minicomputers, such as the Prime 750 or DECVAX Super Mini, are mini versions of the larger mainframe machines. They cost between £100 k and £200 k if peripherals, software and a graphics capability are included; operate in the same way as the mainframe machines, may have a smaller capacity or slower speed but do not require the continual presence of operators. Microcomputers, such as Superbrains, Sirius or IBM PC, and super micros, such as Piscel or Fortune UNIX systems, are cheap, compact machines which operate on the same principles as a mainframe machine, but with more limited processing capacity. This miniaturization has been brought about by the development of the silicon chip which allows what would formerly have been extensive and complex wiring networks to be accommodated on a chip the size of a finger-nail. The microcomputers typically in use in the transport field have input devices – a keyboard and magnetic disks (known as floppy disks); output devices in the form of a screen monitor, disk and a printer; and a processing unit. They weigh in the region of 20 kg and are capable of operation in a normal office environment. A complete system can be purchased for between £3000 and £4000 at 1984 prices depending on the machine purchased.

The advantages of using a microcomputer are

1   Cheapness, and they can be rendered even more cost-effective if a number of microcomputers use the same printer. Indeed, it is estimated that a micro-system can pay for itself in a matter of weeks if it is used instead of purchasing mainframe computer time at bureau rates.[6]
2   Accessibility, either at or immediately adjacent to the transport planner's work station.

3 Ease of use, which reduces much of the mysticism surrounding computing.
4 Interactive capabilities, i.e. the programs being run can interact with conversational instructions input by the user and output the end product to the screen monitor or printer, as instructed.
5 Increased productivity, by avoiding delays associated with waiting for printout from mainframe batched systems.
6 Use as a terminal to link into other computer systems, i.e. they can send or receive data files to or from other computer systems.

There are, of course, potential disadvantages with using microcomputers, the most obvious of which are the limitations of processor speed and the scale of the transport problem that can be handled. These problems, however, are not as serious as might first appear. For example, an area the size of Norwich (122,000 population approximately) can be studied using a microcomputer and an assignment to a 1500 link highway network can be completed in ten minutes.[7] More serious problems focus on the floppy disk which has limited capacity (about 4000 questionnaire replies) and is unreliable in that the file(s) on a disk can be corrupted. This latter problem can be overcome by adopting a back-up system of disks, by copying each file and keeping one set as a master in the event of the working disk being corrupted. The problem of limited capacity can be partly overcome by incorporating a hard disk into the system.

The level of provision of microcomptuers in a transportation office will obviously depend on the computer resources already available. Where such resources are scarce, for example in developing countries, there is a strong argument for their use to provide a computing capability at low cost. Even where the provision of mainframe computing facilities is good there is a sound case for introducing microcomputers, both as intelligent terminals capable of interacting with a mainframe machine and for use in those situations where the scale of the problem merits the use of a microcomputer and a speedy turnround of work is required.

Standard programs in transportation planning

In the 1960s, numerous standard transportation programs were developed to produce solutions to a given problem in a quick and efficient way, and to save the non-expert programmer from struggling to write an inefficient program to solve the same problem. These programs were written by experts for particular computer systems and tended to be restricted to common problems encountered in transportation planning, for example, the Bureau of Public Roads standard programs for trip generation, trip distribution, traffic assignment, modal split.[8] More recently, suites of programs have and are being developed by transport consultants for use on mainframe, mini and microcomputers, for example, *MicroTRIPS* developed by Systematica[9] and *MINITRAMP* by Wootton Jeffries and Partners.[10]

To run a standard program, it is necessary to input data to the central processor through an input peripheral. The detail and format of the input varies with the type of computer system used. However, the basic elements of the input are similar and, in general terms, consist of details of the problem being processed, program instructions and the data to be processed. The details of the job involved include the identification of the user and the job; the calling into storage of any routines or subroutines required, and the setting up of any peripheral devices to be used by the program, such as line printer, paper tape reader. These details are generally input from punched cards, paper tape, or direct from the terminal keyboard.

The program instructions, setting out the process to be undertaken by the central processor, are then input from punched cards, paper tape, magnetic tape, keyboard or called directly from disk.

The end of the program instruction is indicated by an identifying card (if the input is from punched cards) or data block, and this is followed by the data to be manipulated. The end of the data, and the end of the job is identified by an END card data block.

Survey analysis
This type of standard program has been developed to analyse the extensive and complex data collected in the survey stage of the process and to present it in a form that enables intelligible patterns to be discerned. Prior to the development of the computer, this data had to be processed manually, or by using simple punched card tabulators. Consequently, severe limitations were imposed on the type of study which could be undertaken. Now, using a computer and a general survey analysis program, the transportation planner needs only to specify the type of analysis required in a stylized form of English. The assembler then converts these instructions into a form which can be understood by the computer.

The basic data collected during the survey is punched on to cards or paper tape or entered directly through the terminal keyboard, depending on the type of input used in the computer system and in accordance with a predetermined coding system. It is essential that this coding be kept as straightforward as possible, to keep the cost of checking, punching and coding errors to a minimum. Wherever possible, three simple rules should be followed

1　Use numeric decimal coding
2　Use continuous code ranges, e.g. if the design of the study involves the use of eight journey purposes, then these should be coded 0–7
3　Use a most significant digit to indicate breaks in sequence. External traffic zones are characteristically prefixed by the digit 9, internal zones by 1 and central area zones by 0.

Different computer systems have developed their own standard programs which vary in detail. In general terms, however, the procedures followed are similar.

The analysis of the basic data can most conveniently be considered in three stages. In the first stage it may be edited or added to in various ways. For example arithmetic operations can be performed on the data, while alterations can be made to the notations used. The basic records may also be subjected to checks to establish the relevance and validity of the variables used against a range of values for the same variables, which are specified by the user.

In the second stage, basic tables are formed from selected information in the basic data. These tables can take the form of general exploratory tables, or more detailed analysis of specific problems. Exploratory tables could, for example, analyse trip purpose only, irrespective of interzonal movements, to determine which trip purposes warrant further, more detailed analysis. At this stage, the data can be manipulated and operated on. For example, the rows and columns of separate tables can be joined or merged, or arithmetic operations may be performed on individual rows and/or columns.

The third stage involves the output of the tables produced in stage two. Appropriate headings, text, row and column labels and other annotations are added. The analysed data can be output as 'print-out', punched cards, paper tape, magnetic tape or stored on disk, according to the requirements of the total transportation model. Throughout the analysis reports and error messages are provided on the interrogating typewriter.

Trip generation
Two basic methods are now in use to forecast trip generation – multiple linear regression and category analysis. Standard programs are generally available for both methods and for most computer systems.

The details of standard regression programs vary with the computer system used, but in outline the procedure used is similar and can be broken down into three stages

1   The first step is the reading in of the basic data on which subsequent analyses are to be performed. This data must be stored in a manner which allows the subsequent analyses to take place. Consequently, this stage of the program provides for the transformation of this data into, for example, cross-product or correlation matrices from which regression analysis can proceed. Progress reports and error messages can usually be printed out at this stage.
2   The regression analysis is then performed on the transformed data derived in stage (1). Usually this standard program is extremely flexible in application, and allows the user to carry out analysis with a dependent variable (Y) and a complete set or sub-set of independent variables (X_n). Appropriate confidence limits can be specified for the independent variables and if these are not met, then the 'offending' variables are

eliminated from the set or sub-set.

3   The final stage of the program involves the print-out of the results of the transformations carried out in stage (1) and the analysis performed in stage (2) with appropriate statistical measures of the quality of fit of the regression plane, for example, standard error of estimate; multiple correlation coefficient. Appropriate headings, text and annotations are also added.

Category analysis is a technique for estimating trip generation rates by mode of travel and journey purpose, using measured trip rates current today and a minimum of land-use and planning data. Indeed the information required about socio-economic characteristics is compatible with that available from the Census.

In general terms, the standard programs for category analysis calculate person trip productions and attractions in each traffic zone, a group of zones, for a range of modes of travel (usually three) and journey purposes (usually six). The program can be used to make predictions for any future year and for any land-use plan for which the appropriate data is available.

Trip distribution

The problem of estimating future interzonal traffic flows is of great importance in the transportation planning process, and numerous models have been developed to distribute these interzonal movements. However, two basic distribution models tend to be widely used and standard programs are generally available for them. They are the *gravity model* and a growth factor model known as the *Furness forecasting method*.

The standard programs for the Furness method can be basically subdivided into three stages

1   *Input stage* which reads in and stores the data necessary for the subsequent computational procedures. The input data required consists of an origin and destination matrix of the existing traffic flows from one zone to all other zones. Normally, origin and destination data output on magnetic tape by the survey analysis standard programs for a particular computer system will be accepted as input for the Furness distribution model standard programs written for the same computer system.

In addition to the origin and destination matrix, estimates of the future growth of traffic productions and attractions must also be supplied.

2   *Computation stage* which calculates future flows between zones by an iterative process in which the sum of all traffic movements is made to agree alternatively with estimates of future traffic originating and terminating in each zone, until both estimates are satisfied or 'in balance'. Using this method the predicted trip interchanges retain approximately the same proportion of trips produced by the originating zone and attracted by the terminating zone.

It is normal to specify at the input stage the number of iterations or percentage accuracy required from the computational stage of the program.

3   *Output stage* which prints out, or records, the output from the Furness distribution model standard program and takes the form of an origin and destination matrix of future interzonal movements, with the required headings and annotations.

The gravity model is possibly the most widely used and best documented trip distribution model and has a whole range of standard computer programs available. The input required for the basic gravity model recommended by the Bureau of Public Roads, USA is a good example and consists of

1   Trip productions and attractions for each zone, usually by journey purpose. At the calibration stage, this data is derived from the observed origin and destination matrix. When future zonal trip interchanges are forecast, however, this information is derived from the trip generation stage of the process.
2   Minimum path travel times between zones, including time spent travelling within the zone of origin and destination. (Minimum time path routes from one zone centroid to all others are referred to as 'trees'.) This information is normally derived from the 'tree-building' program associated with the traffic assignment stage of the process.
3   Initial or assumed travel-time factors for each one-minute increment of travel time.

Before the gravity model can be used to forecast trip interchanges it has to be made to fit the present-day situation. This fitting procedure is known as calibration, and in outline involves

1   Calculation of present-day trip interchanges using the gravity model formula, data concerning zonal trip productions and attractions derived from the observed origin and destination matrix, and the initial, assumed, travel times.
2   Comparision between the number of trips attracted to each zone as derived from the gravity model, and the observed number of attractions extracted from the original origin to destination data. If there is any discrepancy between the two sets of figures then the program adjusts the zonal trip attractions by a process of iteration, using the ratio of observed trips to calculated trips.
3   Calculation of a new set of trip interchanges using the adjusted zonal trip attractions.

When the trip length frequency curves* derived from observed and estimated

---

*Trip frequency curves take the form of a graph, with the percentage of total trips plotted against travel time, or distance. In the calibration stage of a gravity model programme they can be considered to be in close agreement when (a) visual inspection reveals a close relationsip, and (b) when the difference between average trip lengths is ± 3 per cent.

zonal interchanges are in close agreement, the gravity model is said to be calibrated, and ready for use to predict future zonal trip interchanges using future estimates of zonal trip productions and attractions derived from the trip generation stage of the process.

If the comparisons are not in close agreement then adjustments are made to the initial travel-time factors by multiplying the travel-time factor used by the ratio of the percentage of survey trips to the percentage of estimated trips derived from the gravity model. This calculation results in a new set of travel-time factors, which are then used in place of the initial set of travel-time factors. The process of calibration is repeated until a satisfactory comparison of trip length distribution curves is achieved, and the model can then be used to predict future zonal trip interchanges.

Other types of gravity model use different measures of travel resistance in their basic structure. For example, straight line or road distance between zone centroids is often used instead of travel-time factors. However, the basic standard computer program procedure involved with the Bureau of Public Roads gravity model can be considered typical.[11]

Traffic assignment
Traffic assignment attempts to predict how a given volume of traffic is or will be distributed over the road system of a town or urban area. To date, two methods of assignment have standard computer programs available for use with a range of computer systems. These are 'capacity restraint' and 'all or nothing'.

Capacity restraint
In general terms, the capacity restraint program requires as input (a) a description of the road network in terms of zone centroids, links and nodes (this description should include link speeds and capacity and traffic volumes); (b) future estimates of zonal trip interchanges in the form of an origin and destination matrix.

The operations then carried out by the program are

1   The calculation of minimum paths between zone centroids, a procedure referred to as 'build trees'.
2   The loading of interzonal trips to the minimum path 'trees' in specified percentage increments, and for a specified number of iterations. Following the specified number of iterations, the program then takes account of vehicle interaction on the network, and calculates new travel speeds for all roads, according to the assigned traffic volume, link speeds and capacities. Using the new link travel speeds the minimum path trees are calculated. These are not necessarily the same as the previously used trees because of the introduction of new travel speeds on the links of the network.
3   The loading of the remaining interzonal movements to the network using

the new 'trees', in specified percentage increments, and for a specified number of iterations. This procedure is followed until all the interzonal trip interchanges have been assigned to the network.

The output available from such a standard program is comprehensive, but is rarely asked for in its entirety because certain of its aspects are expensive of computer time. For each assignment directional traffic volumes, overloading and turning traffic on each link can normally be requested. Traffic routes from each zone can change with each iteration, and these changes can be printed out if required. However, the number of routes tends to be large, with the result that only certain routes are selected for printing out in this manner.

In addition to printing the route, standard programs generally print the increment in traffic using the route, and the total time. However, route printing is expensive of computer time and its use is mainly confined to selected link assignments.

Other information such as total vehicle miles, total vehicle hours, average vehicle speed, is also normally included in the print-out.

All or nothing assignment
The input required for a standard program for all or nothing assignments is similar to that required for capacity restraint: (a) a description of the network in terms of zone centroids, links and nodes, including link travel speeds; (b) an origin and destination matrix derived from the survey analysis stage if existing flows are to be assigned, or from the trip distribution stage if estimated future zonal interchanges are to be assigned.

The program operates by calculating minimum path trees between zones, then loading interzonal movements to these paths.

The output produced can include journey times between zones, minimum path trees, total turning movements, and the loadings on individual links. It is only on inspection of individual link loadings that 'overloads' are revealed, and this problem is overcome by revising the link travel speeds on the appropriate links, and re-running the program until an acceptable assignment is produced.

Modal split
Early procedures for estimating notice of travel mode were fairly simple in concept and utilized the standard programs for multiple linear regression and category analysis already described.[12] Indeed, such models are still used in situations where only poor data and inadequate network models are available. However, given good disaggregate data and adequate network models, then conventional practice is to estimate a logit model using maximum likelihood.

MicroTRIPS[23] and MINITRAMP[24]

A number of suites of transportation programs are available in the UK today, and two of the most flexible and widely used are *MicroTRIPS* and *MINITRAMP*. Both follow the general procedure and principle outlined above, but differ in the detail of their application. To give an indication of their basic characteristics and the operational requirements and constraints, they are summarized here.

MicroTRIPS

This is a comprehensive transport planning suite developed by MVA Systematica, the computer services company of The MVA Consultancy Group. It runs on most mainframes, mini or microcomputers which support Fortran, and it handles problems of up to 300 zones and 2000 links on a microcomputer with 64 Kbytes of core, and larger problems on computers with more core, for example, 2000 zones and 4700 links on a microcomputer with 256 Kbytes of core. The individual programs are fully interactive and can be controlled by 'conversation' with the user through the terminal. A separate program TTY (Terminal Evaluation and File Transfer for Microcomputers) is also available which allows the microcomputer to act as an intelligent terminal to the mainframe and provides for the either way transfer of large volumes of data between the mainframe and the microcomputer. On larger computers the package is known as *TRIPS* and offers additional facilities as well as larger capacity. The following only relates to *MicroTRIPS* as it operates on microcomputers.

The suite consists of sixteen core programs and it can be supplied as software, or as a complete package including a suitable microcomputer and printer. The sixteen core programs fall into four main groups – highways, models, public transport, and matrix handling.

Highways
MVHNET reads and edits a file of highway link records describing a highway network with up to thirty-two link types. It then builds a binary network file which is subsequently used for tree-building and assignment. Preload link volumes and observed capacities can be added to the network at this stage, while the user can optionally obtain a print-out of the network description, including link characteristics, and average distances, speeds, times, capacities and pre-load volumes in the network.

MVROAD is a highway assignment program capable of

1 Printing a network built by either *MVHNET* or *MVROAD*
2 Building and printing up to twenty-five test trees incorporating turning movement penalties
3 Building, and optionally saving, all trees and printing up to twenty-five selected trees incorporating turning penalties

4 Carrying out an all or nothing assignment or a capacity restraint assignment
5 Saving loaded networks and saving the 'skimmed' cost matrix

The capacity restraint assignment can use one of three restraint techniques – iterative, volume averaging or incremental – and up to ten iterations are allowed. Summary statistics are produced.

MVSELC is capable of carrying out an analysis of

1 Selected links in the highway network, whereby a printed report and/or a matrix of trips that use any one or all of the links in a specified set of links is produced
2 Selected sub-areas within the study area, whereby a single sub-area trip matrix is produced for the defined sub-area
3 Turning movements, whereby a printed report of link flows and turning volumes for each selected node in the highway network can be provided.

MVPLOT is a plotting program which has been designed to be used with A3 flat bed plotters that can be driven directly by microcomputers (although other plotters can be used). Any network produced by *MVHNET* or *MVROAD* can be plotted provided a grid co-ordinate file is constructed defining the location of the nodes in the network.

The plot may have the links annotated with any of the link characteristics, i.e. speed, distance, time, volume, volume/capacity etc., and some of these attributes may be expressed as bandwidths to provide visual emphasis.

The program will allow for 'windows' to be plotted in the network and for an automatic expansion of a plot to occupy up to sixteen sheets of paper if the network is too dense to be plotted on a single A3 sheet of paper.

Models
MVTEND is a trip end estimation model which has been designed to cater for a wide variety of model formulations including a household level regression or category analysis model of trip generations and a zonal level model of trip attractions. Alternatively, trip generations may also be calculated directly at the zonal level.

The household allocation model calculates the number of households in each of up to six household classifications and three car owning groups. Households are then distributed among these car ownership/household categories using a Furness procedure.

Trip generations and attractions are calculated using zonal land use data and the calibrated model relationships. A trip end file is produced as output which contains one record per zone, each record containing up to three sets of generations based on car ownership and availability, and the total attractions for the zone. Trip attractions are calculated using a regression model, and are controlled to total generations. The output is suitable for the direct input of trip ends in the distribution model program *MVGRAM*.

MVGRAM is a sophisticated self-calibrating gravity model program which can operate in one of three modes:

1 *Calibration*   One trip matrix can be calibrated per run. Either a negative exponential or gamma deterrence function may be estimated. Listings can be derived for the deterrence curve parameters; an indication of the degree of convergence achieved for each row/column balancing iteration; parameter closure statistics; standard deviations between observed and estimated matrix cells; observed and estimated mean trip lengths and mean log trip lengths and the trip length distribution plot of observed and estimated matrics. Calibration may be done using the partial matrix technique where unobserved intra-zonal movements are synthesized using the calibrated deterrence function.

2 *Forecasting*   Up to three matrices can be forecast in a single run with three sets of productions balanced against a combined set of attractions. The deterrence function(s) can be mathematically defined or be defined by the user. Listings can be obtained for the input trip ends; the deterrence curve parameters used; an indication of the degree of convergence achieved for each row/column balancing iteration; estimated mean trip length and mean log trip length; the trip length distribution for the estimated matrix and the number of trips in the output matrix. A k-factor matrix may be used to apply localized modifications to the distribution if desired. As with calibration, the partial matrix technique can be used.

3 *Growth factoring*   Up to three matrices can be growth factored in a single run with three sets of productions balanced against a combined set of attractions. The 'target' productions and attractions are taken in conjunction with the observed productions and attractions to provide the growth factors. Listings can be obtained for the input trip ends, an indication of the degree of convergence achieved for each row/column balancing iteration and the number of trips in the output matrix.

MVSPLT is a modal split program using input diversion curves or logit parameters. It takes as input up to three trip matrices (i.e. for up to three car ownership/availability groups) and splits them into two output trip matrices – the first for public transport (mode 1); the second, private transport (mode 2). The calculation of the modal split is done using a mathematical function or a user supplied curve defined as a series of points. Each input trip matrix must be complemented by two cost matrices: one for mode 1, the other for mode 2.

Public transport
MVPNET builds a description of a pattern of public transport services, so that within the *MicroTRIPS* suite an overall public transport network is described by

1   A network of links with associated link types, times and distances as built

by the highway network program (*MVHNET*)

2   A set of one way lines describing public transport routes and service characteristics produced by *MVPNET*

The program reads, checks, edits, and produces summary statistics of public transport service routes which are described to the program as a series of consecutive nodes on the network with associated line number, mode, headway, turn-round time and the company identifying code. Up to 100 nodes can be used to describe a line. Circular lines are allowed.

MVPATH is a public transport path building program. It determines from an input network file (from *MVHNET*) and the input binary public transport lines file (from *MVPNET*) the minimum impedance routes based on in-vehicle time weighted by mode; walking time weighted by link type; and waiting time weighted by mode. Transfer time between modes can be penalized or prohibited. Parallel lines of the same mode may have their headways combined, to produce lower waiting times. The programme can either build and print selected paths or produce a full paths file.

MVPASS is a public transport trip assignment program. It is used to assign a trip matrix to the public transport paths produced by *MVPATH*. Trips are assigned to parallel lines of the same mode in proportion to their relative frequency. Listings include passenger flows by link and line as well as summary statistics by mode and company.

MVPSKM is a public transport path 'skimming' program which can be used to accumulate zone to zone sums for up to six elements from the paths built by *MVPATH*. The following elements of journey time and cost may be 'skimmed'

1   Time, summed for line of selected modes
2   Distance
3   Number of transfer
4   Walk time
5   Wait time
6   Fare, as a function of distance on each line of selected modes

Matrix handling

Five programs are available to build, manipulate, modify and print matrices.

MVTRIP builds trips matrices from trip records or can restore a matrix from a 'dumped' card image file. *MVMNIP* manipulates up to ten matrices to give up to ten new matrices, transposes matrices, creates a trip end file from matrices and 'dumps' a matrix into card image format. *MVMOD* modifies cells conditionally in up to ten matrices, modifies matrix diagonals, merges matrices into one file, and generates test matrices. *MVSQEX* expands or compresses up to ten matrices. *MVPRIN* prints matrices in a variety of formats, prints trip end summaries and prints trip length distribution histograms.

In addition, a suite of survey analysis programs (*MicroSURVEY*) is available for (a) editing, correcting, manipulating and tabulating survey data, and (b) the application of expansion factors and regression analysis.

Users of *MicroTRIPS* also receive a subroutine library which allows users to interface their own programs to *MicroTRIPS* data files and which offers other helpful facilities.

MINITRAMP

This is another comprehensive suite of programs for the analysis of traffic surveys and land use transportation studies, developed by Wootton Jeffries PLC. The suite runs on a wide variety of mainframe, mini and microcomputers and makes the following minimum demands on computing facilities

1   The equivalent of 64 Kbytes of random access memory
2   Five logical files
3   A printer
4   An elementary Fortran compiler

At the present time, the *MINITRAMP* suite consists of the fifteen programs outlined below. Only two main types of binary file are used – a matrix file and a network file. Figure 35 shows the programs and files forming the *MINITRAMP* suite.

Canal is a trip end estimating program that uses category analysis. The program accepts a detailed definition of the study area in terms of planning parameters and produces generations and attractions by traffic zone.

The program falls into two parts, the first deals with household and employment distributions and the second with the trips generated by those households. The household and employment distributions program allocates the households in any traffic zone to six family structure and three car ownership categories. Each of these categories is assigned an income distribution of the Gamma type. The allocation of the households to the 0, 1 and 2 + car owning groups is carried out by conditional probability distributions which are defined in the calibration phase. The only figures required for the calibration are the proportion of 0 and 1 car owning households, which is usually available from census data or a household survey.

The employment data is supplied to the program by eight employment types and is also classified by employment density. Students are regarded as one of these employment types.

In the trip generation and attractions program, trip rates, measured as trips per household or trips per employee, are supplied for each category and for each mode and purpose for which trip ends are required. The trip generation rates are expressed in the form of linear relationships with income.

The program can be used to establish the household income for each zone

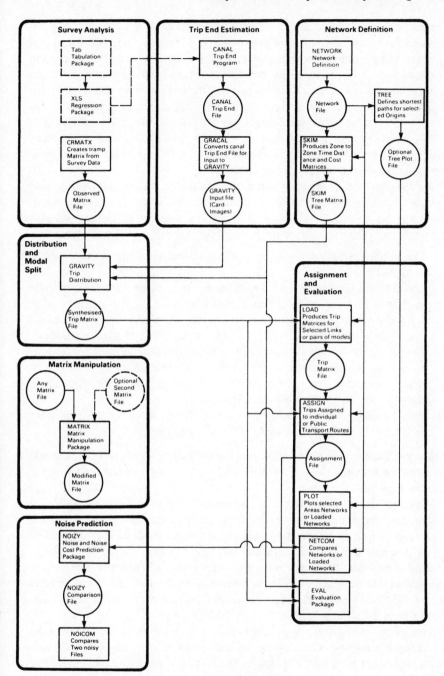

Figure 35 *MINITRAMP: Programs and files*

Source: Wootton Jeffries, *MINITRAMP*, Woking, Surrey (1984)

from existing car ownership data, calibrate trip ends to observed data, or forecast future trip ends. It produces trip generations and trip attractions for each zone and summarizes the results by sector. Trip ends can be balanced to control totals, while trip generations and attractions can be produced for up to three modes of travel and six purposes. They may also be classified by car ownership. Growth rates in real income and the projection period are parameters that can be varied when using the program to forecast future traffic.

The future planning data required for each zone is the number of households, population, employed residents, area and the number of employees in up to eight different employment categories.

NETWORK is a program which defines both private and public transport networks, the former as roads, the latter by routes. It accepts a definition of the transport system, checks the data and builds a network in a form suitable for further processing. The transport system is defined to the program by

1 *The modes* included in the system, which may be highway or public transport
2 *Links*. Every intersection where routes merge, diverge, cross or terminate is defined as a node and given a unique number. Other nodes may be defined where it is necessary to simulate access to the system. A link exists where there is a road or other form of service between adjacent nodes.
3 *Turn penalties* which allow turn prohibitions and delays at intersections to be simulated by specifying the three nodes that define the turn.
4 *Routes* in a public transport system, which are defined by the sequence of nodes and links through which it passes.
5 *Zone connections* which attach zones to the network by artificial links which can have all the characteristics of actual links.

The program may be used to build completely new networks or update an old network. A maximum of eight different modes may be used to define the transport system.

Links are defined for each mode of travel. Link data includes mode, the nodes, distance, three speeds or time for each direction, and a capacity index. Up to eight capacity indices may be used permitting the definition of up to 64 speed flow curves for the program *ASSIGN*.

Routes may pass through a maximum of 100 nodes. They are identified by the mode and a unique name. Three frequencies of service can be defined and restrictions may be placed on certain nodes to simulate minimum fares, competing services or fare stages.

There is no restriction on the number of links connected to a zone or node. The program makes logical checks of data and always prints errors. A network without error is written to magnetic tape for storage and may be printed on request.

TREE is a program which finds the shortest path through a transport system on the basis of distance, time or cost. It accepts the network description produced by the program *NETWORK* or that produced by the program *ASSIGN* and determines the shortest path from each of up to eight selected zones to every other zone and prints the path. The path may optionally be plotted by the program *PLOT*.

Up to four different sets of trees may be built in one pass of the program. The trees will then usually be built from different combinations of the modes. Alternatively up to four multiroute trees may be built for each zone.

Additional information that may be required by this program includes generalized cost data for each mode, and a waiting time function and boarding penalty for route modes.

The program is used to build a small number of trees (maximum eight) which are printed and may optionally be output to a 'plot' file for input to the program *PLOT* and subsequent plotting. Trees may be built from zone centroids or from zone connections.

Generalized cost is defined by a cost per mile and a cost per minute. For public transport the fare increment and the cost while waiting may also be specified. Waiting time in public transport modelling is related to frequency of service and independent boarding penalties and waiting time functions by mode may be applied. The network description tape (*NETWORK*) is required as input. Multipath trees can be built by specifying limits within which the link times or costs can vary. Variations are calculated using a random number generator. Capacity restraint trees may be built taking cognizance of unrestrained assignments.

SKIM produces a zone to zone time, distance or cost matrix which is required for the *GRAVITY* model program. It also produces distance or time matrices along cost trees for the program *EVAL*.

The program accepts the network description produced by the program *NETWORK* or that produced by the program *ASSIGN* and determines the shortest path from each zone to every other zone in a similar manner to the program *TREE*. *SKIM* then skims these trees and produces zone to zone time, distance or cost matrices for input to the *GRAVITY* model program. A further option enables the user to output additionally, or alternatively matrices of the distance or time along the trees built, the resultant matrices being suitable for input to the *EVAL* evaluation program.

All the facilities of the program *TREE* are available in defining the criteria for building trees except that trees may only be built from zone centroids. Up to eight skimmed trees may be printed for selected zones. Only one pass of the program is required to build skimmed tree matrices and matrices of the time or distance along the trees built. When matrices of distance or time along the trees are to be produced the user may apply factors to this distance/time by mode. The program produces matrices for highway and/or public transport networks with equal ease.

GRACAL converts the trip generations and attractions as output from the program *CANAL* into a format suitable for input to the trip distribution program *GRAVITY*. Each of the six purposes and three modes from *CANAL* can be assigned to each of up to six matrices for *GRAVITY*. Non car owning generations and car owning generations may be combined or left separate. External zone date may be specified so that a complete input data set for *GRAVITY* is prepared.

GRAVITY is a trip distribution program that estimates the number of trips between zones using a traditional gravity model formulation. The program has the flexibility to produce a trip matrix for a single mode and purpose or a complex modal choice situation Using the technique of maximum likelihood the program can also be used in self-calibrating mode.

The program can fulfil six different functions

1 It can synthesize a set of single mode trip matrices from given trip ends and distribution functions. The synthesis is made using a standard gravity model formulation.
2 It can synthesize a set of dual mode trip matrices from given trip ends and distribution functions. The synthesis is made using a multimode gravity model formulation.
3 It can calibrate a gravity model from an observed matrix and a skimmed tree. The matrix can be partially observed, e.g. from a screenline survey. In this function, the program assumes the observations in the matrix are selected from a Poisson Distribution and outputs the calibration distribution function and an estimate of the total trip ends.
4 It can calibrate a single mode gravity model from a set of trip ends, an observed matrix and a skimmed tree. The matrix can be partially observed, as is the case with a screenline or cordon survey. The program outputs the calibrated distribution function.
5 It can calibrate a dual mode gravity model from a set of trip ends (car owners and non car owners), observed matrices (partially observed) and a pair of skimmed trees (public and private). The program outputs the calibrated distribution function.
6 It can produce a new trip matrix from an existing trip matrix and a set of trip ends using a growth factor procedure.

The six functions are independent of one another.

MATRIX is a very powerful program that allows the manipulation of observed trip matrices or those produced by the gravity model. The program can print, combine, factor, edit, compress, expand, multiply, divide, take the maximum and minimum, or transpose matrices.

LOAD builds all trees according to the specified criteria – time, distance, or cost (multipath if selected) – for private and/or public transport and examines the trips from every origin to every destination and includes them in the output matrix if they

1 Use one or more selected links
2 Use at least two selected nodes

3 Use one or more selected links or have an origin or destination in a selected zone, i.e. cordon

ASSIGN builds all trees according to the specified criteria – time, distance or cost (multipath if selected) – for private and/or public transport and produces either a link assignment or turning movements at selected modes.

EVAL is used to compare a series of proposed transport systems with a 'do nothing' situation. It calculates the increase in consumer surplus, the increase in user costs, the increase in resource costs, and the taxation effects.

PLOT accepts files created by the programs *NETWORK, TREE, MATRIX* or *ASSIGN* and plots networks, selected trees, loaded networks or desire lines, using a pen plotter. It can also produce graphical output in suitable computers.

MATEST is a program which estimates origin destination trip matrices from a series of volumetric traffic counts observed along links in the road network. The program can work in either an update mode, in which an already existing trip matrix is input as a starting point for the estimation procedure or the process can be started from a unit matrix. In an age where there is increasing reluctance to carry out surveys from both a financial and political point of view, this type of technique is becoming increasingly popular.

JAM is a junction delay assignment model which simulates the junction delays in a congested urban network using junction delay algorithms originally developed in the program *JUDY* based on work published by the Transport and Road Research Laboratory. *JAM* is an incremental assignment model in which road traffic is assigned to many different paths, each path reflecting different sets of junction delays caused by conflicting demand for road space at the junction. This program is used extensively for investigating congested town centres and for evaluating different traffic management policies.

INTERTAB is a survey analysis module specifically developed for use on mini and microcomputers. The program allows the user to define his or her own screen layout based on his or her own survey forms and to edit the data using simple English sentences.

SIGNPOST is a program which will accept a road network defined within the transport planning process and using the standard tree building algorithms will produce a consistent set of signposts throughout a road network. This is a particularly important step in implementing any road transport policy and is of most relevance when re-signing whole sections of the network when new motorways are constructed.

VISTA is a combination of computer software and hardware which allows the engineer or analyst directly to extract from video tape a whole series of quantitative parameters, thus reducing the cost of the data collection phase of any study.

Conclusions

The field of computer technology is changing and advancing rapidly. Ten years ago, transportation analysis and modelling was carried out on large, expensive, mainframe computers housed in air-conditioned premises. Today, transportation planners have at their disposal the current round of large mainframe machines, the cheaper and smaller minicomputers which fulfil the same functions as the mainframes, and the small and inexpensive microcomputers which are capable of handling transportation analyses for areas of a limited size. Miniaturization and a significant reduction in cost ensures that accessibility to computing power is significantly better now than ten years ago.

At the same time, the development of an interactive computing environment in association with the use of minicomputers and microcomputers linked to mainframe machines is increasing the capacity of transport planners to evaluate alternative plans. Currently, there are indications that the ready availability of a graphics capability with minicomputers, or microcomputers linked to the mainframe machine, will further enhance the transportation planner's capacity to evaluate alternative transport policies.[15]

Developments in the software field have matched the initiatives in hardware. Suites of inexpensive, flexible standard programs are readily available for mainframe, mini and microcomputers with the result that transport planners with only a limited computing capability are well able to service a complex series of transport analyses and evaluations with a minimum of cost and delay.

References

1   Moore, E. F., 'The shortest path through a maze', International Symposium on the Theory of Switching, *Proceedings of the Harvard Society* (1957).
2   *Manual of Procedures for a Home-Interview Traffic Study*, US Department of Commerce, Bureau of Public Roads, Washington (1954).
3   *Traffic Assignment Manual*, US Department of Commerce, Bureau of Public Roads, Washington (1964).
4   *Calibrating and testing a gravity model for any size urban area*, US Department of Commerce, Bureau of Public Roads, Washington (1965).
5   See for example: Baxter, R. S., *Computer and Statistical Techniques for Planners*, Methuen & Co., London (1976) pp. 336.
    BBC, *The Computer Book: An Introduction to Computers and Computing*, BBC, London (1982).
    Coats, R. B. and Parkin, A., *Computer Models in the Social Sciences*, Edward Arnold, London (1977) p. 130.
    Marshall, G., *Computer Languages and their Uses*, Granada (1983) p. 108.
    Pratt, Terence W., *Programming Languages: Design and Implementation*, Prentice-Hall Inc., New Jersey (1975) p. 530.
6   Queree, C., 'Microcomputers in Transport System Analysis', *PTRC Summer Annual Meeting – Transportation Planning Practice*, University of Warwick (July 1981) pp. 61–4.
7   *ibid.*
8   US Department of Transportation, *Urban Transportation Planning: General Information and Introduction to System, 360*, Federal Highway Administration, Bureau of Public Roads, Washington (1970).

9   Systematica, *MicroTRIPS: Transport Planning*, Systematica, 112 Strand, London WC2R OAH (1984).

10 Wootton Jeffries P L C, *MINITRAMP*, Cemetery Pales, Brookwood, Woking, Surrey (1984).

11 *Calibrating and testing a gravity model for any size urban area, op. cit.*

12 *Modal Split*, U S Department of Commerce, Bureau of Public Roads, Washington (1966).

13 Systematica, *op. cit.*

14 Wootton Jeffries, *op. cit.*

15 I C L, Road Planning P E R Qs U P, *Public Service and Local Government* (September 1984) p. 62.

9 Evaluation of transportation proposals

Introduction

The implementation of transport proposals affects the well-being of individuals and groups in society, and given that they can affect the life chances of large numbers the cumulative consequences are important. Similarly, as the majority of transport proposals are put forward by public agencies, whose concern should be with those who comprise society, rather than particular groups in society, the merits of transport proposals should be judged by their potential effect on all members of society. Against this background, it is argued that transport and other planning proposals which affect the public welfare should be subjected to a 'welfare test', or evaluation.

Evaluation involves the assessment of the comparative merits of different courses of action. Thus it is concerned to analyse a number of alternative plans or projects with a view to identifying systematically and logically their comparative advantages and disadvantages. Evaluation differs from the various types of analytical tests that are applied to each alternative separately, to ensure that plans are internally consistent, e.g. tests to ensure that the capacity of the proposed transport system is adequate to accommodate the predicted volume of traffic. In the words of Lichfield et al., 'Evaluation should be concerned with the assessment of particular consequences of planning proposals for the individuals or groups of individuals who comprise a community'.[1] The prime reason for undertaking an evaluation is to assist the decision takers in forming a judgement as to the most appropriate development. Contrary to some views, evaluation is not decision-taking.

A number of different methods are currently used to evaluate proposals for development, the most significant of which include

1 Financial appraisal, which is concerned primarily to estimate the future streams of capital and operating costs and revenues resulting from the implementation of investment projects
2 Check list of criteria, whereby alternative proposals are ranked subjectively on an ordinal basis in relation to a number of specified criteria
3 Goals achievement analysis, where the extent to which alternative proposals will achieve a predetermined set of goals and objectives is determined

4 Costs in use, which estimates both private and public capital and operating costs involved in urban developments
5 Threshold analysis, where the capital and operating costs of location are investigated and crucial thresholds in relation to the scale of development and the provision of services are identified
6 Cost-benefit analysis, where the social worth of public sector projects is appraised
7 Planning balance sheet analysis, which is a particular application of the cost-benefit analysis approach.[2]

Proposals to improve or extend existing transportation systems can range from limited improvements, such as the widening of a section of road, or the improvement of a junction, to comprehensive proposals which involve the construction of significant sections of urban motorway, the development of new forms of public transport and the close integration of different transport systems. Before decisions are taken to proceed with any proposals, either small or large, an attempt is normally made to evaluate the efficiency of the proposed improvements. The large-scale transportation proposals are invariably assessed by means of a cost-benefit analysis, which aims to compare the costs and benefits associated with alternative schemes. This usually takes the form of an indication of the annual rate of return on the investment proposed, which is derived from a discounted benefit-cost calculation. The smaller scale proposals are generally assessed by less sophisticated methods, and in accordance with Ministry recommended procedures. Again the comparison of costs and benefits is indicated by a rate of return on the investment proposed, based on a simple annual rate of return.[3]

Cost-benefit analysis

Cost-benefit analysis is a practical way of assessing the desirability of projects, where it is important to take the long view (in the sense of looking at repercussions in the further, as well as the nearer, future) and a wide view (in the sense of allowing for side effects of many kinds on many persons, industries, regions), i.e. it implies the enumeration and evaluation of all the relevant costs and benefits.[4]

Cost-benefit analysis is a technique which has been developed predominantly in this century, as an aid to decision making. It is basically a procedure to test the soundness of proposed developments by estimating the cost of a particular proposal, in terms of the value of the resources to be employed in the venture, and comparing these costs with the value of the goods or services produced by the development – the benefits.

In a market economy, where the value of any benefits associated with a particular venture is reflected in the price the consumer is prepared to pay, there is no need to carry out a cost-benefit analysis to decide the most appropriate course of action. However, there is a whole range of developments in our present society for which no direct charge is made, but which are essential to the economic and social well-being of the nation, e.g. schools, hospitals, transportation systems. Such developments or services are group or collective needs, which cannot be easily marketed, with the result that they are invariably paid for indirectly through taxation, and decisions to proceed with a particular venture at the expense of an alternative are often politically motivated. In general terms, guidance as to the policies to be adopted in connection with the provision of these services is obtained at the ballot box in central and local government elections. However, this has resulted in many public expenditure decisions being taken by rule-of-thumb methods, which have led to the neglect of certain types of proposals such as road improvements, while in other spheres public money has been lavished with only the vaguest idea of the returns to be expected.

An increasing awareness of this problem on the part of politicians and economists has resulted in a search for 'tools of economic appraisal to assess the wisdom of alternative courses of action that will be better than political decisions where a market is not, or can not, be used'.[5]

Pioneering work on cost-benefit analysis was carried out in the United States of America in connection with navigational improvement schemes following the River and Harbour Act 1902. At this stage the benefits were considered to be the value of additional commerce resulting from the improvement, while the costs were the actual capital costs of the improvement.

In the 1930s, with the 'New Deal' philosophy and the idea of a broader social justification for proposed developments, the cost-benefit analysis technique was further advanced in the field of flood control schemes carried out under the Flood Control Act of 1936. Under this Act Federal aid was granted to such schemes 'if the benefits, to whom-so-ever they may accrue, are in excess of the estimated costs'. By 1945 the approach to cost-benefit analysis had been further broadened to include both indirect costs and benefits, and an assessment of intangible factors associated with development projects. This process of refining the basic techniques associated with cost-benefit analysis has continued to the present day.

In the field of transport, cost-benefit analysis was first used in the State of Oregon in 1938, in connection with road improvements and a great deal of work has now accumulated on the subject.

In this country it has developed through the traditional M1, and Victoria Line analyses to the more wide-ranging assessment undertaken in connection with the potential impact of the third London Airport and the M25. At the same time, and following the publication of the Buchanan Report *Traffic in Towns*, attempts are now being made to take into account the many intangible social and environmental factors associated with transport and traffic schemes.

General principles of cost-benefit analysis

Cost-benefit analysis attempts to list the costs and benefits associated with the factors which need to be taken into account in making decisions about projects, whose value cannot be assessed in the open market. However, this simple aim poses three main questions which are extremely difficult to answer

1 Which costs and benefits are to be included in the analysis?
2 What value is to be placed on these costs and benefits?
3 At what rate of interest are these costs and benefits to be discounted?

In addition these questions must be answered within the physical, political, administrative and financial context of the time, with the result that a whole series of constraints must be considered to be operating on the process.

In general terms the procedure to be followed involves

1 The definition of the project and the listing of the current costs and benefits to be included. The direct costs and benefits to the sponsor of the project are usually defined quite simply. For example, the costs could involve the amount of capital tied up in the project, and the labour force required to implement the proposals, while the benefits could take the form of increased productivity and profits. However, there is another group of costs and benefits which accrue to persons or bodies other than the one sponsoring the project. These external effects are often difficult to identify and manifest themselves in many different ways. A typical external benefit could result from the construction of a dam to generate electricity which also gives flood protection which is not paid for by those receiving it. A typical external cost could result from atmospheric and water pollution associated with an industrial process.

2 The placing of a monetary value on the costs and benefits associated with the project, in order to arrive at an estimate of the current net benefit. Where the costs and benefits involved can be expressed in monetary terms, all the values used must be reckoned on the same basis, which is usually the level of the market prices prevailing in the initial year. Problems arise, however,

(a) When the scale of the projects is large enough to affect these prices. In such instances it is normal practice to assume a linear relationship between the original and ultimate levels, and adopt a value halfway between the two

(b) When monopoly conditions exist, and distort relative outputs away from those which would prevail under conditions of perfect competition. Accounting adjustments can be made by applying a correction to the actual level of costs

(c) When intangible costs and benefits, which cannot be quantified, are involved in the analysis, e.g. the scenic effect of building electricity transmission lines

3 The choice of an appropriate rate of interest to compare the stream of

annual net benefits with the capital cost of the project. Bearing in mind that the function of a rate of interest is to allocate capital funds between the varying uses to which they might be put, and to reflect society's preferences between present and future consumption, the choice of an appropriate rate of interest is purely value judgement.

In short the 'most that can be said for the doctrine (of cost-benefit analysis) is that by listing the supposed indirect benefits or detriments, it indicates a desire to introduce a semblance of rationality into the spending of large sums of money by public authority'.[6]

Goals achievement analysis and the planning balance sheet

Goals achievement methods

These methods of evaluation originated in the United States in the field of land-use transportation planning. There are four main characteristics underlying this approach

1   Goals and/or objectives are always formulated in advance of the design of alternative plans and the evaluation of the consequences arising out of implementation
2   The objectives are multidimensional, and include economic, aesthetic, environmental and political objectives
3   The method is concerned to compare mutually exclusive plans or proposals, i.e. the plans or proposals evaluated are alternative ways of tackling a particular problem.
4   The objectives used for the evaluation are ranked in order of presumed importance, prior to the evaluation, i.e. they are weighted.

Broadly speaking, the application of goals achievement methods in transport falls into two groups – those involving a simple ranking of plans in relation to the various objectives, and those that use performance measures to assess the extent to which the plans are likely to achieve the objectives specified. Schlager has developed a method of evaluation which falls into the former category where the objectives set are ranked in order of their considered importance, prior to the evaluation taking place.[7]

The most sophisticated and well known goals achievement method is that developed by Hill in connection with transportation plans. This method is usually referred to as the goals achievement matrix,[8] and involves

1   The formulation of a set of goals and objectives in advance of the design of alternatives, and their definition in operational terms, so that a measure can be obtained of the extent to which they are achieved
2   The relative importance of the objectives is then established, and given a numerical value or weighting
3   The level of achievement of each plan or proposal is then estimated for

each of the objectives, and then weighted by the respective numerical values or weightings of the objectives. These values are presented in matrix form

4 The weighted achievement levels of the objectives are then summed to give an overall index of objective achievement for each plan

5 The index value is then adjusted as appropriate to take equity considerations into account

The distributional consequences (equity) are considered by grouping individuals in the community according to criteria which accord with the concept of fairness or justice arising out of the implementation of the plan, for example income level. A set of incidence weights are allocated to these groups in an attempt to represent the community preference in relation to the alternative distributional consequences of the different plans. These incidence weights are allocated by the political decision-takers.

An alternative and simpler goals achievement method for application in transportation planning has been developed by Schimpler and Grecco.[9] Using what they refer to as an effectiveness matrix approach, objectives are given a numerical utility value to represent their relative importance. Effectiveness values ranging from 1.0 to 0.0 are then given to the alternative plans or proposals in relation to each of the objectives (1.0 indicates maximum achievement; 0.0 indicates zero achievement). The total effectiveness of the plan is represented by the sum of the achievement scores multiplied by the utility values given to each objective.

Planning balance sheet methods

These methods of evaluation were developed by Lichfield during the 1950s and 1960s.[10] In essence, this approach establishes a particular framework within which the methodology of cost-benefit analysis can be applied. Lichfield was concerned to ensure that equity and the wider intangible costs associated with a proposed development are taken into account in any evaluation. In brief, the procedure involved is as follows

1 The various groups or sectors who establish and/or run a project are listed vertically in balance sheet form. These groups are referred to as producers/operators.

2 Instrumental objectives are established for the various sectors to represent the criteria by which it is assumed they will judge the alternative schemes.

3 Each producer/operator is paired with appropriate groups of individuals who will consume the goods and services generated from the implementation of the project.

4 Each linked pair of producer/operators and consumers is assumed to be engaged in a real or notional transaction where the producer/operators produce goods or services for sale to the consumers. These transactions

include goods and services which are exchanged in the market place as well as intangibles such as visual intrusion.

5   Estimates of the resource costs involved in producing the goods and services are included in the balance sheet.

6   Those items which can be allocated a monetary value are given it. Those intangibles which cannot be given a monetary value are given a subjective numerical value. Both are included in the same table or balance sheet (usually referred to as Table A).

7   A summary sheet is then produced in an attempt to remove some of the inherent complexities. This sheet is usually referred to as Table B and groups the items into the measured (or monetary) analysis and the unmeasured analysis of intangibles. These latter items are then weighted to reflect their relative importance and the associated 'points' score is presented in a third sheet (Table C) to establish the order of preference for the unmeasured scores.

8   The three balance sheets are then analysed to establish the 'best' plan or proposal.

The advantage associated with this approach is that it makes explicit what intangibles have been taken into account and the relative costs/benefits associated with them. The difficulties arise in giving the intangibles a subjective value, and developing the instrumental objectives by which to judge the alternative schemes. The cost-benefit analysis carried out by Lichfield for the Stevenage Development Corporation is an interesting example of the application of the planning balance sheet method of evaluation in relation to public transport.[11]

Examples of evaluation studies in transportation planning[12]

The M1 motorway study[13]

The M1 study, which was published in 1960, was the first major cost-benefit analysis undertaken in the transportation planning field in the United Kingdom. The study was carried out in two main parts (*a*) an investigation of the traffic implications of the motorway and (*b*) an economic assessment of the traffic implications.

The traffic investigation included an estimate of the number of vehicles of different types which could be expected to divert to the motorway; the journey time and mileage savings involved for this diverted traffic; and the likely changes in the number and type of accidents as a result of the new motorway facility.

The implications of these predicted changes in the traffic characteristics were then examined by economists, who defined their task as the measurement of 'the hypothetical sum that the community would be prepared to pay for the motorway rather than not have it'.[14] In deriving this hypothetical sum, Beesley and Reynolds, the economists involved, examined

1   The benefits to traffic diverted to the motorway
2   The benefits resulting from reduced congestion on the existing road network
3   The benefits derived from the change in accident characteristics
4   The benefits to traffic which were estimated would be induced to travel because of the lower cost of travel after the motorway was constructed. This type of traffic is referred to as generated traffic.

The study found that the major benefit likely to be derived from the construction of the M1 was a reduction in journey time, and it was assumed that changes in the amount of time spent by vehicle occupants travelling as part of their work could be valued at the average hourly earnings of the persons involved. Journeys other than those carried out in connection with employment were more difficult to value. To overcome this problem a range of assumed values was adopted for leisure time savings.

Another benefit assumed to derive from a reduction in the time taken to complete a journey was the reduction in the size of vehicle fleets necessary to carry the same ton mileage. This assumption is open to criticism on the grounds that given fixed working hours, and vehicle operating regulations, small changes in journey time would not be sufficient to allow the same vehicle to make additional journeys.

Further benefits were assumed, resulting from changes in fuel consumption, and vehicle operating costs, and an estimate of the annual value of the reduction in accidents resulting from the construction and use of the motorway. Changes in fuel consumption were calculated net of tax on the grounds that indirect taxation merely represents a transfer from one sector of the community to another, while the valuation of accidents was based on a consideration of loss of output, medical expenses, damage to property and administrative expenses.[15]

Benefits received by generated traffic, which came into existence only because of the reduced costs of road transport, were considered to be of less importance than existing journeys which were being made at the original higher level of transport costs. Consequently they were valued at half the average benefits per vehicle mile experienced by the existing traffic.

This type of analysis of the benefits associated with the construction of the M1 did not take into account external effects such as changes in the environmental standards, which cannot readily be quantified or valued.

The financial cost of the construction of the M1, estimated at £23.3m, was considered to be a reasonable measure of cost, which included the opportunity cost (or alternative benefits rejected). The annual rate of return on the capital invested was used as the simplest method of comparing costs and benefits. Table 16 illustrates the estimated net annual savings to be derived from the construction of the M1.

The annual rate of return derived from this analysis varied with the hourly rate assumed for non-working time (which ranged from zero to 50p per hour). If non-working time was valued at zero the annual rate of return was found to be 3.8 per cent at 30p per hour it was 6.2 per cent, and at 50p per hour it was 7.8 per cent. Although now out of date this study is a classic in the field.

	Changes in £000s per annum	
	Benefit	Cost
Savings in working time by traffic transferring to motorway	453	
Reduction in vehicle fleets	80	
Change in fuel consumption for vehicle mileage transferred to motorway	117	
Change in other operating costs of vehicle mileage transferred	200	
Cost of additional vehicle mileage incurred in transferring to motorway		229
Reductions in cost to vehicles remaining on old roads	128	
Benefits for generated traffic	113	
Savings in non-work hours (dependent on hourly rate chosen)	0–938	
Reduction in accidents	215	
Maintenance costs of motorway		200
Totals	1306–2244	429
Net annual savings per annum	877–1815	

Table 16　*Estimated savings and increases in annual costs resulting from construction of the M1 motorway*

Source: *The London-Birmingham Motorway – Traffic and Economics*, Road Research Technical Paper No. 46, HMSO.

The Victoria Line cost-benefit analysis[16, 17]

The Victoria Line analysis undertaken by the Road Research Laboratory and the London Transport Board marked an important advance in the development of cost-benefit techniques by attempting to take into account the value of social benefits derived from the construction of the Victoria Line underground railway. On a purely commercial basis the Victoria Line was an extremely unattractive proposition, which at the then current fare levels was estimated by Foster and Beesley to be likely to run at a loss of £2.14m per annum. However, they went on to argue that the benefits likely to be derived from (a) the reduction in journey time and costs, and the improved comfort and convenience experienced by those persons diverted to the Victoria Line

(b) the reduction in journey time and vehicle operating costs experienced by those not diverting to the Victoria Line (c) generated traffic attracted to the Victoria Line which would not otherwise have travelled – must all be considered in an attempt to assess whether the benefits associated with the project were in excess of the costs likely to be incurred.

Two values for time were used in assessing the benefits likely to be derived from reduced journey times – a value for work time and a value for non-work time. The work time value was based on a sample of the hourly wage rate of those likely to be affected by the Victoria Line (36p per hour) while the non-work time value was taken somewhat arbitrarily at 25p per hour. It was estimated that 95 per cent of the journey time savings would be derived in non-work time.

The improved comfort and convenience likely to be associated with the Victoria Line were imputed indirectly, by estimating and giving a value to the increased probability of getting a seat on the Victoria Line. Foster and Beesley argue that given a valuation of time, and observing how many people chose to transfer from a fast service with low seating probability to a slower service with a better seating probability a value can be set on the rate of substitution of comfort for time. Rather than use the yearly return on outlaid capital as a crude measure of costs and benefits the present discounted net value was used to express the comparison of costs and benefits. The reasoning behind the choice of this method was that it takes several years to construct an underground railway over which time the capital cost of construction is spent. But for this same period of time no benefits will result until the line (or sections of it) are completed. Thus a method of evaluation is required which takes account of the time at which the costs and benefits accrue, and the most appropriate was considered to be the present discounted net value.

For the purposes of the study a range of discount factors was taken, 8 per cent, 7 per cent and 4 per cent. Using the 6 per cent factor as an example it simply means that £1 benefit realized today is equivalent to £1.06 of benefit in one year's time. Assuming a fifty-year operating period for the line and using this discount factor, both benefits and costs in the future discounted back to the time of the study.

Table 17 sets out the costs and benefits measured by Foster and Beesley using the 6 per cent discount factor, and expresses the total as an annual rate of return of 11.3 per cent over the period of construction and operation on the present value of the capital invested.

General criticisms of the method adopted are (a) it does not take into account all the social consequences (b) the valuations were undertaken in the context of current vehicle taxes and fare levels.

The third London Airport (The Roskill Commission)
The cost-benefit analysis undertaken for the Roskill Commission on the third

	Present discounted value at 6% £m
(A) Costs – Annual working expenses	16.16
(B) Benefits – Traffic diverted to Victoria Line from private motor vehicle, buses and underground, including time and comfort savings.	29.34
(C) Traffic not diverted to Victoria Line (includes comfort and time savings for bus, rail, motor vehicle and underground).	44.79
(D) Generated traffic, includes time, fare and other savings	11.74
(E) Terminal scrap value	0.29
(F) Total Benefits (B + C + D + E)	86.16
(G) Net current benefit (F – A)	70.00
(H) Value of Capital expenditure	38.81
(I) Net Benefit (G – H)	31.19
(J) Social surplus rate of return	11.3%

Table 17 *Victoria Line – Social benefit and loss (five and a half years' construction, and fifty years' life assumed.)*

Source: Foster, C. D., and Beesley, M. E., 'Estimating the social benefit of constructing an underground railway in London', *Journal of the Royal Statistical Society* (Series A 1963).

London Airport is acknowledged as being one of the most sophisticated analyses undertaken in Britain, although, strictly speaking, it was not a proper cost-benefit analysis. Rather, it was a comparison of the costs of the four alternative airport sites on the short list, i.e. Cublington, Foulness, Nuthampstead, and Thurleigh.[18]

The decision to undertake a cost-benefit analysis as part of the Commission's work was justified on the grounds that a systematic analysis of the entire problem was essential and that it would help avoid subjective judgements on issues which aroused deep emotions.[19] The Commission accepted without question that there was a demand for a third London Airport and undertook the cost-benefit analysis specifically to assist with the comparison of the four alternative sites. Thus 'Only inter-size differences require to be looked at. The objective must be correctly to identify and measure those differences'.[20] Twenty major items were considered (see Table 18) including construction costs, passenger user time, airspace movement costs, and the disbenefits associated with intangibles such as noise, loss of landscape and rural amenity. The costs were discounted at 10 per cent and the base year used for discounting was 1982. Business travel time was initially valued at 46 shillings per hour (230p) rising to 72 shillings per hour (360p) by

	Cublington		Foulness		Nuthampstead		Thurleigh	
	High time values	*Low time values*	*High time values*	*Low time values*	*High time values*	*Low time values*	*High time values*	*Low time values*
1 Airport construction	18	18	32	32	14	14	0	0
2 Extension of Luton	0	0	18	18	0	0	0	0
3 Airport services	23	22	0	0	17	17	7	7
4 Meteorology	5	5			2	2	1	1
5 Airspace movements	0	0	7	5	35	31	30	26
6 Passenger user costs	0	0	207	167	41	35	39	22
7 Freight user costs	0	0	14	14	5	5	1	1
8 Road capital	0	0	4	4	4	4	5	5
9 Rail capital	3	3	26	26	12	12	0	0
10 Air safety	0	0	2	2	0	0	0	0
11 Defence	29	29	0	0	5	5	61	61
12 Public scientific establishments	1	1	0	0	21	21	27	27
13 Private airfields	7	7	0	0	13	13	15	15
14 Residential conditions (noise, off site)	13	13	0	0	62	62		
15 Residential conditions (on site)			0	0			5	5
16 Luton noise costs	11	11	0	0	8	8	6	6
17 Schools, hospitals and public authority buildings (including noise)	0	0	11	11	0	0	0	0
18 Agriculture	7	7	4	4	11	9	9	3
19 Commerce and industry (including noise)	0	0	2	2	1	1	2	2
20 Recreation (including noise)	13	13	0	0	7	7	7	7
Aggregate of intersite differences (costed items only) high and low time values	0	0	197	156	137	128	88	68

Table 18 *Summary cost-benefit analysis: differences from lowest cost site in £ million discounted to 1982*

Source: Table 12.1 *Report of Commission on the Third London Airport*, HMSO, London (1971).

the year 2000, at 1968 prices, while leisure time was valued at 4 shillings and 7 pence per hour (47p). Subsequently, two values of business and leisure time were taken (a high and a low value) in an attempt to offset criticisms about the way in which time was valued by the first exercise.

Table 18 summarizes the differences from the lowest cost site (Cublington), and itemizes

1   Airport construction costs, including site preparation, the building of runways, taxiways, terminal buildings and other facilities
2   The cost implications for Luton Airport of the choice of an inland site as opposed to Foulness, i.e. if an inland site were chosen Luton would close and the assets be disposed of
3   The cost of various airport services, such as taxi-ing distances
4   The cost of delay caused by different meteorological conditions at each site
5   The costs arising from the different flight paths followed to reach the four sites, from a defined cordon boundary
6   Passenger user costs
7   Freight user costs
8   The cost of providing road and rail surface links to the four sites
9   Air safety costs, e.g. protection against bird strike
10 The cost of redeploying defence, and other government and research establishments
11 The cost implications for private and test flying
12 The cost of noise
13 Compensation paid to residents whose property falls within the designated airport sites
14 The cost implications of noise and other effects of the airport on schools, hospitals, public buildings, commerce, industry and recreation

It can be seen from the aggregate costs of intersite differences that the ranking of the four sites was, in order of increasing costs

	High time value	*Low time value*
Cublington	0	0
Thurleigh	£ 88m	£ 68m
Nuthampstead	£137m	£128m
Foulness	£197m	£156m

The cost-benefit analysis adopted by the Roskill Commission, although acknowledged as being extremely thorough in its attempts to quantify intangibles, has been heavily criticized on a number of counts. Professor Sir Colin Buchanan, who was a member of the Commission commented on the cost-benefit analysis in his minority report, as follows

As the (CBA) Team progressed, with even more ingenious methods of surmounting this or that difficulty or criticism, so I become more and more anxious lest I be trapped in a process which I did not fully understand and ultimately led without choice to a conclusion which I would know in my heart of hearts I did not agree with.[21]

He went on to question

1 The basis on which some of the figures such as the value of gliding and user travel costs had been estimated
2 The validity of aggregating the 'costs' of twenty items including direct costs which would have been paid, such as construction costs, and indirect costs which would not have been paid, such as noise costs
3 The application of the cost-benefit analysis in a land-use planning vacuum, i.e. the airport was considered in isolation from the land-use planning policies for the South-East. Indeed, he states

Where I begin to get into difficulties . . . is over the aggregation of the costs to produce a batting order . . . as the items included in the analysis become more numerous and of greater diversity, and as they become involved with questions of who pays and who benefits, so does the credibility of any terminal summation become more and more strained. . . . I have to confess that the process has been stretched beyond my ability to understand what the total really means. I have the feeling that the whole cost/benefit approach has been pushed too far and too fast beyond the fairly easily quantified problems that are its usual domain.[22]

E. J. Mishan, in a review of the first cost-benefit analysis undertaken by the Commission, commented that '. . . for Britain at least the Report has aimed at a level of sophistication that will not be easy to exceed. . . . The theoretical underpinning is respectable, and the tone is suggestive of a determination not to forsake principle for facility of calculation. The so-called intangibles are believed in principle to be quantifiable, and the research team has not yielded to the temptation to hand back part of its brief to the political process, which had offered it to the economists in the first place.'[23] However, he then went on to criticize the analysis on the following grounds.

1 The choice of a relative costs evaluation rather than a cost-benefit analysis carried with it the presumption that a third airport at any of the four short-listed sites could be justified on economic grounds
2 The questionable basis on which the value of travel time and airline operation costs had been calculated
3 The methods employed in the Report do not meet the conditions of an ideal cost-benefit analysis, i.e. that it must be independent of existing institutions
4 The social costs incurred through the provision of air travel facilities, and the issue of equity, such as loss of life and destruction of natural beauty, are largely ignored. Indeed, Mishan comments that if alternative, and, in his view, more plausible estimates of the value of passengers' travel time in the future are taken, then '. . . the cost differences between the four

sites as a proportion of total resource costs become so small as to be unreliable for the purpose of economic ranking'. He also states '. . . because the benefits are registered largely as market phenomena, and the disbenefits largely as "intangible" the asymmetry of treatment tells heavily in favour of the benefits'.[24]

The impact of the M25[25]
The impact study undertaken by the Standing Conference on London and South East Regional Planning is wider than the traditional cost-benefit analysis and was concerned with establishing the likely consequences of the M25 on

1 Locational pressures and choices in the South-East, especially from industry and commerce
2 The current strategy for regenerating inner London and concentrating growth at specified locations in the rest of South-East England and restraining it elsewhere

The study took as its starting point the hypothesis

. . . that a major infrastructure investment which links the main radial routes from London in a ring around the periphery of the metropolis will significantly alter the pattern of accessibility in the South-East region in a way which will change locational perceptions and decisions. This could result in a significant increase in development pressures in certain parts of the region, including the Metropolitan Green Belt where strict restraint policies apply.[26]

In reviewing the potential impact of the M25 the issue was set within

1 The national economic policy context, where the aim of government to confine assistance to projects which will strengthen the national and regional economy and provide more secure jobs, was accepted.
2 The regional economic policy context, where the economic objectives underlying the Strategic Plan for the South East 1971 were accepted as the development of growth areas to provide adequate labour markets without posing journey to work and congestion problems. However, the government's attitude towards, on the one hand, the need to balance the demands for land release for economic development and, on the other, to preserve and enhance the environment, was also taken into account.
3 The wider economic context, where the following changes in the economic climate were considered to be particularly pertinent to the M25 impact study, viz., structural changes in employment, especially the decline in manufacturing employment; the prolonged recession which has highlighted the widening gap between the declining and growth sectors in the economy; and changes in travel costs where the increasing costs of public transport relative to retail prices indicate that travel to work by the private motor vehicle might become more attractive in the future.

The policy constraints on development of the Metropolitan Green Belt, high quality agricultural land, and areas of landscape quality were taken into account, as were the existing development commitments, especially industrial, warehousing, office, retail and housing commitments.

The study considered in detail the likely changes in road accessibility, traffic flows and travel times as a result of the construction of the M25, using of information derived from the TRRL, the Lichfield/Goldstein/Leigh study of the M25,[27] and travel time and traffic flows provided by the Eastern and South Eastern Road Construction Units and the Greater London Council. The TRRL study considered accessibility in terms of car travel time between zones to four types of opportunity (jobs, retail jobs, employed residents and people) in 1976 and 1986. It found that Central London will remain the area with the greatest accessibility to all four types of opportunities, although the M25 will only marginally increase its accessibility. By contrast, significant improvements in accessibility are forecast for a band around London centred on the M25 – especially in the east with the completion of the M11, and around Watford, St Albans and Welwyn Garden City.

Substantial travel time savings are expected on all cross-London journeys using the M25, for example, 30 minutes saved between Watford and Brentwood; 25 minutes saved between Watford and Reigate. By contrast, time savings on trips between Central London and locations outwith the M25 are likely to be much less, although the changes will vary depending on the origin and destination.

Increases in traffic flows are forecast for most radial routes outside the M25, while within the M25 many routes will be relieved of traffic. In total, it is expected that London will be relieved of 3–5 per cent of its total daily traffic (2 million vehicle miles per day) and a substantially higher proportion of heavy goods vehicles. However, the cost of this relief is seen in terms of pressure for development on locations within easy reach of an M25 junction, especially at the junctions with the main radials. Indeed, it is expected that

1 Pressures for industrial development will focus on the most dynamic growth industries in towns just beyond the Green Belt
2 Accessibility changes are likely to have the greatest effect on the location of warehousing where transport costs are a significant element of total costs, with pressures for development concentrating to the east and northeast of London, and around Watford/St Albans/Welwyn Garden City
3 Pressures for office development are expected to focus on existing centres in London which are subject to less restrictive development policies, i.e. Romford, Croydon, Hounslow, Uxbridge and Barnet. In addition, given the importance of good accessibility to specialized and local clerical staff in office location decisions, some pressure for development in towns where accessibility is forecast to increase most is expected, e.g. Harlow, Sevenoaks, Watford

4   Pressure already exists for the establishment of freestanding retail developments (hypermarkets and superstores) in the area of the M25 and well into the built-up area of London. Increased pressure for such developments are expected, especially in the vicinity of the M25 junctions with M1, M40, A3, A21 and A2. However, as the majority of the desirable locations for this type of development are in the Green Belt, pressures may be diverted to locations in outer London where policies are less restrictive

The conclusions reached by the impact study are that there is a real threat that the M25 will reinforce the dispersal of economic activity from London to easily accessible locations close to the M25, and reinforce the polarization '. . . into a prosperous, buoyant west side and a declining east side'.[28] Indeed, the study states unequivocally that the two main concerns which the M25 gives rise to are

(i)   the nascent conflict between the motorways transport function, the economic objective of assisting industrial and commercial development as part of the nation's recovery from recession and the maintenance of the Green Belt, and

(ii) the finding that the main development pressures which the motorway is likely to accentuate occur mainly in the western sectors, while the main opportunities and needs for new investment lie in inner London and the eastern sector.

Without some clear statements of policy there is a real danger that the regional strategy will fail in these key respects.[29]

The M25 Impact Study presents a marked contrast to the highly technical approach adopted in connection with the third London Airport. It could be criticized for being subjective and lacking rigour. An alternative view is that it acknowledges the realities of politics and a rapidly changing world. As such, it provides an indication of the likely impact of the M25 – as the study team point out 'The investigation has been carried out as a monitoring exercise, not as a finite study. It is seen as providing the basis for a continuing examination of the development impact of the motorway . . . to be reported on annually.'[30]

Evaluation and accessibility and environment

The Buchanan Report expressed the relationship between accessibility, environment and cost in the form of a rough and ready law: 'In any environmental area, if a certain standard of environment is adhered to, the level of accessibility that can be obtained depends on the amount of money that can be spent on physical alterations.'[31]

Having stated this 'law' the report outlines a technique which allows the three variables – environment, accessibility and cost – to be measured so that qualities of different highway networks can be compared, and the most efficient arrangement identified. However, environment and accessibility as defined in the report are comprised largely of intangible and unquantifiable elements, such as comfort, convenience, appearance, which are difficult if not impossible to value.

In an attempt to illustrate how this problem could be overcome the report took Newbury as a case study, listed all the important identifiable benefits associated with the three alternative town centre schemes put forward, and attempted to give them a numeric value to represent their various qualities. The costs of the three different proposals were measured in terms of the net capital cost of preparing land for building, i.e. cost of acquisition, clearing and servicing minus the value of the land for building purposes. The cost of building was excluded on the assumption that at the time of development the cost of the buildings is equal to their value if cost is taken to include the developers' profit, so that their net cost is nil.

The benefits associated with the accessibility were considered under

1   The safety of the layout for vehicle operation (40)
2   The distribution of parking and loading facilities (25)
3   The suitability of internal routes to allow direct access from one area to another (20)
4   The convenience of the layout for vehicle users (15)

The maximum numeric values given to each of these aspects were 40, 25, 20 and 15 respectively, and a subjective assessment was made of the weighting warranted by each town centre scheme. From this an Index of Accessibility was derived. The benefits associated with environment were considered under the safety, comfort, convenience and appearance of the particular area for the people living and working there. Again the respective maximum numeric values were 60, 15, 15 and 10, and subjective assessments were made of the appropriate weighting to be given to each alternative town centre scheme. Using these weightings an Index of Environment was derived.

The next stage of the process involved the calculation of one index to reflect both the level of environment and accessibility for each scheme (the Index of Environment and Accessibility). These indices were then compared with the Index of Environment and Accessibility derived for the present-day situation to obtain a measure of the benefits associated with the alternative schemes. The measure of each benefit was then related to the cost of implementing the scheme (i.e. benefit divided by cost) to represent a rate of return on the investment.

Table 19 illustrates the relative costs and benefits associated with the three alternative proposals for Newbury. On cost grounds alone scheme B has the highest rate of return, and should be implemented. However, there is a need to decide whether the extra benefits derived from scheme B warrant the additional expenditure over scheme A.

Scheme	Index of environment and accessibility	Benefit	Cost	Benefit/Cost
No change	11	nil	nil	0
(A) Limited improvements	22	11	2.7	4.1
(B) Improved primary network	57	46	3.4	13.5
(C) Improved primary network and internal circulation	72	61	5.6	10.9

Table 19 *Benefits and costs – Newbury*

Source: Appendix 2, *Traffic in Towns*, HMSO (1963).

This is achieved by relating the incremental costs to the additional benefits derived to obtain a measure of the rate of return on the extra cost involved.

Table 20 shows that in the Newbury case study scheme B, which costs £0.7m more than scheme A, has an increased Index of Environmental Accessibility of 35, and the rate of return on the additional investment is 50. Thus scheme B on both its benefit/cost ratio, and incremental benefit/cost ratio has the highest rate of return.

Scheme	Additional benefit	Incremental cost	Benefit cost
		(£m)	
No change	—	—	—
(A)	11	2.7	4
(B)	35	0.7	50
(C)	15	2.2	7

Table 20 *Incremental costs and benefits – Newbury*

Source: Appendix 2, *Traffic in Towns*, HMSO (1963).

This technique can be criticized on the grounds that it is subjective, and the allocation of numeric values arbitrary. However, in its favour it does attempt to take account of the many external factors which are difficult to quantify, while with time and when sufficient schemes have been examined in this way a consensus of opinion could well develop about the weighting system to be adopted. In the words of the Report 'however immature the analysis technique may be at this stage, its use will lead to surer judgement. And as the technique matures and experience and data are accumulated, so will rational decisions be assisted in the wise use of public investment resources.'[32]

The Canterbury Traffic Study[33]

The Canterbury Traffic Study, carried out by Buchanan and Partners, was primarily concerned with selecting a major east–west traffic route through or around the old city. The study, although interesting in its own right as a traffic study of a small town, is particularly noteworthy for the attempt made to integrate an economic evaluation with the wider considerations of environment, along with the lines indicated in the *Traffic in Towns* Report. The main evaluation was of three alternative highway routes compared with the original development plan route of an inner ring road. In addition to the economic evaluation, separate assessments of movement, accessibility, and environment were made.

The economic evaluation was based on a comparison of the capital costs of the new parts of the network, including acquisition costs, with the estimated user cost savings resulting from the extra investment. A discounted cash flow technique was used to produce a benefit-cost ratio. In addition to this indicator, three other indices evaluating the movement-network performance, accessibility and environment were also produced. The movement-network performance compared alternative networks by ranking them – as Good (*A*), Acceptable (*B*), and Unacceptable (*C*) – on their ability to accommodate traffic. Similar rankings were made for accessibility and environment. Each network was compared

1   In terms of local accessibility for vehicles to enter and move about the central area, with particular concern for short journeys, the effect on public transport, and response to possible changes in demand after the design years.
2   For the impact on pedestrian movement, noise, severance, and the effect on historic settings and visual character.

The four evaluations, i.e. benefit-cost ratio; movement-network performance, accessibility and environment were then compared to help form a final conclusion. Table 21 summarizes these evaluations.

It is clear from this table that no one scheme is superior to the others on all counts, and as a result an incremental comparison was made. Thus the surface rail route, although cheapest in terms of capital outlay, was inferior to the inner sub-surface route in every evaluation, and was consequently eliminated. The inner sub-surface route was then compared with the sub-surface rail route in an attempt to determine whether the extra environmental benefits were worth the extra costs and worse economic, movement and accessibility performance. Since, however, the environmental benefits of the rail route were only marginally greater than the benefits for the inner sub-surface route, this latter route was preferred.

Although this approach to evaluation can be criticized on the grounds that the economic evaluation was narrow in comparing only user cost savings with capital cost, that intangible factors such as comfort and convenience were not

	Inner sub-surface route	Surface rail route	Sub-surface rail route
1	2	3	4
MOVEMENT			
Network performance	A	C	B
ACCESSIBILITY			
For commercial and private vehicles	A	C	B
For public transport	B	C	B
Adaptability of networks	A	B	B
ENVIRONMENT			
Effect on pedestrian movement	A	B	B
Noise and severance	B	B	A
Effect on historic settings and visual character	B	C	A
COSTS			
Capital cost (net)	£2 250 000	£1 600 000	£2 500 000
Benefit/cost ratio	1.34	0.86	0.65

A = Good   *B* = Acceptable   *C* = Unacceptable

Table 21   *Canterbury Traffic Study Evaluation Summary*

Source: Table 12, *Canterbury Traffic Study*, Buchanan and Partners.

included, and that the 'double-counting' of certain costs and benefits has taken place, nevertheless *The Canterbury Traffic Study* demonstrates a considerable conceptual advance in its attempts to integrate intangibles within the evaluation.[34]

Although there is no compulsion for social and environmental factors to be taken into account in transport evaluation exercises, the fierce opposition that investment into transport infrastructure often arouses, results in such factors being included as an integral part of the evaluation. Indeed, the government has issued a sound state of the art review on the environmental evaluation of transport plans, on which local authorities often base their approach to environmental evaluation.[35] In the United States, following the introduction of the Environmental Policy Act 1969, environmental amenities and other factors must be given appropriate consideration in decision making – an initiative which has led to the development of specialized techniques to assess environmental impact. While such techniques are intended to be applied to major developments with potentially great environmental consequences, such as the proposed coal mining developments in the Vale of Belvoir, they are equally applicable to major transport proposals. Broadly speaking, the application of these environmental impact techniques falls into two stages – first, analysis, which measures the environmental effects such as air pollution, noise and visual intrusion, and second, evaluation. Needless to say, the second stage of the process is more difficult, involving as it does subjective judgements, concerning the trade-off between increasing air pollution, noise, visual intrusion and employment, for example. It is claimed that the objective underlying environmental impact analysis is to indicate to the decision makers the likely consequences of their decisions.

In the United States, a formalized technique of environmental impact analysis, referred to as the Leopold matrix, has been developed.[36] This technique involves

1 A consideration of the technological possibilities of achieving the objective
2 The establishment of the alternative ways of achieving that objective
3 The identification of existing environmental conditions which might be affected by the proposed development

For each possible technological means of achieving the stated objective, a matrix (the Leopold matrix) is prepared. On one axis are the actions resulting from the technological solution which impact on the environment; on the other axis are the existing environmental conditions which might be affected by the different elements of the technological solution. A modified and simpler version of the Leopold matrix has been suggested by Potter for use in the UK.[37, 38]

The economic evaluation of transportation proposals

Road proposals[39, 40]

The Department of Transport has produced several documents dealing with the techniques and problems associated with an economic assessment of road improvements. These have invariably been based on work done by the Road Research Laboratory, and current developments tend to be an elaboration of earlier work done by D. J. Reynolds.[41]

Three main stages are involved in an evaluation of the economic benefits associated with road improvements (a) the estimation of the cost involved in an improvement scheme (b) the estimation of the benefits, and their monetary value, derived from an improvement scheme (c) the relation of the costs involved to the benefits derived.

Costs

The capital costs involved in any road improvement scheme should include the construction costs of the road, at the price level obtaining on the date on which the improvement is carried out, the cost of land acquisition, compensation, legal and administrative procedures, and maintenance costs. Land which has been acquired some time in advance of the date on which the improvement is to be carried out should be valued at its present alternative use value, while maintenance costs likely to prevail in the future should cover such aspects as the cost of periodic resurfacing, cleansing, lighting, verge maintenance and traffic control. If a complete discounted flow calculation rather than a first year rate of return is to be calculated then interest costs on work in progress should be omitted.

One further cost, which is often ignored in road improvement schemes, is the cost of delay and accidents imposed on road users while the improvement is being carried out. These costs are especially important if a discounted flow calculation is to be used as immediate costs are discounted less heavily than future long-term benefits.

Benefits and associated monetary values
'Road improvements are designed to bring benefits to road users in the form of cheaper, quicker and safer travel.'[42]

The relevant benefits include those resulting from the saving in time, and the reduction of accidents, and also a number of environmental or amenity benefits, such as the reduction in traffic noise or fumes. These amenity benefits are often difficult to quantify and impossible to put a monetary value to. Consequently they are generally excluded from an economic assessment of most road improvement schemes.

In considering the benefits derived from a road improvement four main categories of traffic must be distinguished – traffic already using the road to be improved; traffic likely to divert to the improved road from other roads; traffic which will remain on roads from which traffic will be diverted; and generated traffic. For all these categories it is essential to estimate the likely traffic flows, in terms of an annual average daily flow (be it 24, 16, or 12 hours), or an annual average hourly daily flow, to calculate the benefits due to changes in journey speed.

The average 24-hour flow can be derived in a variety of ways, for example by using continuous automatic counts for one year, or four one-week continuous automatic counts at three-monthly intervals, supplemented by manual counts.[43]

For evaluation purposes it is also necessary to have some measure of the likely future growth in traffic. The Road Research Laboratory has established that current growth rates in p.c.u.s. are in the region of 5 per cent per annum compound, and in the absence of known local factors recommend that this growth rate should be used. However, for long-term improvements reference should be made to the latest available estimates on vehicle ownership and traffic growth.

Savings in the operating costs can be subdivided into journey time savings and vehicle running costs. In assessing the journey time savings it is necessary to estimate accurately the difference in journey times between the existing unimproved and the proposed improved road. This involves measuring present-day speeds on the unimproved road, estimating how these speeds on the unimproved road would be likely to change with the growth of traffic; estimating the speeds likely to be achieved on the improved road and comparing the results to derive the journey time savings which would result from the improvement. Perhaps the most satisfactory method of measuring present-day speeds or journey times on the unimproved road is the moving observer method previously described.[44]

Comparison of costs and benefits
There are two methods of presenting the final results comparing the costs and benefits associated with improvements. The simpler method involves the use of a 'first year rate of return' in which the costs of construction are discounted forward to the year of completion, and then compared with the benefits derived for the first year of operation of the completed scheme. The ratio of the annual benefit to the construction cost is expressed in percentage terms as the annual rate of return.

In equation form the rate of return may be expressed as

$$R = \frac{O + A - M \times 100}{C}$$

where R = rate of return in per cent
   O = savings in annual labour, vehicle time and operating costs
   A = annual savings in costs of accidents
   M = additional maintenance costs per annum
   C = capital cost of improvement

A more complicated approach can be adopted which takes account of the fact that future costs and benefits are worth less in the future than they are today. Using this technique, costs and benefits are calculated for each year for, say, thirty years and discounted back to the present day to give the net present value. The net present value is expressed as a percentage ratio of the discounted capital cost. If the net present value is positive it can be argued that the proposal is worth while.

Algebraically the present discounted value is expressed as

$$P_0 = (B_0 - C_0) + \frac{(B_1 - C_1)}{(1 + i)} + \ldots\ldots + \frac{(B_n - C_n)}{(1 + i)_n}$$

where P_0 = the present value of the investment in year 0
B_0 and C_0 = benefits and costs in year 0
   $B_1 - B_n$ = benefits in years 1 to n
   $C_1 - C_n$ = costs in years 1 to n
      i = the discount rate per annum
      n = the number of years for which the return is to be calculated

The present discounted value should always be accompanied by a 'first year rate of return' calculation, which should ideally be in excess of the rate of interest used in the present discounted value calculation. If the first year rate of return is less than the rate of interest used in the present discounted value calculation then the scheme should be postponed. This will have the effect of increasing the discounted value.

In an attempt to improve and standardize evaluation technique the Department of Transport has developed a computer-based cost-benefit analysis program known as COBA. The program is available for both mainframe and microcomputers. The method was first introduced in the early 1970s and has been continuously updated and revised. It is now in its ninth version, which was introduced in 1981.[45] Briefly COBA compares the cost of road schemes with the benefits derived by road users and expresses the results in terms of a monetary value, known as the Net Present Value (NPV). It is a partial technique in that it is an economic appraisal which does not attempt to measure value of money over the whole range of costs and benefits. Thus a number of costs and benefits incurred through constructing or improving a length of road, including environmental factors, are excluded from the analysis. Initially COBA was intended to be used on interurban roads, but the latest version (9) is capable of application in urban areas.

COBA is principally concerned with estimating benefits as they accrue to the users of the road system. Since road users are not required to pay directly for these benefits they have to be estimated on the 'willingness to pay' principle, and COBA therefore uses a consumer surplus approach, i.e. the difference between what people are prepared to pay for a given quantity of goods or services and what they actually pay. The estimation of benefits is achieved by evaluating one or more proposals to improve a road network with the existing situation, i.e. it compares a 'do something' situation with a 'do nothing' situation. The approach followed is illustrated in Figures 36 and 37, and the method is used to assess the need for improving a route; to compare alternative solutions to the problem; to determine the priority to be given to a scheme and to assess its optimal timing. The user is required to provide as input to COBA (a) a description of the highway network to cover both the existing and improved situations and (b) traffic flow data. The network is described in terms of links and nodes and the program can handle a maximum of 250 links and 150 nodes.

Traffic flow data can be entered for a single year or several years. If flows are specified for a single year, then the year should normally be the survey year. It should not be earlier than the base year of the traffic growth profile in COBA 9 (1976). The data is input as a fixed trip matrix, i.e. it is assumed that the pattern of trip making will not be affected by the proposed improvements, although the actual routes taken will change as a result of the improvements. The fixed trip matrix is then assigned to the existing and improved networks for analysis by COBA. It is important that there are no

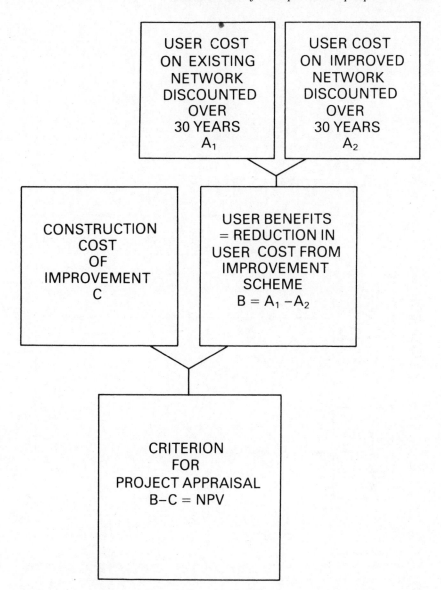

Figure 36   *Outline structure of COBA evaluation system*

Source: Department of Transport, *COBA 9*, London (1981)

USER COSTS

1 hr, 12 hr or 16 hr flow on each link

converted by program into total yearly flow by multiplying factor which depends on the day, month, location and length of the survey

total yearly flow on each link

program divides flow into different vehicle classes eg cars, buses, light goods using information input by user

yearly flow for each vehicle class on each link

program increases flow yearly by a factor for each vehicle class

yearly flow for each vehicle class on each link for each year of 30 year evaluation period

program divides by 8760 to give annual average hourly flow for each vehicle class then divides flow into different flow groups (or levels of flow) to represent peak periods, night time flow etc.

hourly flow for each flow group and vehicle class on each link in each year*

description of each classified junction including layout, turning proportion of traffic, geometric delay etc.

description of each link including length location accident rate bendiness, hilliness speed limit etc.

VEHICLE OPERATING COSTS

speed is related to volume of traffic on a link so is different for each flow-group. Also depends on type and

VALUE OF TIME

EXPENDITURE

profile of scheme construction costs

profile of maintenance expenditure costs (traffic and non-traffic related)

profile of total scheme costs over evaluation period

program discounts total costs at 7% to Present Value Year (1979)

total discounted scheme costs

ACCIDENTS

LINKS

JUNCTIONS

total no. of vehicle kilometres on each

flow through each junction

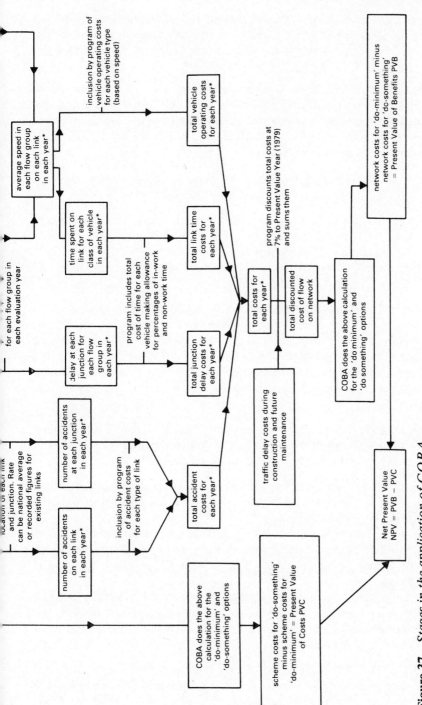

Figure 37 *Stages in the application of COBA*

Source: Department of Transport, *COBA 9*, London (1981)

major discrepancies between the assignment and COBA networks, and that they agree at least in relation to overall journey speeds and times. In addition, the user is required to input to the program the following details relating to traffic flow.

1 The proportions of the various vehicle categories (car, light goods, goods vehicles 2-axle twin wheels; goods vehicles 4-axle twin wheels, buses and coaches) presented as a weighted average which takes into account the lengths of network links and the total flow throughout the year. The weighted average is calculated from

$$\frac{n_1 L_1 + n_2 L_2 + \ldots + n_n + L_n}{q_1 L_1 + q_2 L_2 + \ldots + q_n + L_n} = \frac{\Sigma\, nL}{\Sigma\, qL}$$

where $n_1\, n_2 \ldots, n_n$ = the number of vehicles per day in any category on links $1, 2 \ldots, n$

L_1, L_2, L_n = the length of each link

$q_1, q_2 \ldots, q_n$ = the total number of vehicles per day on links 1, 2. . . , n

Where 12- or 16-hour classified traffic count data for August and a neutral month are used to determine the vehicle category proportions, then the measured proportion of different vehicle categories should be adjusted by appropriate factors provided with COBA.[46]

2 The road types (i.e. main urban, interurban and recreational/interurban) which are used by the program to adjust for seasonal changes in traffic flows.

The basic unit for traffic flow calculations in COBA is the Annual Average Hourly Traffic Flow (AAHT). This is required for every link in the network and it can be derived in one of three ways

1 Direct input in AAHT from an assignment model or national data, which is then modified by the program to take account of seasonal flows by vehicle categories

2 Input of an all vehicle 16-hour manual classified count which is then modified by the program to take account of the different proportions of vehicle categories, and seasonal flows by road type and vehicle categories

3 All vehicle 12-hour manual classified count which is expanded to a 16-hour count by the application of an expansion factor and then manipulated by the program in exactly the same way as the input 16-hour count data

Taking the fixed trip matrix and the given assignment in an initial year, COBA then estimates the effects of daily and seasonal flow variations on total user costs through the application of speed flow, junction delay, accident and vehicle operating cost related formulae. Using the traffic growth forecasts built into the program·it can repeat these calculations for each of the thirty years built into the evaluation.

User costs are derived by taking account of

1 User's time, where working time and non-working time are valued differently
2 Vehicle operating costs
3 The cost of accidents

Construction costs and highway maintenance are also taken into account.

Costs and benefits are aggregated and compared by reducing them to a common value for the selected present year (1979) by discounting. Thus in the first year after the present year chosen for the calculation, all costs and benefits are reduced by the factor $1/(1 + r)$ where r is the appropriate discount rate to give the Present Value Costs (P V C) and Present Value Benefits (P V B). In the second year, the factor is $1/(1 + r)^2$ and so on. The current discount rate with COBA is 7 per cent and the present year is 1979.

The Net Present Value is calculated by subtracting the Present Value Costs from the Present Value Benefits (i.e. $NPV = PVB - PVC$). In purely economic terms, a scheme is considered viable if it has an N P V greater than zero, i.e. its discounted benefits are greater than its discounted costs. If the N P V is negative then the preferred solution in economic terms is the 'do nothing' solution, which in effect acts as a baseline against which the costs and benefits of the 'do something' solution are measured. If there are a number of 'do something' options, the economically preferred solution is the one with the highest N P V. Generally, N P V results are presented to two significant figures to avoid the impression of spurious precision. Indeed, COBA 9 recommends that given the uncertainty implicit in the long forecasting horizon associated with a long-life investment such as a trunk road, high and low traffic and economic growth rate forecasts should be used to set bounds on the uncertainty. This inevitably complicates matters for the eventual decision-takers, especially in situations where the incremental analysis is sensitive to a number of factors, such as forecast turning movements. However, this type of analysis inevitably focuses the decision-takers' judgement on the key variables.

The Department of Transport recommends that, although COBA is applicable to the majority of schemes in the trunk road programme, there are situations where alternative approaches are appropriate. Thus, for example, for schemes costing less than £1m a less sophisticated approach to economic evaluation is appropriate, such as the first year rate of return. Similarly, for larger schemes where the improvement to the network is likely to generate additional trips, variable trip matrix evaluation techniques may be applied, although in doing so the values and principles used should be consistent with COBA.

Over the years, COBA has been criticized on a number of counts, many of which were considered by the Advisory Committee on Trunk Road Assessment in 1977 (the Leitch Committee).[47] Heggie, in particular, was critical of the earlier versions of COBA on the grounds that

1   The method of forecasting future traffic volumes, which relied on the extrapolation of past trends, was conceptually deficient and therefore was not an appropriate basis on which to base policy formulation
2   The inclusion of all time savings in the analysis, however small, gave too great an emphasis to these small time savings and hence to minor road improvements in urban areas
3   The exclusion of a consideration of environmental matters ignores the environmental case for urban by-passes
4   If, by including the intangible factors such as the environment benefits and costs in any analysis the tangible monetary effects of a road scheme become less important, the value of discounting is called into question.[48]

COBA 9 addresses the first of these criticisms in that it now uses two approaches to forecasting car ownership – the first based on the TRRL model, which is a modification of the logistic curve formulation used in earlier versions[49] (the extrapolation of past trends). The second model uses data produced by the Family Expenditure Survey and attempts to identify the causes underlying decisions about car ownership and seeks to quantify their effects. Two sets of car ownership forecasts are produced for each model on the basis of optimistic and pessimistic assumptions about future levels of, for example, economic growth and petrol prices. The upper and lower forecasts from each model are then combined to form the upper and lower limits of future levels of car ownership. Similarly, optimistic and pessimistic assumptions are made about the future level of real income and the price of fuel, and these are used to produce upper and lower estimates of car use. The car use estimates, in terms of average distance travelled, and car ownership estimates are then combined to produce upper and lower limits to the range of forecasts for car traffic.

By contrast, COBA 9 still takes all time savings into account, no matter how small, and it does not consider environmental factors. Thus the criticisms levelled against earlier versions of COBA by Heggie are still valid. However, COBA 9 recommends that 'COBA . . . must be seen as only one element in the appraisal process, to be used along with assessments of environmental and other considerations'.[50] The Leitch Report illustrates a framework against which such an environmental analysis could be undertaken. The framework is based on Lichfield's Planning Balance Sheet.[51]

Railway operations
With exceptions the evaluation of rail schemes has to date taken the form of disinvestment rather than new investment proposals. Economic assessments

have generally been undertaken with a view to closing down services rather than developing new routes. The techniques used in these evaluations are based on marginal cost accounting principles, and show the net financial benefit to British Rail resulting from line closures.

A good example of this type of evaluation is the work undertaken by Foster on two suburban railway lines in Greater Manchester, on which services would be withdrawn if only commercial considerations were taken into account.[52] As part of the analysis, account was taken of the effect of improving the rail service, and providing feeder bus services. The results of the evaluation are summarized in Table 22.

	Present Value £m
Disbenefits to road users through additional congestion	14.8
Disbenefits to former rail users transferring to bus	0.7
Changes in road accident costs	0.3
Resource costs of replacement bus services	1.3
Resource costs of replacement car journeys	1.9
Avoidable costs of rail services	− 6.0
N P V of improved service	+ 13.0

Table 22 *Costs and benefits of withdrawing rail services in Manchester, 1973–97*

Source: Foster, C. D., *Social Cost-Benefit Study of Two Suburban Rail Passenger Services*, British Rail, London (1974).

The figures show the present value of the six major items considered for the period 1973–97, discounted to 1973 at 10 per cent p.a. The costs and benefits are calculated on the basis of a comparison between improving and withdrawing the services. It can be seen that the disbenefit to existing road users makes the biggest contribution to NPV. With the exception of the social cost-benefit analyses undertaken in connection with the closure of certain lines in North Wales, social factors such as time loss and inconvenience to passengers are excluded from such economic assessments.

Work done in connection with the Victoria Line underground railway, and the *Liverpool Outer Rail Loop Study*, have indicated in broad terms the approach which should be adopted in evaluating in economic terms rail investment proposals.

In such schemes the capital and operating costs should ideally be compared by some form of discounted cost flow calculation. However, such a calculation requires an estimate of both rail and road conditions well into the future, which may be impossible. As an alternative a simple annual first year rate of return can be used. The capital and operating costs of new rail proposals are generally easier to deal with than the associated benefits. Capital costs should be discounted back to a common base year, and operating costs will vary with the predicted level of traffic, and the increase in labour costs.

The benefits derived from such proposals are more difficult to cope with. Time savings, diverted and generated traffic benefits can be derived comparatively easily, but benefits associated with changes in comfort and level of service are much more difficult to assess and quantify. Other aspects which should be included in an evaluation of this kind include changes in income received by the public transport operators, and changes in central government revenue from indirect taxation such as fuel tax.

As with road proposals the cost-benefit analysis is only one element of an appraisal framework, and, ideally, any comprehensive evaluation should attempt to take into account the likely impact on intangibles. For example the Glasgow Rail Impact Study attempts to assess the likely impact of a series of underground and suburban rail improvements on a range of factors including travel patterns, competing modes of transport, travel by the disadvantaged, land use, and the environment.[54]

Evaluation of complete transportation network proposals

There are no absolute standards by which a transportation plan can be evaluated. It can only be compared with the estimated results likely to be achieved through the adoption of some other plan. This alternative plan can range from a 'minimum' plan in which nothing is done, at one extreme, to a comprehensive set of proposals at the other. General comparisons with the base year situation can be achieved by analysing simple tabulations such as trip totals by mode and purpose, and total interzonal movements.

A basic appreciation of how the proposed transport systems are likely to function can be derived from an examination of the 'loads' assigned to the different 'links' of the system, and comparing them with estimated capacities. In this particular respect an automatic data plotter operating in conjunction with computer output can quite rapidly plot a network of some size, showing link volumes or volume/capacity ratios.

To date, the techniques adopted in an economic evaluation of transportation proposals for the large conurbations have regarded the total movement demands as a function of the proposed transport network. This contrasts with the simpler analyses already outlined where, with the exception of generated traffic, trips have been considered independent of the network and the benefits were derived direct from statistics relating to vehicle miles and time. The evaluation of user benefits derived from a complete transportation plan is more complex, and one possible approach could involve

1   An estimation of the volume of traffic moving between any two zones, for any given time period, both with and without the new transportation proposals
2   The calculation of the mean of the two volumes estimated above
3   The multiplication of this mean by the cost differential (i.e. the cost without, minus cost with)
4   The summation of the total derived in (3) above, for all possible combinations of movement, to give the total direct user benefit during the chosen time interval.

This technique utilizes the reduction in cost of travel likely to result from the transportation network proposals as a measure of the benefits users will receive, and cost in this context includes fares, vehicle operating costs, time, comfort and convenience.

In the analysis three types of journey should be considered

1   Journeys unaffected by the new proposals, i.e. journeys between the same origin and destination, by the same route and mode. These journeys will obtain some benefit (or incur further costs) depending on the ease (or increased difficulty) with which these trips can be made. This benefit or loss will be equivalent to the cost differential derived from the cost of trip making before and after the new proposals are introduced.
2   Journeys generated by the new proposals, i.e. trips not previously made, but which, because of the improved facilities, are now completed. As in the M1 and Victoria Line studies such trips are considered to benefit less than the already existing trips, and would be likely to be valued at 50 per cent of the cost differential.
3   Journeys which have changed their destination as a result of the improved facilities provided by the transport system, i.e. journeys which formerly went from A to B, now go from A to Z because under the base year situation it was difficult or impossible to get from A to Z, but the new proposals incorporate a link which allows journeys from A to Z to be incorporated.

This type of analysis is crude in the extreme, and presupposes that all travellers have the ability to estimate in advance the likely cost of any action they consider undertaking. However, from a practical point of view an averaging process is necessary, which reflects the different preferences and values of different people.

One further complication arises from the fact that the same journeys can have different costs at different times of the day, by different modes of travel and for different journey purposes. For example, a journey in the peak period may cost (in cost-benefit terms) considerably more than the same journey at midnight, while a journey undertaken for leisure purposes may 'cost' less than the same journey undertaken for business reasons.

To overcome the problems associated with journeys undertaken for different purposes, by different modes and at different times of the day, involves the same considerations, i.e. cost differential before and after the transport proposals should be introduced by the main journey purposes, such as leisure, to work, and commercial, and by the major modes of travel, such as public and private transport and for the most significant time periods, such as peak and off-peak periods.

The problems associated with the consideration of the same journey by different and competing modes is, however, slightly more complex, as each individual user will assess the cost of travel by competing modes in the light of his or her own preferences. It is assumed that he or she will only transfer to an alternative mode if the cost is less by that mode than the mode being used. Thus the benefit associated with a change of mode can be considered to be a function of both the cost of the previous mode, as well as the cost of the alternative mode. This could be taken into consideration, by relating the benefits derived from a change of mode to the ratio of the journey volumes using the competing modes before and after the introduction of the transportation proposals being evaluated.

The capital and operating costs involved in the implementation of the proposals, and the value of individual time savings can be deduced in the same way as they are estimated for normal road improvements.

The comparison of costs and benefits associated with complete urban transportation system proposals is usually expressed as a one-year rate of return since the expense and time involved in the production of a present discounted value is likely to be prohibitive.

References

1   Lichfield, N., Kettle, P., and Whitbread, M., *Evaluation in the Planning Process*, Pergamon Press, Oxford (1975) p. 5.
2   See Lichfield *et al., op. cit.* (1975) Chapter 4, pp. 48–77 for a review of the alternative approaches to evaluation.
3   This chapter provides a very general introduction to the evaluation of transportation proposals. A number of texts deal with the topic in greater detail including:
Harrison, A. J., *The Economics of Transport Appraisal*, Croom Helm, London (1974).
Heggie, I. G., *Transport Engineering Economics*, McGraw Hill, London (1972).
Hutchinson, B. G., *Principles of Urban Transport Systems Planning*, McGraw Hill, Toronto (1974) Chapter 10, pp. 255–325.
Wohl, M. and Martin, B. V., *Traffic Systems Analyses*, McGraw Hill, New York (1967) Chapters 7–10, pp. 180–321.
4   Prest, A. R. and Turvey, R., *Cost-Benefit Analysis: A Survey*, Surveys of Economic Theory, Vol. III, Macmillan (1967).
5   Peters, G. H., *Cost-Benefit Analysis and Public Expenditure*, Eaton Paper No. 8 (1968).
6   Peters, G. H., *op. cit.*
7   Schlager, K., 'The Rank Based Expected Value Method of Plan Evaluation', *Highway Research Record No. 238* (1968) pp. 153–6.
8   Hill, M., 'A Method for the Evaluation of Transportation Plans', *Highway Research Record No. 180* (1967) pp. 21–34.
'A Goals-Achievement Matrix for Evaluating Alternative Plans', *Journal of the American Institute of Planners*, 34 (1968) pp. 19–29.

9   Schimpler, C. C., and Grecco, W. L., 'Systems Evaluation: An Approach Based on Community Structure and Values', *Highway Research Record No. 238* (1968) pp. 123–52.

10 Lichfield, N., *Economics of Planned Development*, Estates Gazette, London (1960) pp. 273–9.
     Cost-Benefit Analysis in Urban Development, Research Report 20, Real Estate Research Program, University of California, Berkeley (1962).

11 Nathaniel Lichfield and Associates, *Stevenage Public Transport: Cost Benefit Analysis*, Vols. 1 & 2, Stevenage Development Corporation (1969).

12 See the following for more detailed reviews of the scope of cost benefit analysis in transport:
     Barrell, D. W. F., 'Cost-Benefit Analysis in Transportation Planning', *Oxford Working Papers in Planning Education and Research No. 10*, Department of Planning, Oxford Polytechnic (April 1972).
     Barrell, D. W. F. and Hills, P. J., 'The Application of Cost-Benefit Analysis to Transport Investment Projects in Britain', *Transportation*, Vol. 1 (May 1972) pp. 29–54.
     Gwilliam, K. M., 'Economic Evaluation of Transport Projects: the State of the Art', *Transportation Planning and Technology*, Vol. 1 (December 1972) pp. 123–42.

13 Coburn, T. M., Beesley M. E. and Reynolds, D. J., 'The London–Birmingham Motorway – Traffic and Economics', *Road Research Technical Paper*, No. 46, HMSO (1960).

14 Coburn, T. M., Beesley, M. E. and Reynolds, D. J., *op. cit.*

15 Reynolds D. J., 'The cost of road accidents', *Journal of the Royal Statistical Society*, Series A, General (1956).

16 Foster, C. D. and Beesley, M. E., 'Estimating the social benefit of constructing an underground railway in London', *Journal of the Royal Statistical Society*, Series A, General (1963).

17 Foster, C. D. and Beesley M. E., 'The Victoria Line: social benefit and finances', *Journal of the Royal Statistical Society*, Series A, General (1965).

18 Roskill, Mr Justice, 'Report of the Commission on the Third London Airport', *Commission Papers and Proceedings*, Vol. VII, Part 2, HMSO, London (1970).

19 Roskill, Mr Justice, *Final Report of the Commission on the Third London Airport*, HMSO, London (1971) p. 11.

20 *ibid*, p. 118.

21 *ibid*, p. 155.

22 *ibid*, p. 155.

23 Mishan, E. J., 'What is Wrong with Roskill?', *Journal of Transport Economics and Policy*, Vol. IV, No. 3 (September 1970) pp. 221–34.

24 *ibid*, p. 232.

25 Standing Conference on London and South East Regional Planning, *The Impact of the M25*, Report by the Industry and Commerce Working Party of the Regional Monitoring Group SCLSERP, London (July 1982).

26 *ibid*, pp. 3–4.

27 Nathaniel Lichfield and Partners, and Goldstein Leigh Associates, *M25 London Orbital: Property Market Effects*, Lichfield and Partners, Grafton Road, London (January 1981).

28 Standing Conference on London and South-East Regional Planning, *op. cit.* (1982) p. 53.

29 *ibid*, p. 54.

30 *ibid*, p. 57.

31 Buchanan, C. D., *Traffic in Towns*, HMSO, London (1963).

32 Buchanan, C. D., *op. cit.*

33 Buchanan, C. D. and Partners, *The Canterbury Traffic Study* (October 1970).

34 Barrell, D. W. F., 'Cost-Benefit Analysis in Transportation Planning', *Oxford Working Papers in Planning Education and Research*, No. 10 (April 1972).

35 Lassiere, A., *The Environmental Evaluation of Transport Plans*, Department of the Environment, HMSO, London (1976).

36 Leopold, L. B., Clarke, F. E., Hanshaw, B. B., and Balsley, J. R., *A Procedure for Evaluating Environmental Impact*, US Department of the Interior, Geological Survey, Circular No. 645 (1971).

37 Potter, A. F., 'Keeping Track of Environmental Impact', *New Civil Engineer*, 12–13, (2 January 1975).

38 See Hothersall, D. C. and Salter, R. J., *Transport and the Environment*, Crosby, Lock-wood, Staples, London (1977) Chap 1, pp. 1–23 for a review of impact assessment.

39 Dawson, R. F. F., 'The Economic Assessment of Road Improvement Schemes', *Road Research Technical Paper* No. 75, Ministry of Transport (1980).

40 Department of Environment and subsequently Department of Transport, *COBA Versions 1–9*, Department of Transport, London (1972–82).

41 Reynolds, D. J., 'The assessment of priorities for road improvements', *Road Research Technical Paper*, No. 48, HMSO, London (1960).

42 *Research on Road Traffic*, Chapter 15, HMSO, London (1965).

43 See: *Research on Road Traffic*, Chapter 2, HMSO, London (1965).

44 Wardrop, J. G. and Charlesworth, G., 'A method of estimating speed and flow of traffic from a moving vehicle', *Proceedings Institution of Civil Engineers*, Part II (1954).

45 Department of Transport, *COBA 9*, Assessments, Policy and Methods Division, Department of Transport, London (1981).

46 Department of Transport, 1981 *op. cit.* Para 4.5.8.

47 *Report of the Advisory Committee on Trunk Road Assessment*, Department of Transport, HMSO, London (1977) (the Leitch Report).

48 Heggie, I. G., 'Economics and the Road Programme', *Journal of Transport Economics and Policy*, Volume XIII, No. 1 (January 1979) pp. 52–67.

49 Tanner, J., *Car Ownership Trends and Forecasts, L R 799*, TRRL Crowthorne, Berkshire (1977).

50 Department of Transport, *op. cit.*, (1981) Introduction.

51 Leitch Report, *op. cit.*, (1977) Appendix 6.1.

52 Foster, C. D., *Social Cost/Benefit Study of Two Suburban Rail Passenger Services*, British Rail, London (1974).

53 Ministry of Transport, *The Cambrian Coast Line: A Cost Benefit Analysis of Railway Services on the Cambrian Coast Line*, HMSO, London (1969).

54 Gentleman, H., Mitchell, C. G. B., Walmsley, D. A., and Wicks, J., *The Glasgow Rail Impact Study*, Supplementary Report 650, TRRL, Crowthorne, Berks. (1981).

10 Conclusions

Introduction

The traditional land-use transportation studies have generally used travel demand forecasting models derived from a base-year data set which establishes patterns of future travel behaviour aggregated from household level to zonal level. These travel patterns are then related to a representation of the existing and proposed transport networks and the particular spatial characteristics of the area being studied. These modelling procedures are known as 'aggregate sequential models' or 'the four stage sequential sub-modal approach', i.e. trip generation, trip distribution, modal split and traffic assignment. While it has been claimed that this approach may be interpreted as a behavioural representation of the travel choice process,[1] overall it has been heavily criticized on the grounds that it does not represent the reality of decision making with regard to choices about travel; it has an inadequate theoretical basis; it fails to address adequately relevant policy issues; and it is only capable of simulating travel demand rather than explaining it.

In the face of these criticisms a number of researchers have developed or extended new approaches to the travel demand forecasting process. The most significant developments include land-use allocation models, disaggregate behavioural choice models and activity analysis. This chapter briefly reviews these developments and offers an indication of where the transportation planning process is likely to move in the future.

Land-use allocation models

Historically the transportation planning process has developed using a sequential series of models to deal with individual parts of the problem – trip generation, trip distribution, modal split, and traffic assignment. The major shortcoming of this approach is that in separating the process into elements or stages, it becomes divorced from reality. In the real world, factors such as residential population, employment, retailing and transport are interlinked. Thus problems and possible solutions concerning one factor affect other factors. In an attempt to consider these interrelationships, a range of integrated models have been developed. These models are transport planning-related land-use models and they were initially developed to prepare land-use inputs to the transport models described in earlier chapters. The great advantage of these integrated models is that they may be used to estimate a land-use allocation and the associated travel demands simutaneously. In addition, they require much less information to be input exogenously and are sensitive to some of the major policy variables which affect development.[2]

The most well known and widely used of these models is probably the Lowry model, or variations on it. This integrated model was developed in 1964 by Ira S. Lowry.[3] It has subsequently been developed by Garin,[4] who incorporated spatial sub-models into the framework and expressed the Lowry algorithm in vector and matrix format. It uses economic base theory to link population, employment and transport to produce a land-use transport model.[5] Briefly, economic base theory divides the employment of a region into basic and non-basic employment. Basic employment manufactures goods consumed outside the region, and its growth is linked to external factors in the economy. Non-basic employment exists to serve the local area, and its growth is dependent on the needs of the local population. The main assumption underpinning the Lowry model is that changes in a region depend on changes in basic employment. Thus the manufacturing industries which employ the basic work sector export their goods out of the region. This results in a flow of money into the region which is used in part to pay for the services needed by the basic employment sector and their dependents, such as retailing, education, transport and banking.

The basic characteristics of the Lowry model, which uses the location of basic jobs in the region to forecast the location of other factors, are best described in a series of stages

1 Locate the basic jobs in the region.
2 Use the attraction constrained gravity model to locate basic workers to residential zones.
3 Calculate the non-working population of each residential zone, i.e. immediate family of basic workers, pensioners, unemployed, sick. This is derived on the assumption that non-workers are proportional to the basic workers living there.

At the end of this stage, the model has estimated the total basic population of each residential zone which is dependent on basic employment.

4 Calculate the number of non-basic workers required to provide the services required by the basic population. (Lowry's original model was concerned with the retail sector.) This is derived on the assumption that the non-basic workers needed in a zone are proportional to the basic population.
5 Use the production constrained gravity model to locate non-basic workers to non-basic employment zones.
6 Use the attraction constrained gravity model to locate non-basic workers to residential zones.

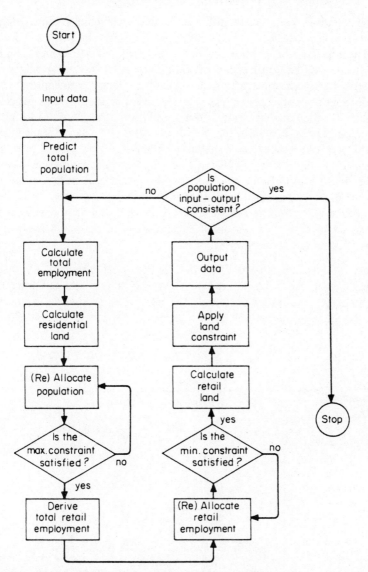

Figure 38 *The structure of the original Lowry model*

Source: Reproduced, with permission, from Reif, B., *Models in Urban and Regional Planning*, Blackie, Glasgow and London (1973)

7 Calculate the residential population dependent on non-basic workers for each residential zone and the non-working population. This is again derived on the assumption that it is proportional to the non-basic workers living in each zone.

At this stage, each residential zone has two components of population – basic and non-basic.

8   The non-basic population of each zone calculated in 7 above also requires services. If the non-basic population is large, then these services will be provided by a second increment of non-basic workers to employment and residential zones, i.e. Stages 4–6 above are repeated. This process will increase the non-basic residential population of each zone and, again, if the increase is large, Stages 4–6 are repeated. The model continues with this iterative process until the last increment of non-basic workers has a service requirement which is small enough to ignore, and there is a stable co-distribution of all employment and residential population, within the overall constraint of land availability.

9   The output from the Lowry model is the location of non-basic employment; the total population of each residential zone and the work and service journeys between zones.

Figure 38 illustrates one version of the Lowry model showing the sequence of stages and the iterative approach. Figure 39 shows the structure of the Garin–Lowry model which avoids the need for iteration by using matrix algebra. Despite the benefits associated with this integrated land-use trans-

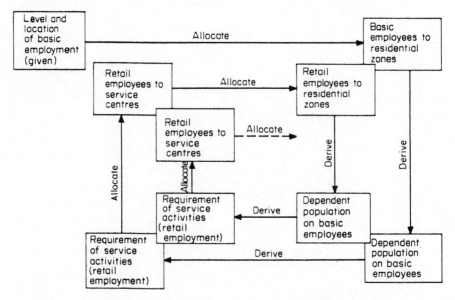

Figure 39   *Functional structure of the Garin-Lowry model*

Source: Reproduced, with permission, from Reif, B., *Models in Urban and Regional Planning*, Blackie, Glasgow and London (1973).

port model which is easy to use and requires relatively little input data there are a number of disadvantages, the most significant of which are

1 The model does not describe the changes which take place in a region over time, i.e. the model is an end-state model which predicts for a specified point in the future. It makes no attempt to predict the situation in intervening years.
2 The model assumes that at the end of every forecast period all the regions' elements and activities are in equilibrium. In reality cities and regions are invariably in permanent disequilibrium, due to the time lag between cause and effect.
3 The model is theoretically suspect in that economic base theory, on which it is based, ignores the direct links between the basic and non-basic employment centres.

Despite these criticisms the Lowry model (or variations of it) is widely used, and a new generation of models has developed around the basic underlying principles in ways which attempt to offset the weaknesses identified with the original model. For example, Echenique has suggested a dynamic and disaggregated formulation of the model, where changes over time in the distribution of basic employment are taken into account.[6] Wilson has developed a disaggregated residential location model based on Lowry which takes account of different household income groups, different wage levels by type of employment, different house types and variation in house price by location, although there are data problems associated with calibrating a model of this type.[7]

Variations of the model have been applied in the Nottinghamshire–Derbyshire; Bedfordshire and Lancashire areas of England.[8] However from a transportation planning point of view, the problems associated with the output relate to the limited number of trip matrices produced, i.e. work journey, and service or retail journeys, while modal split and assignment procedures still have to be applied in the same way as in the aggregate demand forecasting approach.

Dissatisfaction with the aggregate demand forecasting approach and the use of land-use allocation models has encouraged the development of activity systems analysis and disaggregate behavioural approaches to transport modelling.

Disaggregate behavioural travel demand models[9]

The aggregate sequential approach to transport modelling is criticized on a number of counts, the most significant of which are

1 It is concerned with groups of people aggregated into geographic units and is thus primarily a correlative process
2 It is expensive and time consuming

3   It does not represent a coherent theory of travel behaviour
4   It fails to address adequately the range of relevant policy issues
5   It is unable to predict what use might be made of new or improved transport facilities
6   It is unable to predict what effect certain restrictions might have in deterring travel
7   It is geared to a twenty-year time horizon rather than the here and now dynamic interrelationships between activities and travel
8   It is naive in breaking down the total demand for travel into a series of independent elements
9   It is capable only of simulating travel demand, with few if any explanatory powers

In short, it is argued that '. . . since travel is usually a derived demand, it can be expected that the decision-making process over all aspects of a trip is generally a considerably more complex procedure, one which cannot be adequately modelled through the use of simple sequential procedures'.[10] In an attempt to offset these disadvantages, disaggregate behavioural models have been developed at the level of behavioural unit (the individual or household). These models assume a theory of behaviour which is (a) partially economic and partially psychological, and (b) based on the concept of a rational individual choosing a method of transport which minimizes the disbenefits of travel (disutility). The disutility function includes a component which attempts to take account of idiosyncratic characteristics of individuals.

The basic differences between aggregate and disaggregate models can be summarized as follows

1   Aggregate models are estimated with a dependent variable representing a group of observations. By contrast a disaggregate model is estimated with a dependent variable which represents an observation of a single occurrence.
2   Aggregate data is grouped in zones or over categories of households. Disaggregate data takes the form of basic individual observations, although some of the information contained within the observation may be at some level of abstraction. For example, it might be based on a classificatory system where the absolute value of a characteristic is replaced by a group average value, such as income classes. While the dependent variable in a disaggregate model is the individual observation, some of the independent variables in the model can be represented by aggregate data.

The advocates of disaggregate models argue that travel demand is highly complex and that trip ends are spatially disaggregated from specific origin to specific destination. Thus, while work trips are generally fixed from home to work, other trips are home-based at one end but have a variety of destinations at the other end. Similarly, the time at which a trip is made can be influenced by the effect of, for example, peak periods and congestion. While the starting and finishing times for workers are generally fixed by the employer, the traveller can choose to arrive early and/or leave late. Indeed, the introduction of flexitime working is designed to encourage more flexible arrangements for working. Other optional activities are less constrained in terms of timing than the work journey and the trip-maker can invariably exercise a considerable degree of choice as to when such trips are made. At the same time, a wide variety of modes of transport are available to make trips – motor car, motor cycle, public transport, walking, cycling. Thus, for any given trip the traveller is required to exercise choice – initially whether or not to make the trip and, subsequently, a series of choices about destination, time of travelling, mode and route.

Trips are rarely made for the sake of travelling. Rather trips are normally undertaken for a purpose connected with the activity at the destination end. Thus, travel is a derived demand and as a result the trip-maker's behaviour need not be the same for different trip purposes. Equally, there is little chance of substituting one trip for another given that they are undertaken for different purposes.

It is claimed that the aggregate sequential approach to transportation planning over-simplifies this complex situation by representing trips as single, one-way by the dominant mode from origin to destination. Even the simple work journey trip is really a chain of two trips, i.e. home–work and work–home. Under different conditions more than one activity can be undertaken giving as many as six trips in a complex tour, e.g. home to work; work to library; library to shop; shop to sports centre; sports centre to public house; public house to home. In complex tours such as this, the trips to and from each activity are generally interdependent, and decisions made about the early trips influence decisions on the remaining trips, and vice versa. In the above example, if the library closes later than the shop then the order in which the library and shop are visited might vary or the mode of travelling between the two might be changed.

In disaggregate models this complexity is accommodated by treating trips as tours with an origin, a mixture of different destinations, travel models, routes and purposes and a range of times when the journey can be made. Simple tours have two identical legs, such as home–work, work–home. For more complex tours the dimensions of choice are significant. Fortunately, the majority of urban trips are of the simple two-tour variety. The theoretical basis on which these behavioural models are founded is that the trip-maker's behaviour is conditioned by the principle of utility maximization, subject of course to any resource constraints, i.e. the trip-maker will attempt to maximize the benefits that he/she can obtain within the limitations of the available resources – usually time and money. In this context, the travel demand of a single consumer is seen as involving choice and it is assumed that '. . . travel choice can be better described as a probabilistic choice from a set of mutually exclusive and exhaustive alternatives. . . .'[11] Thus, it is not surprising that much transport research effort in recent years has focused on improving the operationalization of probabilistic choice models, the most common of which is the logit model, as set out by Richards and Ben-Akiva[12]

$$P(i:A_t) = \frac{e^{U_{it}}}{\sum\limits_{j \in A_t} e^{U_{it}}}$$

where t = a behavioural unit (in the case of this study, a person)

$\quad\quad$ = 1, 2, . . ., T

$\quad A_t$ = the set of relevant alternatives for behavioural unit t

$P(i:A_t)$ = the probability that behavioural unit t will choose alternative i out of the set A_t

$\quad U_{it}$ = the utility of alternative i to behavioural unit t

The utility U_{it} is a function of the characteristics of alternative i, e.g. travel time, parking, congestion and the socio-economic characteristics of behavioural unit t which is usually expressed as income. It can be expressed as

$$U_{it} = U_i(X_i, S_t)$$

where X_i = a vector of characteristics of alternative i

$\quad S_t$ = a vector of socio-economic characteristics of behavioural unit t

Despite the advantages claimed for disaggregate behavioural models they are criticized on a number of grounds. Heggie, for example, claims that the results of studies carried out by people like Richards and Ben-Akiva (1975) do not prove that such models are behaviourally sound and policy relevant.[13] Rather he argues that such models '. . . characterise certain aspects of behaviour which are modelled as if they were a true and exhaustive statement of the relevant behaviour being modelled', when in fact '. . . the formal mathematical equations only bear a passing resemblance to the descriptive characterisation of travel behaviour'.[14] He goes on to state that 'The authors simply assume, or implicitly believe, that their results are policy relevant . . .' rather than attempting to prove the point by comparing deductions about policy options with empirical results derived from time series data.[15] In summary, he claims of disaggregate behavioural models 'Although the authors of these new models can take some comfort from the fact that their models are more realistic and do embody a number of useful new policy variables, they cannot yet claim to have fully developed a satisfactory practical travel demand forecasting procedure'.[16] As an alternative approach he offers activity systems analysis.

Activity systems analysis

Work has been undertaken in developing descriptions of travel activities based on actual behaviour. The approach also attempts to take account of non-rational behaviour, habit, resistance to change and internal and external constraints.[17] Central to this work is the concept of an activity analysis framework, as developed by Chapin,[18] Hagerstrand,[19] and Jones[20] among others. This approach emphasizes the derived nature of travel by studying it within the context of daily household activity patterns.

Heggie puts forward an activity analysis approach towards travel behaviour which involves three main stages

1 Describing clearly travel behaviour
2 Characterizing urban travel behaviour, i.e. incorporating limiting assumptions
3 Modelling the behaviour[21]

Describing urban travel behaviour

The description of urban travel behaviour is considered under five main heads – household structure, household characteristics, adaptability, temporal, income and spatial constraints, and the psychology of choice.

Household Family circumstances are considered to impose constraints on behaviour, to place extra demands on time and create problems of interpersonal synchronization, e.g. families with small children find travelling more difficult than families without. Heggie argues that in attempting to describe travel behaviour, it is important to take account of the stage in the family life cycle reached by the household, and suggests that the following groups are representative of that family life cycle in an English provincial town.

Group I	Young adults, whether married or not, without children
Group II	Families with dependent children, the youngest aged 7 years or less
Group III	Families with dependent children, the youngest aged 12 years or less
Group IV	Families with dependent children, the youngest aged 13 years or more
Group V	Families of adults, all of working age
Group VI	Elderly

The basis for this classification is that each group exhibits distinct travel characteristics which differ markedly between groups and are consistent within groups.

Household characteristics The characteristics of the household are considered to be important determinants in travel behaviour. Heggie suggests that the most important characteristics are ownership (which opens up a wider range of choice for location of home and work); neighbourhood car sharing (which relaxes a constraint and enables the car to meet increased household demands); the pattern of driving licence holding (which affects the claim on the use of the car) and access to public transport. He also makes the point that these household characteristics are not entirely dependent on the stage in the family life cycle.

Adaptability The average household is extremely adaptable in responding to changes in environmental and transport circumstances, which Heggie argues should be taken into account in any transportation planning analysis.

Temporal, income and spatial constraints Overall costs, despite having some fixed points, are considered to be generally more flexible than time constraints, while the effects of spatial constraints are obvious. They all interact in a complex way and it is argued that the overall effect of cost and time changes in trips cannot be ignored in any behavioural choice model.

Psychology of choice The trip-maker tends not to have a complete knowledge of all the possible choices open to him/her. Thus in describing choice, thresholds of trade-off between the relative attributes of competing alternatives may have to be explicitly included in the analysis.

Characterization of urban travel behaviour

If a realistic formal model of travel choice is to be developed, then the important aspects of travel behaviour developed from the description stage must be included, although some aspects can be omitted by introducing limiting assumptions. Heggie considers that travel behaviour can be characterized in terms of three major components

1 Constraints on behaviour, many of which are associated with the stage in the family life cycle
2 Mechanisms for response, where the individual can respond to a stimulus to travel by (a) selecting his or her preferred solution (provided it lies within his or her area of choice), or (b) adapting his or her preferred solution if it does not fall within his or her area of choice, to ensure that it does, e.g. combining a work trip with a shopping trip, or (c) altering the constraints that define his or her area of choice, e.g. by having young children looked after to allow the mother to do the shopping alone
3 The process of choice, which will be influenced by the level of knowledge possessed by the household of competing alternatives.

Models of behaviour

The problems of modelling this characterization of travel behaviour are acknowledged as being formidable. The difficulties of formulating a finite set of mathematic equations to represent the complex processes of choice are seen as being almost insurmountable and not practical, although the possibility of using mathematical programming is seen as one way forward. However, Heggie suggests that a more radical approach has to be adopted whereby the individual is required to provide the decision-making input to the model using a method known as the Household Activity Travel Simulator (HATS).[22]

This method involves the household and allows for interaction between different household members. It utilizes existing constraints on household behaviour. It takes the household's existing pattern of travel as its starting point, and it confronts the household with discrete and realistic changes in travel circumstances.

HATS is applied by using display boards in group in-depth interview situations. Activity travel diaries recording all 24-hour activities are completed prior to the in-depth interview, and relate to a specified period. These are translated into diagrammatic temporal representations of a given day as each member of the household builds a detailed picture of how and where time was spent throughout that day. Travel is seen as a special activity which links other activities. The interview procedure is shown in flow diagram form in Figure 40. Location, mode and route information is recorded on a detachable map on the upper part of the board. Once the basic information has been collected the interviewer can discuss with the respondent the reasons underpinning the decisions concerning their activity patterns, and any possible constraints and linkages involved can be amplified.

In addition to using HATS as a recall mechanism, it can be used to examine how household members might adapt their behaviour in response to specific changes in land use and/or travel characteristics. Thus, the interviewer can introduce a policy change, such as the elimination of an existing bus service, and explore with the household the ways in which it would adjust to the change. The resulting change in activity patterns is recorded on the board and the rationale for the change explored in depth. At the end of the process, the interviewer possesses a detailed record of individual activity patterns for each member of the household, both before and after the proposed policy change.

HATS can be criticized on the grounds that

1 The surveys carried out are limited in number because of the in-depth interviews. Therefore, the output will be either expensive to produce if it is to be statistically reliable, or it will be unreliable statistically.
2 It relies on current knowledge of alternatives, therefore it cannot deal with long-term responses to policy.
3 It does not incorporate a financial budget constraint.

However, the method, which involves a combination of group interview and display equipment produces a survey procedure with built-in checks. By reconstructing existing patterns of behaviour respondents familiarize themselves with the equipment and concepts. At the same time, it ensures that

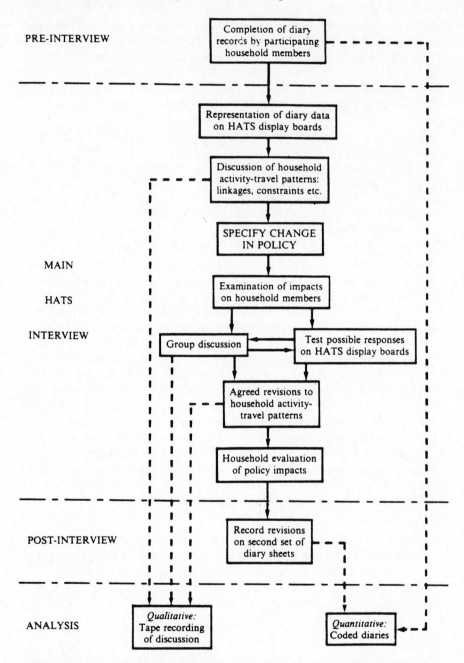

Figure 40   *HATS interview procedure*

Source: Jones, P. M. *et al., Understanding Travel Behaviour*, Gower, Aldershot (1973) Figure 8.3

subsequent discussion focuses on modifications to established patterns of behaviour, rather than on a hypothetical assessment of the effects of a policy change divorced from reality. The survey board is a good vehicle for identifying the feasibility of policies and the consequences of implementing those policies, which requires the respondent to consider the direct and secondary repercussions of any change. In the words of Heggie

> The issue is then quite simple: is it better to have a statistically valid sample (in terms of sample size) which must then be manipulated by a behaviourally unsound model, or to have an unsound sample that is manipulated by a model that is behaviourally correct? There can be no clear cut answer, although the former procedure is almost sure to be wrong.[23]

Conclusions

Historically the transportation planning process developed using a series of models – namely trip generation, trip distribution, modal split, and traffic assignment. More recently, given the inherent disadvantages of treating the process as a linked sequence of events rather than an integrated process, and to attempt to give the process a sounder theoretical basis, efforts have been made to develop and apply disaggregate behavioural models. Arising out of this work the traditional sequential aggregate approach has been improved by the introduction of the concept of generalized cost. At the same time, a range of probabilistic disaggregate behavioural models has been developed and applied in practice which are more realistic than the sequential aggregate approach. This has led to a greater understanding of the interrelationship between activities and movement, but such models are criticized on the grounds that there is no proof that they are behaviourally sound, and the formal mathematical equations do not satisfactorily describe the characteristics of travel behaviour. As an alternative an activity analysis approach such as HATS is considered to be more soundly based in a behavioural sense, although the possibility of using this approach in conjunction with formal mathematical models holds out hope for further development in the future. In short, the three major approaches to forecasting future demands for movement are all deficient in some respect, while the travel output from land-use allocation models is sufficient only for the very broadest of transportation studies.

Despite the disadvantages associated with the aggregate sequential approach, it still has much to offer practice. Given that land-use transportation studies are only aids to decision making; given that decisions to proceed with or reject transport infrastructure investment are political; given that the shortcomings of this approach are well understood and can be taken into account in reaching any decision, and given that the process as a whole is now well understood and readily available in the form of standard computer packages, there is every likelihood that this approach will characterize the land-use transportation planning process into the 1990s although behavioural disaggregate models are likely to be used increasingly in parts of the process. On the research front the evidence suggests that the probabilistic disaggregate behavioural models will attract further attention and improve our understanding of the interrelationships between transport, activities and the reasons why people choose to make the trips they do.[24] At the same time, there are indications that

Future developments may have to turn aside from the usual scientific paradigm and move in the direction of using actual individuals, or groups of them, as a substitute for the normal optimisation rules that are held to capture the essential ingredients of human behaviour. Models of behaviour . . . may thus have to become less mathematical and more human if they are to give realistic insights into the manner in which individuals arrange their various activities in both time and space.[25]

In addition, the world recession and the associated cuts in public expenditure are likely to lead to a greater concern with the management of transport systems and economic, fiscal and pricing issues.[26]

References

1   Wilson, A. G., *Urban and Regional Models in Geography and Planning*, Wiley and Sons, London (1974) p. 129.
2   See: *Journal of the American Institute of Planners*, Volume 31, No. 2, (1965).
       Highway Research Board, *Urban Development Models*, Special Report 97, Washington DC (1968).
       Chapin, F. S., and Kaiser, E. J., *Urban Land Use Planning*, University of Illinois Press, Urbana (1978) Chapter 15, pp. 543–601
    for a review of the characteristics and capabilities of a number of land-use allocation models.
3   Lowry, I. S., *A Model of Metropolis*, Technical Memorandum RM–4035-RC, the R A N D Corporation, Santa Monica, California (1964).
4   Garin, R. A., 'A Matrix Formulation of the Lowry Model for Intra-Metropolitan Activity Allocation', *Journal of the American Institute of Planners*, Vol. 32, No. 6, November 1966 pp. 361–4.
5   See Reif, B., *Models in Urban and Regional Planning*, Leonard Hill Books, Aylesbury (1973) Chapters 12–13, pp. 170–217 for a clear summary and review of the Lowry and Garin-Lowry models.
6   Echenique, M., *Urban Systems: Towards an Explorative Model*, CES UWP 2, Centre for Environmental Studies, London (1969).
7   Wilson, A. G., *Entropy in Urban and Regional Modelling*, Pion Ltd., London (1970).
8   See Batty, J. M., 'Some Problems of Calibrating the Lowry Model', *Environment and Planning*, Vol. 2 (1970) pp. 173–85.
       Batty, J. M., 'The Development of an Activity Allocation Model for the Notts/Derby Sub-Region', *Regional Studies*, Vol. 4, No. 3 (1970) pp. 307–32.
       Cripp, E., and Foot, D. H. S., 'A Land Use Model for Sub-Regional Planning', *Regional Studies*, Vol. 3, No. 3 (1969) pp. 243–63.
9   See Stopher, P. R., and Meyburg, A. H., *Urban Transportation Modelling and Planning*, Lexington Books, Lexington, Mass. (1975) for a brief history of the development of disaggregate behavioural modelling.
10 Richards, M. G., and Ben-Akiva, M. E., *A Disaggregate Travel Demand Model*, Saxon House, Farnborough (1975) p. 7.
11 *ibid.*, p. 21.
12 *ibid.*, p. 29.

13 Heggie, I. E., 'Behavioural Dimensions of Travel Choice' in Hensher, D. A., and Dalvi, Q., (eds.), *Determinants of Travel Choice*, Saxon House, Farnborough (1978) pp. 100-25.

14 *ibid.*, p. 102 and p. 106.

15 *ibid.*, p. 102.

16 *ibid.*, p. 103.

17 See Heggie, I. G., *op. cit.* (1978).
    Jones, P. M., 'Destination Choice and Travel Attributes', in Hensher, D. A. and Dalvi, Q., (eds.), *Determinants of Travel Choice*, Saxon House, Farnborough (1978) pp. 266-311.
    and Jones, P. M., Dix, M. C., Clarke, M. I., and Heggie, I. G., *Understanding Travel Behaviour*, Gower, Aldershot (1983).

18 Chapin, F. S., *Urban Land Use Planning*, 2nd edition, University of Illinois Press, Urbana (1965) pp. 221-53.
    Chapin, F. S., *Human Activity Patterns in the City*, John Wiley and Sons, New York (1974).
    Chapin, F. S., and Kaiser, E. J., *Urban Land Use Planning*, 3rd edition, University of Illinois Press, Urbana, (1979) pp. 194-230.

19 Hagerstrand, T., 'The Impact of Transport on the Quality of Life', *Transport in the 1980-1990 Decade*, 5th International Symposium on Theory and Practice in Transport Economics, OECD, Paris (1974).

20 Jones, P. M., 'Modelling Travel Behaviour in a Human Activity Framework', *Transport Studies Unit Research Note No. 1*, University of Oxford (1975).

21 Heggie, I. G., *op. cit.*, pp. 100-25.

22 Jones, P. M., 'HATS: A Technique for Investigating Household Dimensions', *Environment and Planning A*, 11 (1979).

23 Heggie, I. G., *op. cit.*, p. 124.

24 Stopher, P., Meyburg, A. H., and Brog, W., *New Horizons in Travel Behaviour Research*, Lexington Books, Lexington, Mass. (1981).

25 Heggie, I. G., *op. cit.*, p. 124.

26 National Research Council, *Urban Transportation Planning in the 1980's*, U S Department of Transportation Special Report 196, Washington DC (1982).

Index